# A Year of Days

William Flynn

ISBN-13: 978-1523222629

To all who share the path of recovery with those who seek it

# ACKNOWLEDGMENTS

Special thanks to my friend Mark C. with whom this journey started. Also many thanks to Mike T., Brandon J., John McD., my sponsor and irrepressible friend Stan T. as well as the many other men in my local area who participated in the early text messages that were the beginning of this project. Thanks also to the many friends who helped me continue this project and encouraged me by sharing their own experiences and thoughts.

Many thanks to the thousands of people that have shown their support on the "A Year of Days" Facebook page and who continue to offer encouragement, insight, and their own thoughts and experiences while helping to share the message of recovery with others. Without the bright light of your support this book might not have emerged. As always, in recovery and in life, I stand on the shoulders of those who have gone before me.

Lastly, particular thanks to you the reader. The experience and happiness of sharing in your journey is a privilege and unexpected joy. I deeply appreciate you and your desire for life in recovery. I hope to continue writing in ways that might be of some small benefit to you and others who find themselves on the path of recovery.

# January

"The bravest thing I ever did was continuing my life when I wanted to die."
— Juliette Lewis

"Above all, don't lie to yourself. The man who lies to himself and listens to his own lie comes to a point that he cannot distinguish the truth within him, or around him, and so loses all respect for himself and for others. And having no respect he ceases to love."
— Fyodor Dostoyevsky

"There are two ways to be fooled. One is to believe what isn't true; the other is to refuse to believe what is true."
— Søren Kierkegaard

# January 1

I like the idea that the act of starting to take action is, by itself, a major milestone in my recovery. In active addiction, I spent a lot of time talking about things that were going to happen, but never actually taking the first steps (or sustaining an effort) towards making them happen. It is easy for me to be so focused on the difficulty of achieving a goal that I forget it is attained in small steps over a period of time. The fuller understanding of the reality that, for a man like me in recovery, I must take meaningful action each day has done at least two important things for me. It has helped me to be regularly active in my recovery in ways that I can identify clearly. It also affirms my commitment, providing an example and validation of my efforts that I can look to as a clear sign of progress. Taking some form of meaningful action each day not only places me on the path of recovery, but also ensures I'm moving along it in the right direction. Because of this simple process of daily action I am more present in the journey as it is taking place each day rather than being stalled and unsettled while fixated on a distant goal that at times can seem unattainable.

# January 2

In the past I have been hypersensitive to criticism, ever fearful of failure and being not good enough. The result was a pursuit of a twisted perfectionism, excessive and extreme, yet easily tossed away at the first sign of failure. If I couldn't be perfect, then why try at all? This foolish approach often justified and excused my self-destructive behavior. It offered what became a familiar and comfortable way to always have a good reason to get loaded. Today I'm more mature and easy going about things, I still have that perfectionist trait, but it's tempered with the realism and understanding that what is important is that I honestly make my best effort. When I do my honest best I achieve a result that improves as I learn from my experiences. It allows me to understand that progress toward my goals is what I am really pursing, not some unattainable ideal. Being open and accepting of my imperfections removes the twisted escape clause that for many years I used as an excuse to not try at all. When I make an honest effort at life I do so with my Higher Power's help, it opens the door to trusting the results and relieves me of the burden and trap of mistaking me for my Higher Power.

# January 3

It seems that so much in life is what I chose to make of it and the most important parts need to be made anew each day. For some reason this has been a difficult lesson for me to learn. For many years I approached my relationships with other the same way I would my possessions. Once I had them I didn't need to work for them anymore. Recovery has shown me that my relationships, like many tasks in life, must be worked on regularly if they are to continue to remain healthy. My relationships with others who are close to me in life are the ultimate opportunity to practice how to live in the moment. I must be willing to be present in a steady reliable way if they are to remain meaningful and close. I often hear the idea that God speaks to us through others. If this idea has any truth, then in a way, God is often found in the person whom with I'm speaking at any given moment, and it's my chance to choose to hear the message, participate in a spiritual moment of life, or not. At times doing this requires much patience and compassion, but I rarely fail to be rewarded when I approach life in this manner. The hustle and bustle of the modern world crowds my day, but it's easy to find moments of peace and calm when I chose to seek them.

# January 4

Daily contact with spirituality reminds me of my powerlessness and willful desire to be in control. The art of building and participating in a relationship with my Higher Power, with the spiritual world, is something I'd like to conveniently schedule and complete each day, ticking the box that it's done and then move on to my next task. It hasn't worked that way for me. Instead it's more like the weather or perhaps bird watching. I have to keep my eyes open and be ready to notice when it happens. I have to ask myself what just happened, what does it mean, is there a message for me in it? I can prepare myself each morning to be present, aware, open and receptive but the how and when of it all is not mine to control. Perhaps it's like having an umbrella I carry each day, ready to receive the rain when it occurs and pausing to hear a theme in the sound of the raindrops. Increasingly I am aware of how recovery allows me to understand and engage in my own human nature by connecting spiritually to the world around me. I am, have been, and will always remain a product of the natural world around me, never the reverse.

# January 5

My first reaction to the reminder in recovery that I could, and someday would, enjoy solitude instead of suffering in loneliness, was one of skepticism and doubt. My understanding of what it really meant was frail and incomplete. It was clear to me that rather like sobriety itself, knowing of it and having it were two very different things. Years of feeling apart from the world around me, a feeling that was exaggerated and exacerbated through addiction and its constant feelings of shame and guilt, had become a grinding reality that left me with a defeated soul and a sense of crushing isolation that never fully left me. It has taken time and the daily repetition of certain activities, as well as cleaning house through a continued working of the steps, to become able to accept myself enough to truly understand and enjoy solitude. The comfort I receive in solitude is from the connection with my Higher Power and the proper alignment of my will which provides the surety of knowing I am a part of life today. I am no longer separated and trapped by the loneliness and despair of selfish isolation. The understanding of who I am, and seeing my place in life, connects me always to the spirit of the world around me.

# January 6

In the modern fast food world of instant access and entitlement the foolish, immature and youthful cry of "I want it all and I want it now" is easy for me to carry into life as an expectation. For many years I stood on the shores of life trying to fight and control the tide. Often I fooled myself into thinking I was at times winning, but ultimately in the end I always lost. I lost because there was no peace or lasting value to be found when I was living in denial to escape from the reality of life. My immature nature, one that wiggled and squirmed to avoid growing up, balked at the powerful feelings and discomfort of true relationships. The insightful and often painful reflection of being open, honest, and caring were easily chased away by my drinking and addictions. While, as Samuel Johnson notes, becoming a beast avoids the pain of being a man, I have found that the contentment of being a truly human man is found in both the pain and joy of living each day in reality and acceptance. The nature and path of life is beyond my control but each day I can chose to live my small part fully—to take another small step forward as a man who is doing only what he ought to do. This is the measure of my value today.

# January 7

The true understanding and implication of my powerlessness and ultimate inability to control life is easy for me to lose track of. Remembering that my own plans and designs are like grains of salt on the table of God's world helps me to be happy and right sized. Learning how to let go and become able to overcome the fear of not participating in the illusion I create of being in control has been difficult and is often hard to sustain. However, it's always impossible for me to maintain the illusion of control—sooner or later I'm always shown the truth by life's endless ability to have its way with me. My own efforts to control it are suddenly feeble and puny when life flexes its real strength and confronts me with the choice of either staying the course and riding it out or escaping and hiding from its reality. Having the courage to accept life on life's terms allows me to let go of my own tightly held ideas or expectations and instead make room to see what God has planned for me. I'm much more content when relieved of the frustration, disappointment and burden of trying to force my outcomes on life and instead can relax and enjoy the ride, regardless of its flavor.

# January 8

The notion of powerlessness while at the same time intrinsically being "a part of," is easy for me to connect with when I am conscious of my connection with the natural world. For example, I am easily inspired by Mt Rainier on a clear day when I take a moment to stop and appreciate it—to connect to it with my own natural spirit. Finding and accepting my place in life is a central part of my spiritual awakening. The busy modern world is often not so easy or tranquil. It has taken years of work in recovery to learn how to rely on spiritual support and faith to help solve my problems. Like a storm, they will eventually pass, but when life is raging, blowing or just drearily raining I must take shelter. My spiritual faith has grown stronger over time—like the shelter of a shipwrecked man. It has evolved from a few flimsy rough branches and sail cloth into a sturdy safe home. Today I can take refuge with my Higher Power, withstanding the storms of life that remind me of my powerlessness. When the rains pass and the sun returns there may be unwanted repairs to make and work to do. There is no avoiding the storms of life, only the choice of how I accept, face, and endure them. Understanding that I have a place and that my life is a part of God's natural order, always interwoven with the lives of others and the world around me, means I need never again face life alone.

# January 9

Fear remains a common foe in my daily effort to live and grow spiritually. It is very often the root cause of my agitation or discomfort. Sometimes when I pause and remember to think about my problems from the point of view of fear I can quickly identify what particular thing is causing my discomfort. Other times it's not clear exactly what I'm in fear of—but it is enough to simply recognize and acknowledge the feeling. Today, because of the experience of working and living the steps, I can face fear with faith. I have trust in my Higher Power and that I am living a good life. A life that is rooted in personal honesty and doing what I ought to. Before I had any real spiritual awakening this wasn't the case. I was not honest and could find no respite or relief from the fear that drove my insane thinking and actions. My honest connection with a Higher Power opened the door to the arrival of faith in my life. Faith rides with me on the horse of my honest actions in life and allows me to seek the help of God and my friends because I've nothing held back—nothing hidden that causes shame or guilt. Acceptance, and ultimately transcendence, of life's fears is easier when I'm properly prepared and supported. They become a much more natural part of my living and less likely to control or propel me in ways I don't see or understand.

# January 10

For me today, risk is something to be very cautious about. It wasn't always like that. At times I sought risk out irrationally, as a source of excitement or reward, and somehow related it to a perverted sense of manhood. Today I see life more rationally and take risks carefully and thoughtfully. I try to understand how risk is an unavoidable element of living life and that in a way it tests my understanding of, and my reliance upon, a faith in God. Exercising my own "will" that is set into alignment with my Higher Power allows me to take action in life not knowing exactly what the outcome will be. In a way I must accept rational risk when I accept my powerlessness and surrender to God's will. Otherwise all I am left with is my will which, when unchecked, is often selfish, self-centered and self-deceiving. The results of that choice I know already, they came from the irrational risk of believing I was in control of life. So I must have faith and courage to be the man I believe I should be and not balk at action, even if difficult, painful, or scary because the outcome is in God's control and I will always be ok.

# January 11

The topic of truth is one that is often somewhat uncomfortable for me because my experience has shown that the nature of truth can be quite subjective at times. I used to believe it was more simple, clear, definite and always the same. As my courage and ability to see my own truth has grown through the process of a relationship with my Higher Power I have learned that my understanding of what is true for me evolves. It changes and evolves—a fact that has taken some time to become comfortable with. I prefer things that are at times hard and painful (like self-discovery) to be something that I go through once and reach a point of completion so I can say "Ok—that's done" and move on. I have found that often this is not the case with truth. Like the path of spiritual growth, there is no day of graduation in the process of truth. For me it is a practice that I am gaining skill with over time. However, I can always try to be honest about what my truth is today. I have become more comfortable with the understanding that it will change as I continue to grow. Today If I can be honest, open-minded and willing I am always led towards my truth as I know it today. It is always more clearly seen in the accurate reflection of my own journey of self-discovery and development that I discover in the experience of sharing my life with others.

# January 12

I remember it taking me quite a while to begin to understand the extent to which my self-centeredness and maladjusted sense of ego distorted my sense of reality. In the past, when driving at night, I would sometimes believe that when a single street light would randomly turn off it was related to me. That somehow I had caused it—or that it was perhaps a sign of some sort. Of course in reality they go off on their own all the time for a few minutes when they get too hot. In recovery, when I first came to meetings, if two people were talking after the meeting and happened to look in my direction I assumed that they not only had to be talking about me, but it must also be bad! It took time for that "me, me, me" thinking, and the guilt induced sense of impending doom or punishment, to leave me. It took even longer to realize and understand that I am really not that important. I am learning to see my place in the world as just another ordinary man, as nothing too special, and that the world around me isn't a personalized custom version centered on me. Today I realize that I am a part of life, not a recipient of it. I've had to try to learn to "get over myself," adjust my ego, practice humility, and work to understand how being selfish and self-centered blankets my world in ways I never knew.

# January 13

If I had my own way nothing that was hard, soul searching or painful about my problems would ever be my fault. Asking, "Who me?" and then blaming others is my initial reaction most times. It is often hard for me to be honest with myself about my part in things, because I can struggle to see my role clearly. The honesty that comes from the process of self-examination and sharing with others helps me find a fuller truth that I'm not able to see at first. The saying, "If I'm not the problem then there is no solution," confirms that finding and understanding "my part" in my problems is the only way I can resolve them. Always claiming to be the innocent one in my relationships avoids the sometimes painful spiritual growth that being rigorously honest can provide. I will often fight the truth because it is not what I want to hear or believe. I am sometimes in denial or delusional about how I show up in the lives of others and refuse to accept that I may be wrong. There are few better examples of my own self-will being out of synch with my Higher Power than in these cases. Accepting the truth that I always have some part in my own problems opens that door to letting go of false innocence and defiant self-will. It provides a link to the serenity that comes with being in line with God's will by showing me a way to return to it.

# January 14

In thinking about my place in the world there are two important ideas I return to often. That I must take myself and my life seriously and that I do that by accepting the responsibility that life brings through taking the action it requires. In the past I avoided these hard truths. Recovery has shown me that if I don't care enough to treat my life seriously, with value and purpose, then surely I can't expect anyone else to. Today I am fully eligible for all life offers. I owe it to myself to be ok, to recover from the past, to cease being driven by it. If I know I am broken I must work to repair myself, to learn new things, and to understand that it takes practice and that I won't just "get it" and be better. I must have patience and love for myself in my imperfect journey. There is no magic donut—just the hard work of self-improvement and spiritual growth. My immaturity needs to be reminded that all healthy people go through this process and so must I if I am serious about being the man my Higher Power wants me to be. No matter what might have happened in the past I retain a natural human right to my own place in the world and only I can do the work that is needed for me to step into it.

# January 15

Being overly status conscious is the perfect way for me to avoid being "right-sized" and spiritually content. I have found little value in believing I am to be judged by my material successes. In our consumer driven society much of what I hear each day is formed around motivating me to purchase things and the notion that I am the sum of my possessions or achievements. Basing my personal value on the material world is a problem for me spiritually because there is always more to buy, always something better. Questions such as:
How much is enough?", or, "When is enough good enough?" create anxiety and a constant nagging discomfort. Most of the people I know who are very content in life seem to have realized that lasting happiness is rarely found in status or possessions but instead comes from personal acceptance and relationships with others. Today I realize that my Higher Power values my moral worth not my bank balance. I find true self-esteem in words and actions not in my efforts to control a perceived status within society. When I understand that I am just another man with ordinary abilities and faults, just another person in the timeless stream of mankind, I simply have to do my best as I understand it in order to have self-worth and contentedness. Soon I will be gone and the important question for me today is if I will have enjoyed my time and lived well. I will likely leave no grand event or design upon the world and that is just fine if I can smile and know that I was helpful and useful during my brief time here.

# January 16

I'm often reminded of a quote from St. Vincent De Millay, "Pity me the heart that is slow to learn what the quick mind sees at every turn." Sometimes it may be easy for me to understand a simple guidance, direction, or thought—but I will fail to get results from it because my effort isn't wholehearted. Perhaps because a thing is easy to understand I assume it will be easy to achieve. Living in the moment each day and avoiding the captivating and debilitating glare of my minds pursuit of past or future becomes easier when I put my heart into it. Clearly, what is happening in front of me right now, the living of life with others today, is the only place where my actions become real. The internal world of my mind, while vital and useful, can never be a substitute or valid alternative to the external world of my life which is always lived solely in my daily activities. My thinking world has most value when I link it to a valid purpose. If I am obsessing about the past or future it's like walking in circles all day and expecting to get paid—I won't because there is no value to the activity. I can simultaneously create a better future and a better past only by my good actions that take place in the today of life. This is the only way I know that works. It has worked for me since I learned to not only understand it mentally but also how to put it into my heart each day.

# January 17

For me, the understanding of my powerlessness and inability to control life, the honest admission of my faults and limitations that create unmanageability and my acceptance of my place as a common member of humanity, will hopefully continue to lead me towards a place of humility. Humility is not powerlessness or passivity. I still have a great deal of personal power but am learning about its true purpose, value, and meaning as well as its boundaries and limits. Today it is not enough for me to simply coast on the currents of life and hope for the best. I must paddle my canoe in a direction that is healthy and thoughtful. I must use my power of action to actively pursue "the Good Life." My daily relationship with spiritual thinking, even if only brief moments on some days, allows me to gain little insights, to collect and over time shape the small pieces of spiritual growth into a greater understanding of who I am, where I am going, and why I am going there. Most importantly it offers an ability to enjoy the journey. I don't measure the amount of progress I make each day; instead I recognize the value and pleasure of being on a good path. I can never control the absolute course of my life, only the way in which I participate as I move through it. And for me today, that is the best use of my individual power and will, as I attempt to make choices and decisions that sustain and expand my sense of personal integrity.

# January 18

It has taken a long time for me to even begin to understand the role and power of vulnerability in my life. It is easy enough to see how sharing my life and participating with others with empathy and honest communication allows me to be a part of a loving relationship, friendship, or community. It is much harder for me to be truly vulnerable in doing so. Working the steps and slowly building trust with others has enabled me to experience a true connection and belonging that has deepened from expressing my own vulnerability. Honestly exposing my protected feelings, hopes, fears, or helplessness frees me from spiritual isolation and loneliness. It confirms and enables my human value and worth. When I share deeply, or hear a friend do so, then I am really alive in a way that is uniquely spiritual, powerful, and healing. It authenticates my humanity. We have perhaps all experienced the powerful results of having a true "heart to heart" conversation with another—it can be liberating and cleansing while helping to provide clarity and insight. The willingness to be completely open and honest with my feelings in a trusted relationship is never wrong because it is my truth. Being able to accept the risk of real vulnerability can act as a sort of amplifier to the experience of a true connection with someone close to me. It is almost always a powerfully helpful and rejuvenating moment.

# January 19

Sometimes I find that self-realization arrives as a brief flash of insight and clarity, a sort of ""a-ha" moment as the result of my effort to understand. Other times it is more of a creation. I am able to realize something new from some other process or activity. Either way, it is usually the result of active participation and effort. Often the realization comes after the effort is finished—as if the notion had to bake in the oven of my mind for a while before being revealed. I will have moved on, gone for a walk, be reading, or talking with someone and it will arrive slowly a little bit at a time. Gaining an understanding of my life after addiction has been the result of honest self-examination and participation with others during the course of living life sober. In the past, my living activity was misguided into confusion, delusion and mental suffering. Today my living is well directed and healthier. Over time I've grown comfortable and content in living life for what it is each day instead of trying to make every day something exceptional or extraordinary. Today I'm ok with not always knowing what will happen or having to understand all the gaps and blank spots in my day. I can experience doubt or sadness without fear or an urgent need to solve things immediately. I believe that as time goes by I will continue to realize more about myself, my life, and my place in the world as long as the activity and effort of my participation remains steady and well directed.

# January 20

I have learned so much about whom I am and what kind of man I can be through the valuable and rewarding experience of building close friendships with other men in recovery. At first it was with my sponsor as we worked through the steps. Then it was other friends in recovery. As has often been the case in my recovery I needed to learn some new life skills. From a young age my thinking and social understanding was skewed into a "me, me, me" world of isolation and addiction. The belief that I was alone, that I could live alone, became my song. It has often been hard for me to understand that these new skills are real, that they will work for me, that I need them and will value them. Of course I would never have found out for sure if I didn't at least try them. In addiction I didn't have a strong honest relationship with anyone, especially not myself. Having healthy friendships with other men has helped me learn how to have one with myself. Today these relationships that I've slowly built up over the years are so important I would never go without them again. They help relieve me of the isolation, loneliness, and insanity of my disease. They help me understand my Higher Power and provide meaning in my life. Because we truly know and trust each they are like brothers who care only for my best interests. Their motive is my well-being and the bond of friendship. Without these relationships I would not have been able to recover. They have been a vital part of my personal growth and spiritual awakening. In a few years I have gone from crushing isolation and loneliness to a fearless faith in my eligibility for a good life, and today, I am part of a brotherhood that enables my journey.

# January 21

There is a quote by Pythagoras I've always found interesting. He said that "The most momentous thing in human life is the art of winning the soul, to good or evil." The limbo and zombie-like no-man's land of addiction was mostly neither good nor evil for me—it was just endless, pointless suffering. It brought me to a point one day where I was at last able to become entirely ready and willing to cease my defiant hesitation in the face of real change. That was the day the door opened to a new path for me. I was at last able to take myself seriously enough to walk through that door and honestly fully commit to a new life. Since then I have practiced the art of winning my soul to good. By shunning what I know is the wrong path, the good path has slowly shown itself to me—and with practice my ability to follow it has improved. Today I can look back and understand why it was so hard to leave the fog of addiction. I had no comprehension of what a good life really was, or how rewarding it would be, because I had never grown up and tried it. I was confused about the question of what was in front of me instead of simply becoming ready to leave what I had behind me. I remember clearly the exact moment when I said, "No more, I must really make this change." It was a soft acceptance of a truth I'd fought against. I didn't know who I would become, but knew I didn't want to be who I was anymore. It was the moment I won my soul back by taking a stand and simply accepting, with clarity and fullness of heart, and mind, that I was on a new path.

# January 22

The questions of forgiveness and judgment, and recognition of my own belligerence around them, have been a big part of my learning how to let go of resentments. When I look back at my actions in addiction I am reminded of how, when it was something I really wanted, it was easy for me to do things that crossed the boundaries of my morals. Learning to open myself to having new beliefs around old ideas has been a key to my recovery and ability to be content. It took time to really learn how to live free of resentment and in order for them to fade away I had to learn how to stop feeding and exercising the ones I had. Letting go of a perhaps somewhat childish pursuit of self-forgiveness (which I found to be just another form of self-absorption and denial) and learning instead to find true forgiveness for others was also critical. Given the way I was living my life who the heck was I to judge anyone else? My selfish lying actions hurt the very people that I wanted to resent. They should, and often did, resent me and yet I became the "kettle calling the pot black." Most often it was my own actions that put me in a place to be hurt. Other times life just happened, and it sucked, but either way I have a choice to not have my present be defined by my past. The question isn't how the arrow got into my chest, it is how do I remove it and recover. I had to first be willing to accept that I could let go, that I wanted to let go, and then, over time, the work of the steps showed me how. Today, I don't stand outside in the rainy cold wind resenting the winter; I simply go inside and gently close the door behind me.

# January 23

I often think about how the roles of open mindedness and control relate to each other. Letting go of my death grip on control allows me to learn that it's ok to be me, and more importantly, that it's ok for me to explore and learn more about who I really am and who I can become tomorrow. Sometimes my reaction is to cry out "that's just the way I am" or cling to beliefs or ideas about myself that "I know." If I totally control who and what I think I am, the door to growth remains closed. There are things I enjoy so much today that I used to scoff at because I wasn't willing to try them. My need to control tells me, "that's not who you are." In learning that it's ok to be me, that I can choose who I am rather than being held to an ideal that is fixed and unchanging I create the space to randomly try new things. I can be open and accepting when things aren't the way I planned them. These are all opportunities for growth. It is ok for me to grow and my recovery demands it because I can't just sit back and fight the urge to return to my old life. Instead I've got to move forward and live life in a new way. One way for me to do that has been to loosen the grip on my desire to control life around me, to trust my Higher Power and go exploring the uncharted territory of the new world of a sober me.

# January 24

In early recovery I really struggled with the idea of values and morals. Years of addiction had left me confused, fogged, and lost. I had no meaningful connection to who I was, who I had been, or who I hoped to become. I wanted a quick lesson so I could understand and catch up. It took time for me to really grasp the concept and then even more time to learn how only I can choose what my values are. What are the serious things in life for me? What kind of man do I want to be? What do I believe is right and wrong? It took working the steps to really begin to figure out who I was and what I valued, both in myself and of myself, internally and externally. I had ideas about myself that seemed so entrenched but when I closely examined them I realized they weren't really mine. I'd gathered them like the latest fashion—as a way to fit in or as protection and denial from the results of my disease. Today my true morality grows out of my values and how strongly I adhere to them. Learning to believe in and value who I am required me to first determine who I was and then learn how to stick to those values. In the past whatever values I might have had were easily tossed away in the face of my selfish immoral addiction. Today I can stand my ground on things that are important to me. I don't have to convince anyone else of anything. I know what I stand for and am not easily swayed. My Higher Power and close friends guide me as I continue to learn and develop more clarity around the question of what kind of man I choose to be today.

# January 25

Having sober loving relationships has been a powerful experience for me—especially in early recovery. Until recovery, sex was most often objectified for me, almost more of a conquest and rarely a shared spiritual experience. It centered in the physical. As I've opened myself to a true spiritual experience in life the early relationships in recovery seemed like they were almost magic. Because I never went through it when I was young, it was perhaps like having "puppy love" in middle age. I had to learn how to progress through the middle school, high school and college type relationships. It has felt like the end of the world when something so new and powerful didn't work out. Of course not all healthy relationships do work out. The difference today is that I can accept that the ending is ok and not let my own will try to force things like I did in the past, which of course never worked out. Instead I've become better able to move on and learn from the experience. Learning to deal with life's pain is a part of recovery and that has been difficult because in the past I've usually masked it with the escape of using. Because I feel more authentically today, it's very uncomfortable, but still a part of the process of growth. I trust that my Higher Power has a plan for me, and I do the hard work of self-examination, using the support around me, to understand and proactively chose my path as best I can.

# January 26

I can find a certain peaceful melancholy, an acceptance of my small but important place in the cycle of life, when I view myself as a human first and my role as a man second. This human connection, our inescapable nature of being a part of each other, brings me closer to my Higher Power and others. Young and old, men and women, the church bells ring for all our ears. The rain falls equally on us all, and the generations before and hence are all my family. I belong here today in my space in the cycle, my turn of the wheel. Pondering the grand scheme of things helps keep my life right sized and in perspective. There is a mysterious joy and wonder to life that I don't need to fully understand, but can simply accept and enjoy. The crushing isolation of addiction is gone and I am a part of the world today. Instead of battling the world to force my place in it as a man I can sit easy in the saddle of my life as I ride with life trusting the plan a Higher Power has for us all. Today, I can be a part of this great, endless, life cycle around me because I choose to be—by living like I know I ought to. Accepting my powerlessness over the natural order of the world frees me to enjoy it and brings me a closer connection to it. The natural mystery of my soul and my understanding of faith and spirituality are connections I share with the world around me.

# January 27

Sometimes I find myself seeing all the faults of the world in everyone I meet and nobody it seems measures up to my expectations. It is an approach that ensures I remain bitter, resentful, angry, irritated, and sick. In these times I must remind myself that expecting perfection creates fertile ground for my disease to bloom. Holding the world, and its imperfect people, to an absurdly high standard (one that I can never manage to achieve for myself of course) is a sure way to remain disappointed. The way of God's natural world seems to be one of progress through a messy imperfection that never gives up. Expecting perfection returns me to familiar feelings of disenchantment, isolation, and loneliness. I must remember that I am powerless to control much of what happens in the world around me. Having tremendous expectations and standards for the world is also rather ironic given my own past. How can I possibly expect to be the judge of other people's behavior given my own glaring imperfections? In recovery I have learned that it is only in having acceptance of my own faults that I can find relief from the faults of others. So being able to have acceptance and love for the imperfect world around me always begins with doing so first with me. Recognition of nature's relentless drive that keeps us all going, imperfect and struggling, opens me to a subtle awe and appreciation of my Higher Power's world.

# January 28

Thinking about how I can no longer avoid the suffering that is a natural part of life reminds me of the story in the Big Book when following the tornado the alcoholic happily says, "Ain't it grand the wind stopped blowing," and yet doesn't acknowledge the damage caused. Living life without the escape from reality that addiction offered required me to grow up in many new ways. Today, I am accountable for my actions. The personal integrity of living true to my morals and values has become a reality that I enjoy and seek. Today I can fully participate in the full range of life; socially, physically, mentally, and spiritually. At first it was often raw and overwhelming at times. There is suffering all around me, and as is the case with most things, it's easy for me to take things to the extreme. At first I seemed to feel it all and either run from it or try to fix it, and then cry out, "it's not fair" or "what's the point!" Recovery and working the steps remind me that the problems of the world aren't my duty. It is grandiose indeed for me to begin to even think so. However, doing my small part in life is my duty. There is joy and suffering, excitement and drudgery, happiness and sadness, all of which I have learned to experience with increasing comfort as my emotional maturity has grown. Today, I understand that suffering is something I can have compassion about. I can stand with my friends as they experience it but can never remove it or control life. I have an understanding that we must all be free to follow our own path in its fullness. I cannot, nor should not, cheat myself or others out of the full measure of life, even when it is to suffer. There is no right way for me to thwart God's plan.

## January 29

The desire to control and manage the outcomes and results of the decisions or actions I take is always present—and naturally so. Part of learning how to live my life on a daily basis involves taking action as best I can and leaving the results up to God. Sometimes it seems God isn't on the same page as I am. I've learned to let it be and not leap in and force things when they don't go what I think are my way. Experience has shown me that it will work out in God's time and way, which typically has a result that is ultimately much better than the one I had conceived. I'm often reminded by my persistent desire to future trip, or when I get stuck dwelling on the past, that life is lived only in today. Only in the today of life can I seek and find peace and serenity. Developing trust in my Higher Power has given me the hope, faith, and certainty that there is a plan for my life. This is much different from life in addiction with its wild, flailing, and ineffectual efforts to force my will on the world around me. Today I see that there are two paths I can follow. Each day I must simply stay on the correct path and not worry too much about exactly where it leads. I know precisely where the other path leads and I chose to avoid it. So today, I slowly and steadily walk this new path and grow in ways that aren't measured quickly—but every now and then I reach a clearing, a place of perspective, and see how far indeed I have come by living focused on one day at a time.

## January 30

For many years, living with addiction meant I was living various roles that I would act out. Living a double life for so long meant that I really lost myself as the substance abuse continued to further blur the lines between reality and my own delusions. In fact, because I started so young I never found my true self and instead became many shallow versions of the man I thought would be best for the moment. In recovery, learning that it's ok to be me is a hard thing when I don't know who "me" is. As I sobered up it felt like I was a stranger to myself, perhaps like a sort of amnesia of the spirit and soul. It took building and participating in honest friendships, working the steps a few times, and gaining some insight about myself and God in order to clear the insane thinking. Only then was I was able to begin to learn about who and what I really am and who I want to be. The process has freed me from that constant subtle fear I used to have. Today I have nothing to hide. It is ok for me to be me and I'm no longer a stranger to myself or ashamed of whom I am. By becoming vulnerable to the truth, with myself and close friends, I have gained a tremendously strong and peaceful clarity of mind and spirit. Life is much easier when I'm not constantly trying to figure out who I should pretend to be. Instead, I can have the trust and faith to just be me, safe and secure in the knowledge that just being me is all that is ever really required.

# January 31

The understanding of how the mental, spiritual, physical, and social aspects of recovery are inseparable elements of a single process has taken time to show its true importance to me. My mind and body perform different tasks and yet are totally dependent on each other. If one is unhealthy the other suffers also. The ideas of unity and integrity run throughout recovery in many ways. Just as I'm often reminded that recovery is a "we" program, that I can't do it alone, I also realize the importance of meeting the various needs of my whole self. I can't only work on one area. I must try to keep all areas of my life in balance and aligned with God's will. There are many ways my addictive selfishness can show itself. Do I take myself seriously enough to be physically healthy? Am I worth being emotionally healthy? Do I deserve to be spiritually healthy? These are fundamental questions of self that my relationship with God helps me answer. How can I be of service to others if not yet to myself? The importance of the question of how seriously I take my recovery is shown to me regularly in the suffering of others and my chance to be of service to them. This of course is also of service to me. I feel I must make a good effort in all areas to be ready, willing, and able to do God's will. Otherwise I am left with just my will which, to put it mildly, hasn't worked out very well for me in the past.

# February

"Hope is a waking dream."
— Aristotle

"I like the night. Without the dark, we'd never see the stars."
— Stephenie Meyer

"We need never be hopeless because we can never be irreparably broken."
— John Green

# February 1

The idea that it is only the experience itself that creates growth wasn't what I wanted to hear in the beginning of my recovery. My family relations were adrift and distant. I was largely unemployable with serious financial and legal problems. I was full of guilt and resentment. The wreckage of the ship of my own life was staring at me, sitting there washed up hopeless and lost, as I shuffled around on the shores of a new sobriety. It was there that I found the "child" of my recovery inside myself. It has been the experience and process of raising this new child that has enabled my growth as a man. At first recovery was frustrating, demanding, irritating and relentless. It was confusing and hard work. There were little moments of joy and hope that kept me going. In time, recovery became easier and more fun. Working through the steps and having honest open friendships relieved my crushing isolation and feelings of doom and dread. The guilt and resentment faded away as I realized that no one does a math problem correctly before they learn to count. Life was full of painfully incorrect answers for me until I learned how to live it. At first I wanted to just "get it" but that was like hoping to get fed by reading a cookbook. The experience and effort of working and living the steps is what taught me how to cook the meal that is my recovery.

# February 2

Today I was thinking about expectations. Very early in sobriety I was shown the hope that recovery offered. I realized others had done it and so might I. The hope that I could leave the suffering of addiction became a reality as I worked the program. Now I have a reasonable expectation that if I continue to work it, it will continue to work for me. Learning to see where the edge of a hope that is based on a reasonable expectation ends and the willful demand of an unreasonable expectation begins isn't easy. The idea that I can simply enjoy the basic reward of being a good man who is alive in the fold of today, of today and for today, enjoying the simple pleasure of being a useful part of life is a powerful one. It allows me to be comfortable in myself. Yes, I have ideas and goals. And yes, there are things I don't understand. Things that I feel strongly about and yet without acknowledgment and acceptance of my simple daily living of life they mean little. They can easily shadow and distort my today. Today is the only place where I truly live my life. I've learned that rich or poor, young or old, I am where I'm at, and I live my whole life only in today. So... I may as well enjoy it – regardless of its various details. I have found a comfortable and familiar freedom in being able to live in a hopeful today. The measure of my success most often isn't found in quantity, nor outcome, nor even happiness, but in acceptance. If I keep moving in the right direction, even just a little bit, the simple days continue to become an amazing and rewarding journey. The truth of this simple experience allows me continued freedom from the hopelessness of addiction.

# February 3

Compassion—I remember looking it up and reading about it to better understand what it was really about because I felt it was a key for my development of some sort of humility. Humility is an area that I have always struggled with. Compassion is not sympathy or encouragement. It is about an ability to stand with a person who is suffering and share the experience without offering platitudes or advice. It is primarily about being able to share in this suffering, and crucially for myself, to be willing to help alleviate the loneliness and isolation of suffering rather than its cause. The understanding that I can always be compassionate, in all situations, is powerful. My "Mr. Fix-it-all" personality wants to avoid the difficult and uncomfortable empathy of compassion and instead try to repair, change, demonstrate, or manage. I believe that all of nature is a part of God's plan and because of the gift of reason it is perhaps even more especially true of all people. In some way every person I meet is a part of my relationship with God. Having compassion allows me to "see" that all people as have value and that we all suffer in some way as humans. The presence of compassion is vital in my effort to have some humility. Given my past, my daily imperfections and persistently impatient ego, I need a constant reminder that I have no right to judge anyone else or think I'm somehow better or more deserving. Having acceptance of people, and all their glorious faults, allows my life to be much easier and content. I am less disturbed and much more grateful for the way my life is today. It is rewarding to learn that I can help people simply by seeing them in a new way and that a few kind words of shared understanding are often all that is needed to help another person be less alone in their life.

# February 4

The reality of my often excessive sense of self-importance and its ability to ensure I can sustain a state of constant agitation is a simple fact for me. "Don't you know who I am?" or "Are you talking to me?" can easily become my mindset. This cloak of self-righteous indignation and anger is an easy and comfortable one to slip on. It provides a pure and satisfying venting of the chronic lack of humility that keeps me endlessly focused on the faults of others while providing relief from the pain of examining my own faults. It is easy for me to shake my head at this sort of behavior when I see others do it but is rarely so easy to confront when I am its source. Like a petulant child I can mentally stomp my feet and seethe in tantrum—over what? How easily I sometimes let the actions of others control me while I prattle on about my own supposed virtue. The world around me will always have an endless supply of reasons for me to be upset if that is the path I choose. There will always be plenty of people I know who are not "right" in the way I think they should be. One of the questions that annoyed me so much at first—that over time has helped me grow away from a childish obsession with others— was simple but powerful one. Do you want to be right or do you want to be happy? I am happy today by focusing on my own behavior and my own actions in life and by trying to ensure they are in line with what I think is right. That is enough. Today I can avoid worrying about what is right or wrong for others. It is none of my business. Obsession with the flaws of others prevents me from seeing and working on my own.

# February 5

As a man in recovery the question of healthy boundaries in relationships is an important one for me. We all recognize the person who quickly shares too much about their private personal life or is overly concerned with the business of others. Understanding how enmeshment and healthy personal boundaries work has been a very helpful learning process for me. The steps and a sponsor have helped me see things about myself that weren't clear and patterns of behavior that I simply couldn't see. Or if I did see them it was only partially and the true effect they had on my life remained largely hidden. As more was revealed I began to see how impossible it is to have healthy relationships with another until I have one with myself. Of course at first I thought I knew everything about myself and so it was shocking to realize how wrong I was. But until I was willing to become open-minded and do the work I made little progress. An attitude of "that's just the way I am" kept me ill for a long time. The great truth that all addicts/alcoholics are also codependent has meant I need to learn and understand how codependence impacts all my relationships. Until I became familiar and comfortable with solitude I could never get past the bitter loneliness of a self-inflicted excess of sensitivity to how others behave. Through self-discovery and gaining some personal integrity I am able to have appropriate boundaries and in turn have healthy honest relationships with other people. Today, the privacy I enjoy within my own self is a calm peaceful space where I can sit with my Higher Power and enjoy the comfort of having my own valid place in the world. I am relieved of the excessive concern about the opinions of others because I am truly at home with myself.

# February 6

The naivety of thinking I can do life alone almost killed me. The words of the old Simon and Garfunkel song, "I am a rock, I am an Island" come to mind. I think it was about a boxer who was hopelessly beaten, with no chance of winning, who just kept on fighting because it was all he knew. He didn't know when to quit. I can relate! It was tragically sad how the insane alcoholic addict inside of me wanted to idolize and cling to heroic images and ideas that simply weren't true for me (or anyone I knew). The truth for me is that any success I have today is largely based on the efforts of those who have gone before me in recovery, the fellowship of those who are with me in recovery today, and from the help of my close friends. I clearly remember where going it alone got me and it is a place I no longer want any part of. Today it is the attraction of the good life, rather than the fear of the consequences of addiction, that keeps me excited and eager to participate in recovery. Learning to accept that I was eligible and fully qualified for a life free from addiction took more than coming to believe so. It took taking the risk of honestly and fully, yet imperfectly, committing with no reservations to recovery and to God. Only then could I accept the love of recovery enough to participate fully. Understanding something intellectually is never the same as the knowledge and experience I get from doing it. The power of being a part of a group is real and fulfilling. It has taken some time to learn how to be honest, open, and to understand that what sometimes feels like weakness often brings me strength as I become closer to myself through participation in life with others.

# February 7

For me, the understanding of how a relationship with a Higher Power works in my life is a bit like having a garden or the ability to play an instrument—it is perhaps never really complete but hopefully always improves as it grows and changes over time. I've learned that my spiritual focus must be both inward and outward. The ways of the world around me are not the result of my own efforts or my relationship with God. God gives free will to us all and the society that results is one hewn from human choice as much as through divine intervention. It is my thinking that is changed by my relationship with God and in doing so my relationship with the world around me also changes. Slowly building a steady and daily relationship with God has brought me a growing internal peace. It is comfortable. And it allows me to live life in a way that brings me the grace to love and be at peace with myself. Until my own house was in order my relationships with others were always, at least a little bit, warped. And so putting my own spiritual house in order has at last allowed truly healthy relationships with others. The reality of my past becomes less relevant as I see how God works in my present. Today I can relate when I hear some say that they have "...given up all hope of a having better past" and I can be free to have a firm grip on what my role in life is today. By living well on a daily basis I add to my past in positive ways and enable a new future with each new and valuable day. This is very different from how I lived in addiction. I try not to lose sight of how it used to be because it reminds me of how grateful I am to God for who I am today. I see clearly that having an honest, yet often imperfect, relationship with a Higher Power is what has changed my life by guiding my actions, my choices and decisions, and my ability to use my free will in positive and meaningful ways.

# February 8

Accepting that I am imperfect and yet worthy of love was hard for me in early recovery. The addict inside me loved to focus on an epic construction of the complicated and involved story about my guilty actions and the dramatic suffering of the wreckage of my past. The contrast between this elaborate story of my past and an unlikely ideal of some future perfection was a devious way to impede any recovery. It ensured that I would never think myself good enough. When I reframe my thinking about life and other people with the insight that we are all imperfect it enables me to become more realistic about my own defects. Instead of being held back by an unrealistic and convenient misbelief that I must achieve some unattainable goal of absolute perfection I can instead get over myself and begin making small steps of progress in recovery. My addictive thinking loves to frame everything in extremes. The experience of recovery reforms that thinking by helping me correct the self-imposed and false illusion that because of my faults and failings I am somehow unqualified to be a part of life. In recovery I am just an average human doing what I can to live life in a healthy, honest, and yet always imperfect way. My mistakes today are the result of my honest effort to live the good life. And while the echoes of my old addictive thinking sometimes call out to me, I can recognize them for what they are and leave them in the past. I no longer must cling to a false denial about my faults. Instead I can simply try to recognize them, admit them, and move on with a better understanding of how to not repeat them.

# February 9

The process of recovery demands that I make choices about my morals and values. It insists that I be of service to the world around me. Although not doing what I know is wrong is a great starting point, it is not enough. I must also choose to do what I know is right. The human power of choice, our free will, is the result of our ability to reason. Recovery speaks to me about how my out of control selfishness will kill me and that through the gift of reason, "God makes this possible."[1] Sitting on the fence of my morality is a great place to be if I want to remain in, or close to, addiction. The Greek philosopher Pythagoras noted that "The most momentous thing in human life is the art of winning the soul to good or evil" and in step three I chose to align my will with a Higher Power. For many of us, our morals and values largely overlap, but each of us has our own boundaries and limits. Action is what makes my choices more than just thoughts. It brings my thought into life. How I act is the heart of what my life is. It is the only true measure of who I really am today because it involves a connection to something outside of me. Without action my thoughts and ideas remain in my mind and without others they have no basis in reality; which of course is why we are mostly judged by our actions not by our intentions in life. Action is what dispels the fairy tale world of my thinking and creates the reality of my living. I must examine the results of my actions and adjust myself accordingly. Living in recovery gives me the tools, knowledge, support, and most importantly, the vital relationships with others in which my actions become lessons. They allow me to learn the "art" of winning my soul to good.

# February 10

I remember clearly the confusion and hesitation of early recovery. I had deep feelings of failure and inadequacy when, after being sober a while and

---

[1] *Alcoholics Anonymous: The Story of How Many Thousands of Men and Women Have Recovered from Alcoholism.* 4th ed. New York City: Alcoholics Anonymous World Services, 2001. P. 62.

working some steps, I began to understand that what I understood about the recovery was in some ways not very accurate. The realization and full understanding of what was involved wasn't revealed to me until I was well into the process, probably around steps 6 & 7. That unsettling recognition of the full measure of my role in the mess I had made of my life left me shocked, vulnerable, unsure, and at times, quite overwhelmed. The kind leadership and tolerant accepting smiles of those helping me was humbling. Despite my discomfort, I managed to hold onto a quiet calmness and confidence that, as long as I stayed on the path and kept moving in the right direction, it would all be ok. I learned to ignore my disease that would cry out that I was foolish, that it wouldn't work for me, or that I wasn't good enough. It took a long while for me to become comfortable and secure in the understanding that simply being in the process was all that was really required. Today, that remains true. Each day I follow the path of recovery that is front of me as it leads me, often quite slowly, to an increased spiritual growth and insight that confirms I'm moving in the right direction. I still wish that making mistakes wasn't so often the price of learning. My pride still bubbles up and confounds me. However, today it's easier to accept the truth of my imperfections. It is often more important for me to be happy than right. The blinding arrogance and lack of humility that often goes hand in hand with being an addict is still hard for me to avoid, but today I can be aware of it more quickly and thankfully it no longer dominates my life.

# February 11

In recovery I have had to learn healthy ways to handle disagreement with others. Addiction distorted my personality in many ways – both obvious and subtle. The changes often occurred slowly. Gradually they became more obvious as I found myself in increasingly strange situations. As my disease got worse I kept lowering my bottom, my morals and values. The kind of people I was with changed for the worse. In time this gradual erosion left me unrecognizable. I had lost myself and become someone else. The need to service my addiction, as well as the codependent relationships that went with it, eroded my sense of self. Feeling so sick inside at first drove my desire to always look good on my outside and then that too went by the wayside and I didn't care what other people thought. Fearful of losing what I had or needed I often either avoided disagreements and conflict or created them purposefully. I became expert at building resentment while losing pieces of my personality and self-worth. Relationships had to be "all good" or "all bad" with nothing reasonable in between. Recovering from years of such psychological distortion has been slow and often hard at times. Learning to stand up for myself, my values, and what I think is ok, required that I first figure what those things were for me. I had lost them—replaced by the products of my insane thinking. Learning how to have healthy disagreements with people I care about is a part of how I learn who I really am. It causes me to examine my thinking and confirm that what I am saying is what I am really thinking, that what I'm thinking is what I'm really feeling, and that what I'm feeling is what I really believe in. I've learned I must take the process of self-discovery seriously because if I don't take who I am seriously than no one else will. I must remain willing to take the action that goes with being a man who is fully committed to spiritual growth.

# February 12

For me, the question "Am I good enough?" was for most of my life always framed in a comparative way with others. Modern western culture emphasizes a life that is viewed largely through the lens of consumerism and achievement. It promotes a way of measuring my value as a person that tends to be commoditized and valued against external references. In some ways this fueled my addiction. I felt I deserved to work hard and party hard. To take what I could from life at any cost and that cheating was ok if one didn't get caught. It was a framework that said my winning was all that mattered. Pursuing these and various other similar ideas and values, ultimately, didn't end well for me. The program of recovery teaches me that lasting and meaningful contentment is an inside job that cannot be found through material possessions or "achievements." Today I see that having personal integrity must start from within or it is merely hypocrisy. The measure of my honesty begins with a relationship with me and my Higher Power. Only then can I truly find honesty in relationships with others. I must put the horse in front of the cart. Shifting my source of contentment from outside values of consumption (sex, drugs, wealth, status) to inside ones (morals, integrity, honesty, faith) allows me to cease flailing uselessly in an effort to control the world around me and instead be satisfied with my part in it. In addiction I never wanted to go to bed at night, always feeling like I was missing out, that there was more I should be getting. Now I look forward to going to bed because today was good enough. I am no longer, as the AA Big Book says, "restless, irritable, and discontented."[2] This is in part because of my shift in focus from the external to the internal—to the only source of reward that I can directly control—me.

---

[2] ibid. P. xxvii.

# February 13

When I was growing up in Ireland there was a lot of poverty and suffering with many harsh realities that couldn't be avoided and yet most people remained upbeat and hopeful. The old women would have a good attitude and say things like "You are where you're at! And you spend your whole life there—so you may as well enjoy it!" The idea of living in today, and enjoying it despite the circumstances that surround me, is a good one because today is all I really have. I can never go back in time and add more laughter to the days that have passed. I have met many people who are blessed with wealth and security yet some seem unable to enjoy what they have. It is often said that the program of recovery is a simple one—not easy—but simple. The idea of living in the moment, one day at a time, is very powerful but often not so easy for me to accomplish. Like many parts of life, knowledge of what to do is no substitute for doing it. I've often thought, somewhat ironically, that this should be an easy task because during all those years in addiction I was certainly living just for that one day. Of course living in addiction constantly increased the problems that loomed over my life like a dark dread. Each day was really an escape that only partially masked the constant worry and stark fears about my past and future. So it makes sense that in early recovery I would often get stuck obsessing about the past and worrying about the future. Remaining active in recovery allows me to remove the dread and doom of past and future worries. I've learned to enjoy the freedom that living the good life brings me today and I try not to replace it with self-created worries about things I can't control. Today, I am ok with being ok.

# February 14

Nothing skews the meaning of love in quite the same way as Valentine's Day it seems to me. Increasingly I've learned that love is the currency of the relationships that feed my recovery. In the past love was a dangerous word for me. My thoughts, ideas and values around it were ill-formed and sketchy. In places where it was automatic, like friends and family, it became distorted and broken. In romantic relations it was driven by addiction, sex, control, and codependent possession into something tortured and hurtful. The soft vulnerability of any love I once had was beaten, shrunk, and hardened as my addiction became ever more extreme. As I lost all trust in myself trust in others became impossible. There was nowhere left for love to stand in my life. I hated myself—which is perhaps the ultimate sign of the loss of love. If I have no love inside there could be no real love outside.

Recovery began with the restoration of my inside self, integrity of morals and values, and a willingness to hold true to them. Slowly as I began to have trust in myself again, through consistent action that rebuilt self-esteem, I was able to begin to like and respect myself once more. My understanding of the idea and truth of love expanded beyond the childlike notions and beliefs I'd had before. It has opened the door to love in small ways that are simple and easy. Love is not some huge rare event for me today. Like winning the lottery that will change my life forever and make the world always sunny. It is simply the truth I find in living honestly with nature's world and in my relations with those who are sharing today with me. It is available all day to me in the amount I chose to seek it. It validates and confirms my existence as a person in recovery—as another simple human living life simply today in a way that is connected to, and a part of, the world around me.

# February 15

The stark fact of my addiction was that I couldn't figure it out on my own. No matter how badly I wanted to or thought I should, could, or would. Being open minded to new ways of acting and thinking remains important for me today but in the beginning it was crucial in order to get started in actual recovery. I couldn't catch a new life until my hands loosened their grip on my old life and put it down. The right-now and all-or-nothing framework of my life in addiction contrasted absolutely with the slow and steady progress of life in recovery. Finding a safe and helpful way to learn how to be honest with myself, God, and a few close friends was the key to my initial success. Without honesty I could find no true recovery, only a horrible purgatorial place of "half-in half-out" that each day exposed the harsh reality of my own selfishness and fraud. Once I really committed to a truly honest attempt to do recovery fully, and sustained that honesty with no reservations, I became able to remain sober and make progress. I have learned that in my dishonesty with others I was also lying to myself. Dishonesty always cuts both ways and I didn't realize it was preventing my own chance to see the truth about who I really was. Today I have the freedom to improve my understanding of self and what I know to be true. Rather than picking up the nearest convenient answer that I think might work I instead do the work to find my own answer. I don't just tell you what I think you want to hear. I find my own truth today and share it honestly with my close friends and with God. This vital step helps me adjust and confirm the results of my thinking and self-examination. Remaining true to a complete and shared commitment to honesty is the heart and soul of my freedom today.

# February 16

The notion that hatred and fear are inevitably linked is an idea that has taken a long time for me to grasp. In a general sense I've learned how powerful all-consuming emotions are dangerous to my sobriety. It is hard to think of any emotion more powerful or destructive than hatred although fear might be one. In times when I've felt hatred toward someone or something I can also quickly see how I was fearful about some aspect of the situation. I have learned to examine strong negative emotions by asking questions like; what am I afraid of in this situation or how am I threatened? Why do I feel a need to control it? Is the very thing I don't like in someone else a subtle recognition of something in myself? Is it forcing me to confront my part in the situation—a personal failing of some type? Often what I hate in others I also hate about myself, a truth that was hard to see and accept at first. In recovery I remain close to the understanding that just as I can't drink without horrid consequences I also can't indulge in overwhelmingly powerful emotions like hate. There is always space for me to step away from that thinking and I don't have to resolve it in order to take a break from it. Often I find answers in speaking with others. Sometimes, like a dog fighting to hold onto one bone I fail to notice a better bone nearby. Or like a child unable to deal with anger about one situation I redirect it to another. Fear and hatred are rare for me today. If they do arise they often seem centered in my failure to let go of a willful desire to control others or an effort to fight the world around me. When I focus on my own actions and business I can more easily let go of the actions of others. Today I get to choose how I react to life. I am in control of how I feel and how I make choices my life. There is safety in the guidance my Higher Power provides in my life today and I don't have to fear myself, the world, or others.

# February 17

The modern "tough guy" model has never served me well. I've had an enlightenment of sorts in recovery that has taught me how to be more open and kind. Previously my life seemed framed in a kind of battle against the world and against others—a fight to get ahead by "winning." That tough, heroic, and stoic man was a Hollywood creation made for the immature mind of a boy. A mind like mine that was stuck in addiction. My young mind, immersed early into addiction, never grew out of it or saw it for what it was—fiction. The only really tragic and heroic battle I ended up in was with my addiction. It was one that I lost again and again. Childish thinking and methods, I have since learned, don't work well in the real world. Since the time of the ancient Greeks and Romans what is sought and valued in true manhood, are things like virtue, wisdom, temperance, honesty, expression of ones feelings, good deeds, and trustworthiness. My life in addiction had none of these things. My ability to have and hold true to my values and morals was learned in recovery. It has taken real courage to learn who and what I really am, to derive my own answers instead of adopting some trite "answer" of the week" from a movie, a story, the back of a magazine or a stranger at the bar. Those were the sort of values that I swapped out randomly while holding fast to no truth of my own. Being open and vulnerable to exposing my inner self in relationships with others has made me stronger than ever before in my life. The men I most admire today have integrity, compassion, and moral fortitude. They demonstrate a willingness to be open, honest, and vulnerable when they share life with their close friends. These are the relationships that show me how to be a man.

# February 18

The insight, so well expressed by John Lennon, that "All you need is love" has echoed through my lifetime. It is easy for me to think of the generations of people before me who shared a love for each other. Even If I lived alone on a mountain top there would be love; perhaps in my relationship with nature, some of my activities, or the deep meaning I would find in the rare visit of a friend. This reminds me that life's love is always much more than something based solely in the form of a lover, child, parent, or spouse. Love is all around me if I'm open to seeing, feeling, and participating in it. This is an area of profound change for me in recovery. Addiction cut me off from love and instead brought a crushing and empty isolation. I was lost to all honest relationships—especially with myself, and was left with only bitter loneliness and pain. While the connection I feel with the world today is often best expressed in the relationships I have with people who are close to me there is love all around me that I can be a part of. The only thing that blocks me from the love of the world is my own thinking. We all live and we all die but I think love lives forever in our shared human spirit. I am lucky to be a part of life again—freed from the torture of selfishness and addiction. Today I seek honest connections with others because that is where I most often feel the love of my Higher Power. It really is a joy to be alive when I chose to see it that way. Being able to participate in loving relationships with the world around me validates my human experience. In many ways I think of my life as the sum of my relationships with others and I add to the shared value of all life when I participate fully with the love that God has placed all around me.

# February 19

Understanding why I am here in life is a very deep question that is easy for my crazy brain to go nuts over. I know that my life so far has had several stages and some of them seem like completely different lives. Today I'm clearly not the man I was years ago in active addiction. Nor am I the man I was in early recovery or the man I was when raising my children. In review though, my life has always been most content when I had a good reasons for my actions in life – a meaningful purpose that had virtue of some sort. It is easy to look back and see how I lost that sense of personal value and worth when addiction took over. When I had integrity of self how I was living was always enough. When I lost that integrity how I was living was never enough. Today I don't need to solve any great mysteries about the meaning of life or my place in it. Instead I enjoy a simple framework of living life in a general alignment with my Higher Power. Why I chose this approach is extremely clear to me every time I sit in a meeting or talk with another alcoholic. I can also find reminders all day long when I chose to be part of the world around me—on its terms not my own. The simple purpose of being an active and honest part of my own life is an affirmation of why I chose the Good Life today. I remember in my first year of sobriety when my mother was dying. It was a very sad and difficult time but also a source of great contentment and integrity. I was able to get through the "how" of living life because of my faith in the "why" of my living. The pursuit of happiness directly has never provided me much lasting satisfaction. However, the pursuit of being an honest man with integrity has given me deep and lasting pleasure, comfort, and the contentment of internal peace.

# February 20

The role of anger in my life is an interesting, yet painful, subject for review. Perhaps skipping the maturation process from youth to adult because of my early addiction is one reason. Perhaps my experience with addiction itself is another. For whatever reason, my anger and temper was often explosive and all consuming. Some of the consequences of that anger remain with me today, relieved by the daily practice of acceptance and a willingness to seek forgiveness. In the past, unresolved issues of anger seemed to lurk and bubble just under the surface, often emerging suddenly and excessively. For many years it was like that. My relationships with people close to me suffered from my inability to express anger in a healthy way. I would withhold and repress my feelings. They would grow and seethe within me until exploding all at once. In recovery I've learned that pain, fear, anger, and resentment are often all linked together like the layers of an onion. I can never escape the pain of life, but I can learn how to express my fear and anger in a healthy way that prevents it from settling into a resentment that resides inside my mind and soul—poisoning my life. When experiencing anger, I have the choice to do the real work to find a resolution, or instead hold onto it, harbor it, nurture it and suffer it. Learning how to express and discuss my feelings of anger, instead of basking in my own self-inflicted misery, increases my ability to have compassion and empathy for those I am angry with. The process has shown me how suffering is not a valid way of showing I care—it is more of a mysterious form of addiction. It is a great reminder of the truth I know today, that I am a grown up and not a child, and no one else "makes me" feel a certain way. I chose my response to life—no one else does, ever.

# February 21

Doing work today so that I'll be better prepared for tomorrow is a tactic I never warmed up to as a youth. And it certainly wasn't my practice in active addiction. I viewed the hard work of learning, practice, and preparation as a waste of time and something I didn't need to do. I preferred to believe that I could just show up on the day and somehow heroically manage to find a way to "get it done." The irony of how false that idea was (and can still be) strikes to the heart of my selfishness, delusion, desire to control, and false sense of superiority. Being constantly unprepared for life created an endless stream of situations that weren't going well and that I tried to somehow control. I became practiced at trying to control life around me—a frustrating, exhausting, and impossible task. The idea that somehow the rules didn't apply to me made life a constant battle. Honestly accepting the truth of how my life was really going (epic fail) allowed me to have the willingness to work the steps and see how the learning, preparation, practice, and effort I make today is what will benefit me tomorrow. A spiritual awakening arrived only after I prepared a home for it. Learning to take care of only my business each day and doing the next right thing that life brings allows me to become ready to face life on life's terms. Recovery arrives each day at my doorstep. If I am prepared to receive it then there is a chance for learning and growth that I can participate in. I don't get to control exactly where nor how my life will unfold but I can work on being ready for whatever God has coming for me.

# February 22

It is clear that having a Higher Power in my life has dramatically changed my world. The old expression, "When the going gets tough, the tough get going", reminds me that action is required to overcome the fear and restriction—that immobilizing feeling of not being able to go on—that often occurs in difficult times. Life can seem quite hopeless and devastating at times and in addiction those feelings were increasingly present as my disease progressed. It was overwhelming and the only way I seemed able to deal with it was with more alcohol and drugs—a temporary relief that ultimately always made things worse. In recovery these feelings occur less often and are rarely the result of self-inflicted problems. The more I work the program the stronger my connection to God has become. It is easier to see the usually temporary nature and scope of my problems, easier to have hope, and easier to have faith that it will all work out. I have been through many difficult situations and never once has my faith let me down. It may not work out the way I think it will, or want it to, but it always works out. I'm always ok in the end. These past experiences allow and remind me to step back when I'm stuck in the details of a difficult situation and see the big picture—to gain perspective about what is going on and its true importance. That bigger view reduces my problem and helps me to take action. I have friends who know and understand who I am. I have learned to ask for their help—often when I think I don't need or want it. Going through hard times alone rarely works out well for me. My Higher Power is always with me today and like my relationship with friends I must chose to ask for help and then trust both the process and the result.

# February 23

My life became very confused and misdirected during years of active addiction. Twisted relations with others were common and lead to many resentments, insanely overblown obsessions, and often a desire for revenge. The process of recovery offered me insight about the real effect of this sort of thinking and an understanding of how unhealthy and hurtful it was. The integrity, willingness, and humility of step-work helped me reframe my unhealthy thinking and more clearly see my part in the creation of these situations. It is easier for me to let go of these things when I see my own faults more clearly. With all I've done to others—who am I to sit in judgment and angrily demand justice? Do I want to deny my part in these situations while I stew and fight to change the past—or can I move forward? Driving a car each day reminds me that in life the windshield is much bigger than the rear view mirror. I want to move forward and away from a past that I've given up all hope of changing. Self-forgiveness isn't as useful a concept for me anymore because it centers my thinking on and within me—a circular situation that provides no contact with outside reality. My only relief has come from the forgiveness of others and a willingness to seek the same in return. Life is much more content for me when I avoid obsessions that are never ending self-fulfilling cycles of negativity. If I chose that way of thinking there will always be a supply of things I can find to be resentful about—things that fuel feelings of exaggerated insult and twisted revengeful satisfaction. I become truly lost in my own perverse suffering and blocked from recovery. There are an equal number of ways I can find to enjoy healthy thinking that is rewarding and moves me from a dark useless past towards a helpful and useful future. Today I chose brotherly love over bitter angst.

# February 24

We joke at our Saturday morning meeting about the "spiritual donuts." It often reminds me that while there may be spiritual donuts in recovery—there are no magic donuts. While occasionally I have sudden breakthrough realizations that have an immediate and profound effect, more often, the moments of insight are smaller, incremental, and slowly add up to bigger changes in my thinking and behavior. However, they are both almost always centered on some aspect of the process of shifting the locus of control in my life—from the external to the internal and increasing my own understanding of, and capability for, personal honesty. Being honest about my own thinking is a requirement of my conscious contact with my Higher Power. It was never possible for me to have a real relationship with God when I was knowingly dishonest with myself. Personal honesty is what opened the door to a real relationship with God and each day I get a chance to improve my ability to sustain that conscious contact. Like any other healthy relationship in life it takes an ongoing commitment to honesty for it to remain valid. Being overly focused on outside things around me that I want to control precludes me from spiritual growth. Feeding the dog feels good and makes him happy—but it doesn't make me less hungry. I've come to understand that the solution that recovery offers me can reside only within and so that is where the work must take place. The journey of self-discovery, and the resulting insight it provides, always takes place in the efforts of today that help me understand my past and guide my future.

# February 25

When I arrived in recovery my denial about what was really going on in my life was severe and it obscured the truth of my disease. Today, when working with others I rarely spend much time trying to convince them of their powerlessness or the extent of the unmanageability in their lives because the disease itself is always the best convincer. Left untreated, addiction always gets worse—never better. So, over time, pain always becomes the motivation for progress. Recovery starts with the honesty of the first step and I made no sustainable progress until I was able to get honest with others, myself, and my Higher Power. My ability to lie to others and myself was supreme—but I couldn't lie to God. That meant that I either had to have an honest relationship with God—or none at all. The longer I've been in recovery the more I see just how insane I was when I got here. I had no respect for myself, no morals or values I could adhere to, and was unable to see my part in—or accept any real responsibility for—my actions. It was as though I wanted to claim I was possessed or something. That these things "just happened" or "I simply can't control myself" which in time I learned was all complete rubbish. I simply wasn't able to be honest with myself about my lack of willingness to change. There are no "versions" of truth in life, only variations in my ability to recognize it. To this day most of my problems are of my own making and usually stem from a fantastic ability to be in denial or mislead myself. When problems occur am I able to be real about them or do I cloak them because I'd rather avoid the truth? Either way, sooner or later, the truth arrives front and center and I can't avoid it anymore. I've learned that the honesty of my recovery isn't so much about outward "cash register" honesty but instead it is about the much harder journey of inward honesty, the process of discovery around whom and what I am. Am I today the man my Higher Power wants me to be or am I still playing boss?

# February 26

The reminder that the only house I have a duty and responsibility to keep in order is my own seems simple enough. However, my codependent tendency toward enmeshment and poor interpersonal boundaries with others always remains present to some degree or another. The process of recovery enables me to treat my disease and its symptoms. Keeping my own house in order through working the steps teaches me many truths about myself and life around me. Being honest about my own faults teaches me that I have no place, or right—or qualification of any sort—to judge the lives of others. Keeping my own house in order is often more work than I can handle well enough anyway. Until I completed the steps and gained some spiritual awakening as a result I was much more likely to be distracted and consumed by the actions of others. I have learned that on the lake of life I can paddle only my own canoe, everyone else must paddle their own, and their business is not mine. It is still easy for me to drift off into a fantasy about other people's actions and what I think they should be doing. I usually gain nothing but anger, agitation, and irritation for such efforts. Even more absurd is the insanity of my ability to fabricate and obsess about things that aren't real or haven't even happened yet—but I've learned to catch myself and chuckle when I do. The real insight and truth I know is that if I am busy trying to paddle someone else's canoe then there is no one paddling mine. This is a dangerous situation for me because when left without proper direction my life tends to quickly drift off course. The program of recovery has given me much integrity. I am largely whole today. My own house is in order and I stand with healthy boundaries on a spiritual path in life. It is a place that allows me to be of service to others without mistakenly trying to dominate or be in charge of them.

# February 27

The question of "surrender" remains a critical component of my recovery. Perhaps because of its rather dramatic sounding nature and strong connotation of change it appears to offer a sort of reassurance and comfort when claimed. I've learned that surrender is more than simply quitting using and the abandonment of my old ways. It has been partly those things—but equally it is also the taking up of new ways. Surrender means to quit fighting and join the winning team. At first my surrender was more like a sort of prisoner of war scenario. I waved the white flag and was taken into custody but I wasn't willing to fully join the new group. My defiant belief in my own uniqueness kept me sick much longer than I needed to be. It prevented me from becoming "a part of" and I remained victim to that soul crushing spiritual isolation within. It was hard to let go of the thinking and culture created by many years of living in the Hobbesian world of addiction where life is often "nasty, brutish, and short." Surrendering my own selfish self-centeredness and learning how to be of service to others has freed me from the bondage of self. The Big Book of Alcoholics Anonymous talks about how the gift of reason that separates humans from the animals cuts both ways—it will kill me if I let it.[3] Or it can allow me to be an active part of the great miracle of human life by living fully with others. In addiction I chose to

[3] ibid. P. 63.

become more like an animal in order to avoid the pain that is always a part of human life. Concerned only with my own needs and without the support of others I became isolated and weak. I was like a refugee with no place in the world, separated from the community of others that all humans need in life. The program of recovery has allowed me to surrender my life in addiction and rejoin humanity. I realize that despite my imperfect and willful nature there is always a place for me in God's world where I am accepted and "a part of" at last.

# February 28

The program of recovery has opened many new doors for me. My life is much fuller and I participate in more activities, both new and old, that demonstrate to me that I am really living life today. Before, life was living me and it was a constant battle as I fought my way along a narrow and dark canyon of harsh and lonely addiction. Being able to come up and out of that trap of despair and into the real world is exciting and rewarding. It can also be very difficult and painful at times but I understand today that this is a part of the process of life. I don't run and hide from life's difficulties—instead I stand and face them with the help of my Higher Power and other people. The ability to explore my place in the world and to participate in it stems from the self-discovery and strength that recovery has given me. Having honesty, integrity, and faith gives me confidence and purpose and a sense of value and worth that ultimately allows me to accept my eligibility for all that human life offers. Because of my choices today I am no longer cut off by a feeling of not being good enough. My understanding of myself, who I can be, and what my life can become, has grown, changed, and continues to evolve. There will be many more choices in life for me as I continue my own spiritual growth. As an addict I always wanted more of something that could never be attained. Today, the steps continue to show me how to live in a way that brings me more of the wide range of life's possibilities, opportunities and rewards. I no longer fear or feel unworthy of taking my place in life and redeem my eligibility for the options and choices in front of me today.

# February 29

The underlying feeling of not fitting into the world around me was always a backdrop to my addiction and excess. I remember arriving in recovery and hearing people talk about being "comfortable in their own skin" and then wondering what exactly that was all about. It was hard for me to really grasp their meaning because my own discomfort with who I was had always been so pervasive and constant that the idea that there could be an alternative outlook wasn't easy to grasp. I viewed the question in terms of an ability to be less uncomfortable rather than understanding there was another option entirely. For many years I looked for the answers and solution to my life in the excesses of addiction, or in unhealthy relationships with others, rather than looking within. Today I am comfortable with who I am and how I live my life. I can better understand my place in the world, my purpose and meaning as an individual, and am no longer searching in the wrong place for the answers to those questions. By accepting the inevitable nature of human loneliness, that my life will always be framed in the context of my own experience as an individual—and that I must take responsibility for my own brief journey in life—I have at last become able to fully join in life with others. I am no longer trying to share the impossible parts of myself and as a result I am free to share the possible. My doubts and fears, confusion and joy, childish excitements, and comfortable love are all parts of my life with others today. I can enjoy the power of my own humanity and my valuable place in the cycle of life without yielding to fear because I have faith and understanding of my own freedom and its limits.

# March

"Never be afraid to trust an unknown future to a known God."
— Corrie ten Boom

"Faith is not something to grasp, it is a state to grow into."
— Mahatma Gandhi

"Faith is a place of mystery, where we find the courage to believe in what we cannot see and the strength to let go of our fear of uncertainty."
— Brené Brown

# March 1

The expression that "We stand on the shoulders of those gone before us" is something I've heard many times in recovery. There is a great reward in my life today as a result of the opportunity I have to pass along some of what I've learned in recovery. Carrying the message has been very helpful to my own recovery because the experience of working with others ensures that my own understanding of the principles of recovery, and its underlying message of spirituality, continues to grow and deepen. Like many parts of recovery it wasn't easy at first. I had to learn new things and become more open-minded. The vital relationships I have built as part of the recovery process have helped me learn how to be available and helpful while having better boundaries in my relationships. It has helped me learn and examine many truths about myself. It is true that I have been able to recover from a "seemingly hopeless" situation in my life. I can never fully repay the gift that was freely given to me. However, I can do my part to help others, even (or perhaps especially) when I am busy or preoccupied—because often that seems to be when it benefits me the most. Today, nothing helps me more in my life than helping someone else with theirs. Every day I get to be a part of the miracle of recovery in other people's lives and that is a gift—one that I can only keep through a sense of humility and gratitude. This truth is one of the paradoxes of recovery—that I must give it away to keep it. The history of all human nature demands that I participate with others if I want to survive. While addiction lurks comfortably in the modern framework of individualism and self-propulsion the fact will always remain that I need the help of others to avoid it. By helping others I offer myself the chance to overcome my reluctance and fear of asking for the help I need.

# March 2

The challenge of living life on life's terms has many meanings for me today. It directs my thinking toward the possibilities of my life as it is now and not the unchangeable past. Not only can I see the world around me, but I can also see the strengths and weaknesses within me that I bring into each day. Living life on life's terms helps me replace unproductive thoughts about the unfairness in my life with consideration of the opportunities that are available. It demands that I avoid denial or delusion and have clarity about what is real in my life—particularly around my own motives and actions. Ultimately, the viewpoint of life on life's terms replaces my desire to be in charge and reinforces my willingness and acceptance of a Higher Power in that role. While I've given up the idea, or desire, of having a better past I must still deal with its consequences and how my history can still impact the way I chose to live today. I am in charge of how I act and feel—it's my responsibility—and I can't hide from it by indulging in false moral rhetoric, illusion, or diversion. Today, life is not about a search for constant happiness, or my opinion about the unfairness of the past or present, but instead is about integrity and contentment. There is a good life for me to live today, to participate in fully, and the choice is only if, and how, I want to show up for it. Not with conditions or bargains, or only on my terms alone, but as it is presented to me. No matter how I got to where I am today, I am here, and I remain fully eligible for living a good life today.

# March 3

When major events occur in my world, the ones that cause everything to come to a halt and have great impact or change; I am forced to realize my powerlessness in the face of life. Sometimes I am so very intent on trying to get to "my" future that I don't realize I'm using an out of date map. Recovery has taught me to examine my actions and thinking regularly and to be open minded and accepting of change, both around me and inside me, so that I can better understand the course God has for my life. My values, worldview, and other beliefs that are important to my ability to see my path often grow and change slowly. If I take time to listen to the messages in each day I am better able to see the growth. The more I am in tune with myself the better prepared I am for the uncertain and difficult life events that are sure to arrive so that I can learn from them instead of blindly fighting them. In addiction I clung to ideas and thinking that clearly wasn't working but felt I could somehow still make them work—despite all the evidence to the contrary. Learning to be comfortable with not having to know the answer to everything opens an opportunity to understand more about myself and life as it is right now. Today, wisdom isn't a bunch of stuff I've learned, or things I think I already know, instead it is a willingness to say, "I don't know, let's look and see", and to then examine and consider a question in the light of where I am today. This process of learning to look before I leap, of understanding that finding the right action often requires that I first take no action, smooths my progress forward in life. I avoid the shuffle of three steps forward two steps back. I cannot rush my ability to understand God's plan for me nor force its disclosure.

# March 4

Responsibility was a tough word for me from my early teens on. As a youth I was often very irresponsible and as I got older my addiction and selfishness kept me from the growth and maturity of becoming a responsible adult. The best I could manage was a poor and vague sense of responsibility to others and I struggled to connect with my own sense of personal responsibility. I had a childish practice of blaming others for my problems in life and an unrealistic expectation that my own selfish needs should always be met. Recovery has taught me how to have self-respect and be personally responsible for my own choices in life. I must be thoughtful and truly care about my life, my actions, and decisions. If I don't take myself seriously and with respect it is unlikely that anyone else will. I approached life rather like it was a job and I always expected a paycheck—even though I rarely showed up for work! Today I see life as more of a self-service world in which I need to take action. My Higher Power will help guide my action but won't do it for me. Recovery allows me to clearly see how, over time; the small steps of each day become a great distance. In a few quick years I made choices and decisions, guided by a faith in a Higher Power, which radically improved my life and helped me to become much more content. Not all my choices were correct—but many of them were. Today I don't have to be perfect but I must have the courage to act and take responsibility for the results—be they good or bad. I must be willing to accept the risk of an occasional mistake or failure, while taking the action that is the "work" of living life.

# March 5

In active addiction I was beastly. My natural desires and base animal instincts were out of control and excessive. The inability to manage that important balance between the human capacity for reason, judgment and future planning with the desires and drives that are part of my animal nature was a core image of the iconography of my life in addiction. By the time I arrived in recovery any sense of who I was had been shattered as I was confronted with an inability to trust even myself. I was frightened by who I had become and my own seeming indifference and resigned acceptance that this was just how it was. The hopelessness of my situation was brutal. The battle to regain my rational humanness began when I chose to live a sober life and follow the path of recovery. It took a long time to learn how to trust myself again. In early recovery I quickly discovered how powerfully dangerous the emotions that came with sex, anger, resentment and fear could be. It can still be confusing when I deal with parts of life that are more strongly connected to the more natural desires rather than with my thinking brain. However, I have learned that the true success of recovery came for me when I at last became willing to put my heart into it. The true power of my faith and spirituality emerges from the same heartfelt and passionate place in me that my disease did. The ability to access and use my will, my natural human power, in a way that is aligned with God rather than my own selfishness has been one of the great gifts of recovery. I am able to enjoy a lust for life that is authentic and healthy, vibrant and meaningful, and that increases my spiritual connection to others.

# March 6

As a man in recovery, my work at the job of spiritual growth requires that I have the opportunity to learn from the experience of other men. From an early age I felt as though there was a difference, a separation of sorts, between myself and others. That I didn't fit in. I would see others share and bond in ways that I couldn't. I could impress or be funny, strong, compete or be hurtful, but not really connect in a sharing and close way. For much of my youth there was no father figure or older brother and my early family identity role was framed in a confusing and misguided idea of having to take care of my mother and sister. Alcohol solved the problems of isolation, disconnectedness, and confusion. I never really began to learn what it meant to be a man until I became a father and then it was framed in stereotypes like "hard work" or "provider." I still had no real clue about the morals, principles, or values of true manhood in any way that was meaningfully connected to who I really was or my behavior. Recovery has allowed me the time and space to learn how to have honest, open, and vulnerable relationships with other men. I've been able to see what works for others, how it works, and to learn what it is that I value and admire—to deliberately choose what kind of man I want to be today inside and out. I could never have done it alone. I spent quite a while in early recovery being unwilling to open the door to myself with others and as a result made little progress spiritually. When I finally took the risk and did open up it was quickly clear that while it was uncomfortable and difficult I had nothing to fear. Today I continue to benefit and grow spiritually as a result of my close relationships with other men. I have become the close friend I needed to be in order to have close friends. Some of you reading this today are part of this miracle in my life. I'm thankful and grateful to be "a part of" today and no longer so alone in life.

# March 7

For me, there is a strong relationship between fear and faith. My understanding of that relationship often finds daily relevance in my desire to control people, places and things. I've learned to see how my desire to control exists on multiple levels. Sure, there are often outcomes I try to control or make happen but many times I'm not really that concerned about the outcome and yet, because it is so ingrained in me, I still act in a controlling way. It is a part of my nature. It happens without me thinking about it or realizing I'm doing it. It is a stark reminder of my frequent lack of faith and underlying fears. Sometimes the most basic and inconsequential things elicit a desire to control, to make sure it's done right, which of course really means doing it "my" way. Learning to let go and let God work through others means avoiding my desire to correct and direct. It means letting go of my often passive aggressive need to "help" people (do it my way) when "I" determine they need it rather than waiting to see if they ask for help. By controlling people and situations I remove their opportunity to learn their own lessons. I preclude Gods chance to show me new things and I demonstrate my fear and lack of faith. Mostly, it is simply me trying to play God and it usually doesn't work out well for me. The desire to control also cuts me off from hearing life's messages. It consumes and distracts me from living in the moment—especially if the moment is painful, upsetting, or difficult. Learning to be more aware of this has made my daily life much easier. I can 'take it easy" and go with the flow. I can enjoy watching God working in other people's lives as they find their own path without my "help." Letting go is a way for me to spiritually connect more deeply with others from within myself. All I have to do is quiet my mind and mouth, which of course, is often a very difficult task.

# March 8

Learning to have patience and acceptance about my progress in recovery has been hard. My nature is to want things to happen right away and on my time. They say that others notice the changes in us before we do. I've seen this to be true in my journey as well as for others. Often the progress seems small and inconsequential but over time it has added up for me. One day I got a letter that I was on the Dean's list at College. A few years before that the only list I was on was the Judges docket for court! Quickly or slowly, little things or big, the changes occur for me as they do for others who do the work of recovery. However, my faith in this truth is tested when I expect or demand specific results and want them to happen on my time. I've learned that I must do the work and then leave the results up to my Higher Power. This has always been hard for me because it requires faith that what is happening for me today is enough—that I am enough. That despite what problems remain, my progress is enough. Focusing too much on the problems that remain in my life leads me to futility and despair. It blocks me from seeing the real progress that is taking place. Today, the problems that are always present in my life are simply new opportunities for growth. I have seen and experienced the truth of personal growth and the change that living the good life brings me when I am willing to accept and be patient with the progress of my own journey along the way.

# March 9

Who am I really? Who am I pretending to be? Where does the truth of my own understanding rest? In what ways do I show up in the lives of others and how do I cloak myself to create the face I show to the world? The analogy of wearing a mask works well to highlight my search for the truth of myself—of who I really am. From a very early age it became so normal to put on a front. Of trying to shape my outside person to arrive as I thought others wanted. It is part of growing up to some extent of course, but for me, to a greater or lesser degree, it was often a vital survival tool. By the age of normal maturation, the self-discovery period of my teens, my path was redirected by the easy escape of alcohol and an inability to stop looking outward at what I thought I needed to be for others instead of looking inward to see who I really was. I could not stop playing roles, wearing a mask for each moment, because there was nothing behind the mask. Until doing some work to develop and understand who I am and what I stand for all I had behind these roles was an unsure naked emptiness that was afraid of being exposed. The work of the steps in recovery has allowed me to at last "grow up" and initiate the process of learning who I am. Of developing my own beliefs, values, and sense of morality. Today I can stand alone and exposed as myself. At times my old roles still come over me, with predictable results, as I exaggerate, lie and fantasize or pose with bravado, helplessness, self-pity and victimhood. Over time I've been able to shift my reliance away from these old tools and have enough faith in my Higher Power to trust that the real me is always good enough. I understand that when I chose to live with my actions aligned with my values and morals, then God's work is always good enough—and so am I. Today the principles of the recovery guide me each day as I try to do my honest best. That honest attempt, while usually imperfect and faulty to some degree, is always enough for today.

# March 10

The importance of an understanding that as a human being I have value and am entitled to my place in the world is an essential part of my recovery. It places me among others, as a 'part of', instead of isolated, lonely, and apart from. Of course my tendency to take inventory and harshly judge myself and others works against this ideal. It is hard for me to avoid getting caught up in personalities and imperfections. This problem reminds me of the goal of "principles before personalities" that redirects my tendency toward extreme thinking about me and others toward broader questions of morals and values. For many years, being normal or average was like a good coat I refused to wear. I had to be either all or nothing—either I was great or I was awful. Other people also had to be either perfect or they were fatally flawed. This sort of approach to life is a good example of how I was bound by my own distorted thinking. It framed a world I could never be a part of. One of the greatest gifts of recovery is the freedom from the bondage of self that can release me from this kind of unhelpful thinking. Realizing that I am just another man on the journey of my life with nothing exceptionally special about me one way or another—imperfect and flawed as all people are—allows me to see others in a similar light. Within me is the capacity of honesty and faith that I need to direct my own life and my relationship with God, nature, and the world around me. Accepting the truth of my humanity, the simple facts of my species and that I am unavoidably and undeniably a part of the human world today helps me to take my place in it calmly and contentedly.

# March 11

For many years my lack of maturity dominated my thinking in ways that put me at odds with the world. One example was how I would want to be judged by my intentions rather than my actions. It was a great way for me to see myself as being without fault, as having "good intentions', and to avoid responsibility for my actions by claiming, "I didn't mean to do it, it wasn't my fault", or classically, "But you don't understand!" By denying my imperfections and blaming others for them or focusing solely on the faults of others I had a way to divert attention from my own actions and failings. Of course these tactics might work for a while with friends or loved ones but they rarely work for long at work with the boss or in court with the judge. The process of working the steps and being in active recovery holds me accountable for my actions and confronts me with the consequences of my imperfection. In recovery I can grow out of a childish state of blamelessness and take responsibility for my mistakes. I have learned that it is by accepting my failings and the role that they play in my learning experience that I can then begin to make real progress in the area of personal and spiritual growth. I had to get past the idea that mistakes, and their admission, represent some sort of epic failure or life sentence. All people make mistakes and so the question becomes simple enough. Am I willing to learn and grow from them or instead remain destined to repeat them? By demanding and expecting perfection of myself I in some way act as my own God and relieve myself of the duty of taking responsibility for what I really am—an imperfect human. I must remain willing to overcome the false hubris of my own ego in order to engage with the real work that continues the search for truth and progress in my life.

# March 12

Sometimes I see people whose appearance looks like they are stuck in a time warp from the past. It can be pretty funny. Perhaps it's a woman defiantly clinging to an 80's hairstyle or some dude rocking a mullet while driving an old red T-top Camaro. At times my thinking and outlook on life has suffered the same fate. Having the courage to change the things I can and not hold on to old ideas that limit my progress is a message I hear all the time in recovery. It is true for me that it took courage to face the many uncomfortable truths about how I lived in addiction. I often tried to deny or minimize the consequences of my actions. When I sobered up I was faced with the truth about my life in addiction and yet often still mislead myself about much of it. Slowly I took what I felt was a big risk and tried new things. As these small steps begin to work I made progress and gained faith that having courage to seek change would lead me further into a healthy life in recovery. Today my challenges are less extreme, but there remains this constant undercurrent of change and growth that takes place as I paddle along on the lake of life. Some weeks or months are smooth sailing and then change happens and often I must adjust my course or even sometimes my destination. One of the most important things I've learned is that I need only the courage to face today and can let the fear of the future and the pains of the past remain where they are. I can always get through life one day at a time. Sometimes I struggle and regress. I can become frustrated and quit trying for a while but today I'm never stuck in that situation for long. I am able to reach out to friends for help, to find guidance, to pray, and move forward again. This courage to be open to change, to accept and be ok with my constant imperfection, is freeing and exciting.

# March 13

Some days it is all I can do to not regress. The idea of holding the ground I've gained in recovery is useful in several ways. I often say that the best way to move forward is to stop moving backward. Before in life my focus was not just on meeting my needs but exceeding them—and I wanted to do so quickly. The approach of "I want it all, and I want it now" at best always seemed to have a sort of three steps forward two steps back result. The harsh truth was that it became a mostly backward journey as my life in addiction always got worse. Like a desperate gambler I took greater risks trying to regain ground quickly and invariably lost ever more. Today, by focusing on not moving backwards I achieve small steady steps forward that can, most often, be sustained. By focusing on only today my job is easier and I seek quality not quantity. I can pay attention to each day's results without looking too far ahead to some distant prize, goal, or destination. It is when I reach too far that I most often slip. It is by waking up and preparing only for the day ahead that I become ready for what it brings. Sometimes it is grey and rainy and other days it may include a magnificent sunrise. Either way it provides an opportunity to briefly reflect on the progress I have been able to sustain and the distance I have come one day at a time. It reminds me that today I have another chance to take one more step, solid and sure, on my path of living the good life. It has been learning to accept this truth of daily progress that has become my great reward. It is a destination I can reach and enjoy each day—one that gives my life meaning and purpose.

# March 14

The recognition of how I can play the role of caretaker of others in my life links to a paired sense of being the suffering victim—and was a difficult but very important insight for me to grasp and understand. Once I was able to see and accept the message it was very helpful and lifted a huge weight from me. The burden of caretaking others—something I did far too often over the years—put me in a cycle that my inner-addict relished. I tried so hard to create the fictional reality I wanted for myself but when things didn't work out I felt underappreciated and misunderstood. My thinking turned to being the victim as I cradled thoughts like; "I gave up so much" or "I must not be good enough" or "life is SO unfair!" And so then of course I deserved to have my vices—after all I had earned them! Once I understood this pattern of behavior and was able to accept its truth in my life it became clear that it had been distorting my relations with others for years. Learning to no longer play God by trying to control others using a blinded disguise of caring, helping, or saving them—and then later playing victim around the failed results—has been very powerful and changed my life. I have learned the freedom of knowing that only I am responsible for how I chose to feel.

As a healthy grown man no one "makes me" feel a certain way. I am not a victim controlled by a false sense of the power of others or the outside world. Instead I am in charge of my inside world and my own thinking. By learning to have integrity within myself I can allow others close to me. I can allow them to be who they are without it being a reflection on me or some kind of extension of who I am. Today I am in the "sunlight of the spirit" and that simple truth allows me to walk through each day knowing that life, and my place in it, is enough. [4]

# March 15

Today my appreciation and love for life is heartfelt and powerful—a feeling that was absent during my years in addiction when I chased an activity and lifestyle that I knew in my heart was unbalanced and wrong. The idea of allowing my heart to guide me in life didn't sit well with me at first. I had all sorts of belief systems built around thinking the opposite. That my heartfelt feelings should be—if not ignored—then at least not trusted or valued very much. I've learned that the real power in life comes from the heart not the mind. In life when something truly important is going on with another person we have "a heart to heart" about it. We have all talked to someone about knowing things deep in our hearts. When I was a youth I thought I knew what being a man was but instead found only fear and pain that drove me away from my heart's truth and straight into the numbing arms of addiction. I am reminded of a line by the poet Edna St. Vincent De Millay, "Pity me that the heart is slow to learn what the swift mind beholds at every turn." Our passion and drive, our most basic truths, are heartfelt and in addiction my heart was cut off from life and relegated to a malformed place of twisted sex relations and a love of escape through drugs and alcohol. In recovery my heart and its feelings, those oft dreaded feelings, are once again a healthy part of my life. Learning how to slowly allow my heart back into my life has meant learning what it truly means to be a man through both painful and joyful experiences. Without my heart I am trying to find my way in life with a map but no destination. My mind's logic will find a route, but only my heart will show me where I really want to go. Today I believe that a helpful, loving, kind, considerate and thoughtful man cannot exist without a warm and willing heart that helps guide him.

# March 16

[4] ibid. P. 66.

It is amazing and appalling to recall what sort of life my disease led me to and recognize the sad and lonely truth that I allowed it to happen. Things I said I'd never do that became normal. The wretched people and places that became regular haunts. The endless sick routine of the perverted comfort of crushing isolation and unjustifiable self-pity. These were the stages, worsening each time, on my descent into the lost and despairing world of addiction. Yes, I was off track and lost, but the greatest loss was inside me. Who I really am became ever more hidden and overcome, wrapped in layer after layer of mental confusion, irrationality, blind justifications and a numbing loss of self. Years of addiction steadily changed me into someone I have a hard time recognizing when I look back from the world I have today. It all started quite simply, innocently enough, as my mind became clouded— I was duped and the trap was set. As my addiction took over I lost sight of myself and was unable to clearly see how I was being hurt. I couldn't see the real problem inside. And so for years it became ever worse while remaining hidden from me. In recovery, with the acceptance of powerlessness and a sliver of faith, the mental clouds cleared and a new path of self-discovery began. I found an understanding of who I really am. It is a new place I've travelled to inside myself. A place that was perhaps always there but I was unable to find before or during addiction. The core values of being a part of humanity, the ethics and morals of participating in honest, loving, and trusting relationships are things that result from finding my own human self that was lost deep inside, hidden and largely unknown. Learning to trust enough to open myself up and no longer hide who I am has freed me from the bondage of self. I have found the truth of who I am in its reflection in the others with whom I share my life.

# March 17

Being able to admit my own humanness has opened the door to being able to like myself and others through learning how to be accepting and forgiving about my own imperfections and flaws—the good, bad, fun and annoying parts of who I am. It has allowed me to be a friend to myself and others. My old thinking in addiction meant I was alone behind that unnamable wall of separation—alone with myself and crazy ideals of being so great and so awful. I was smug, arrogant and condescending righteous one day yet lost in despair, confusion, self-pity and worthlessness the next. Ultimately, I was a fraud and if anyone got close enough they would see it. A friend was simply someone I was able to take advantage of regularly. The grand illusions about who I was and what I stood for, and the delusions about my own beliefs, rarely withstood any serious scrutiny. The reality and consequences of my addiction proved that. The realization that I didn't have the skills or experience required for a true friendship was daunting. Slowly, through working the steps with my sponsor I learned how to be a friend to myself as well as to others. It began with a commitment to honesty and the willingness to be open-minded about my own faults and failings. I learned to be ok with changing my thinking and beliefs as I became less concerned about the need to cling to being "right" and instead cautiously tried new approaches. The results have been surprising and vastly greater than I ever imagined they could be. Coming to understand that the gift of friendship is its own reward allows me to share and participate fully in the wonderful humanness of life. While I remain imperfect and flawed today, I share in life's rich range of highs and lows with others through and in friendships. They aren't always easy—but they are real. That wall of isolation and those moments of crushing despair and loneliness are gone and instead the weight and joy of my life is shared with others through honest friendships that began only when I opened myself to them.

# March 18

Watching a lovely sunrise this morning reminds me of the singular urgency of living well today. I've slowly learned that the lessons of my past arrive in the toolbox of today only when I am willing to not only see my mistakes but then accept them by letting them go. It is this truth that released me from my self-indulgent pity party and pursuit of the myth of self-forgiveness. Oftentimes, regrets from my past can be like self-directed resentments that allow the past to disturb, define, and distort my present— enabling me to easily repeat them. And if I'm repeating them I surely have not learned from them. The only thing that hurts more than the painful insight of first learning to understand the consequences of my defects is to then knowingly repeat them. Accepting and learning from my past allows me to convert those negative experiences into usefulness in the chance to be of help to others. Rather than bemoan how long it took me to learn some of these things I instead turn to working at finding the willingness to rid myself of defective ideas and thinking—the ones that cause disturbances around and within me. One of the rewards I've found in recovery is the ability to see undeniable positive change and spiritual growth in my life. I've learned that "spiritual" isn't necessarily always about God; it also relates to the energy and vitality of my own actions through being spiritually awake in each day. Today, melancholy and sadness is not a lifestyle choice. It is an occasional period of useful reflection and a path toward perspective. The darkness and doom of addiction has been replaced by an acceptance of my past that enables the bright light of my participation in recovery today.

# March 19

For me, the challenge of having a spiritual experience lay in the acceptance of my powerlessness and disengaging from the arrogance and cynicism of my "know it all" worldview. Making available the few minutes of time to pray and meditate every morning were the first halting steps on a wonderful and rewarding path of personal growth. It has literally changed my life. There are simple facts and truths about life I always wanted to postpone looking at—to avoid and deny a need to come to terms with. Just as facing my own mortality is ultimately unavoidable, dealing with the truth of it seems best done sooner rather than later lest I suddenly feel cheated and deceived at the end while lamenting the wasted valueless days of a life unfulfilled. Each day is a slice of my time, and it is the only time that is mine to use because the past and future yield only memory and fancy. Today is the only true home of the action of my life. Finding the quiet moments within each day to connect with my place in the spirituality of humanity, to briefly join in my powerlessness with God or Mother Nature, is what opens me to a participation in all of human life. The irony is perhaps that only by stopping and sitting quietly in today can I truly make any valuable connection with yesterday and tomorrow. So each day I make time to open my heart to the spirit of life. Over time it has shown me a lifeworld which was once hard to see or feel a part of. It is now all around me, always present and available, and I am a part of it as it is a part of me.

# March 20

The renewal that abounds in springtime reminds me of hope and faith. The world I've found in recovery has been full of examples of letting go of old ideas while preparing the soil of my soul for news ones that I don't fully understand. Of remaining vulnerable while fragile beginnings slowly emerge. Often they are unsure and unsteady and yet still exciting and full of promise. I will see new growth forming but I'm not sure of its ultimate shape or color or if it's a flower or a weed. Some of the lessons of new growth will last for my life time while others bring only brief brightness. And some, for whatever reason, are cast aside. Such is the nature of my progress. My personal and spiritual growth mimics this natural world around me as the hope I discovered in recovery springs eternal. The freedom of gratitude, choice, and open-mindedness allows me to participate in new growth all the time. Of course in order to grasp the benefit of a new life I had to first empty my hands of the old life that I clung to so desperately. At times it has been painful and frustrating work to till the hard ground of my mind, heart, and soul into the fertile soil into which I can plant the new ideas of who and what kind of man I am becoming. My courage to be vulnerable and hopeful is increased when I connect with the truth of regeneration that I see all around me. The specific color and shape of my future remains unknown but the harvest of the cycle of growth is always available to me when I am willing to participate in the good life of my Higher Powers will for me.

# March 21

At times it is bewildering to look back at where my life was when I arrived in recovery. The memory would be hard to believe if I didn't remember so clearly what it was like living that way. Each morning I thank my Higher Power for where I am today. A place that is so far removed from the insanity of active addiction. It is a relief that I am truly grateful for. In the morning as I make my bed, I remind myself that the most critical measure of a successful day is if I make it back to bed sober. The daily recognition and acceptance of the stark truth of where I have been reminds me to enjoy the freedom of today. In the big picture of life I have few worries of any real merit. I can take it easy and enjoy a simple life. Oh how I scoffed at that idea when I arrived. My world then was defined by the fight and struggle of years of insanity and like an animal suddenly released from captivity I didn't know how to live any other way. It took me quite a while to be able to relax and take it easy. It was hard to let go of the emotional charge, the racing highs and lows, the dramatic self-congratulation of another day of pathetic survival or the bitter and self-deprecating anguish of my suffering. This was the TV show of my life of struggle and I lived it all day every day. In recovery I've slowly learned the skillful art of living a new kind of show that takes more than a few drinks to make happen. It has been like learning a trade or a profession, a retooling of my entire approach to life, one that at its core says—enjoy today! Be the man your Higher Power wants you to be today—imperfect yet alive! Instead of the old fantasy world of an imagined life of fulfillment, meaning, and purpose today's life is real. I've learned that I can't make it happen or force it to occur. It happens as a result of the other work I do that keeps my side of street clean and my life on track. All I have to do is remain in the "sunlight of the spirit" and relax.[5] Today, I've learned to enjoy life as it comes to me.

---

[5] ibid. P. 66.

# March 22

There is a comfort and security that comes from truly being a part of a group with other men in recovery. In addition to the comradeship of a common fight for survival and its shared mission of recovery there is also true friendship and love that is valuable and vital. It creates a space in which I can work through the confusion and painful truths that the newfound honesty of recovery brings. Many times we will sit down, talk and listen as we share our experiences and speak our plain truths about the simple facts of what has happened or what we see in a situation or idea. This work is what enables the often painful personal and moral growth that is the part of a spiritual awakening that I cannot find alone. Honesty remains the foundational base upon which my entire program sits. It is the enabling platform that the willingness to do the work of recovery must rest upon. Without self-honesty my efforts fail to add up or build into anything meaningful. In early recovery I was unable to really understand or grasp this fundamental truth. Later, when I did understand it I wasn't really willing enough to honestly attempt it. I could see the path, and the results it brought for others, but remained unwilling to fully commit to it. Actually walking along the same path that others have taken is the action that brought me results that I can sustain and build upon. Just as it had worked for so many before, and others who arrived since, it has also worked for me. Once I honestly went to work at the full time job of recovery, then and only then, did my Higher Power start opening the door to a truly new life. So today I remain at work in my friendships with others who help me face the hard truths about myself. They guide me through the confusion and fear that I cannot get through alone.

# March 23

My sex relations were a great example of how addiction skewed, confused, and distorted my thinking and behavior. Things like love, friendship, lust, sex, intimacy and trust were all jumbled up together and not working very well. For me addiction and sex were closely linked and tied together in a swirl of codependency and fantasy. My ability to love in a healthy way was crippled, but my desires and insane relationships continued. Sex was simply a part of the soundtrack of my addiction. It has been one of the most difficult things to sort out in recovery because it was messed up from such an early age. Like so many other areas of normal maturation that I missed as a youth I never learned the skills needed for real intimacy. Sex was a powerful force that I confused with being a source of the intimacy that I craved so much without realizing that sex alone can never provide true intimacy—it is instead perhaps most often an expression of true intimacy. I confused sex with things like love, a relationship, or safety. I made it more than it was at the same time as treating it for less than it was. It became a source of conquest, resentment, shame, frustration, and at times inadequacy. It could be a weapon or a tool, a pleasure, punishment, or cure and sometimes all of these things at once. Trying to sort out all these things in the fog of addiction was impossible and like everything else in addiction it always got worse never better. It took a long period of sobriety and a lot of work in other parts of my life before I was able to make real progress in the very complicated and emotional area of relationships, love and sex. Like a beginning artist, I had to learn to paint the more basic pictures before tackling the hardest masterpiece of God's world in life. For me, It has taken time, practice, and much hard work to learn that the joy and pleasure of loving, caring, and meaningful sex only occurs as a result of building an honest and healthy relationship that is intimate in others ways first.

# March 24

It is interesting for me to think about how the practical no nonsense side of me interacts with my more artistic and sensitive side. The clichéd ideas of manliness; of being strong, tough, hard, self-reliant, efficient, and always with purpose seem to conflict with other attributes like being sensitive and having feelings, being artistic, caring, understanding or nurturing. It is fair to say that in my years of active addiction I wasn't a very kind and sensitive person. I avoided my feelings at all costs. So when at first I thought about this I focused on the idea of being open to participating in a wider range of manhood. I have always had a tendency to undervalue things I don't fully appreciate or understand and I certainly was never keen to spend time at a poetry reading in a café when I could be at the bar instead. Today I realize it is more than just "ok" for me to have some of these other traits. In fact these are capacities in me that I simply haven't explored or developed. So, I began to see which of these traits from both the thinking and feeling sides that I value. Which ones do I want to have? It was doing work like this that helped me understand how to have and hold values in my life. I learned that today I must take myself seriously enough to find out what my values really are and drop the basket of half-baked random ideas and values that I used when they suited me. I can't be everything to everyone and when I tried I ended up being nothing to myself. Today my values are current and based on my beliefs not the clichés of others or something I heard once that sounded good. Today my balance in life is found in the careful and ongoing selection of what is important to me and not the "balancing act" of trying to meet someone else's vision of life. The nature of being a man resides in my ability to reason with both sides of my brain. In my heart and soul I know my God wants me to live fully and use them both.

# March 25

I have found an entirely new type of freedom as a result of the ongoing self-discovery of my work in recovery. It has brought me an increased understanding and insight of who I am and what I stand for in life. It has given me self-assurance—a comfortable sense of knowing myself. When I speak and live my beliefs honestly there is a simple truth and acceptance about how it feels. Staking claim and taking true ownership of my beliefs as a man has given me relief from the need to please and satisfy the opinions of others in the world. No longer am I trying to make the whole world like me, fearful that if even one person does not then there is either something wrong with me or them. This process self-examination helped me learn to be ok with being me, who I really am today and what kind of man I want to be tomorrow. It enabled me to begin to change and grow toward that goal. I am less fearful of life because I can see in a general way what my Higher Power wants from me and how to do it. Today, I am never perfect but usually I am good enough. I have clarity of purpose and my relations with others have boundaries that I know and like. The opinions of most others no longer hold sway over me—I can hear them and not have to agree, disagree, correct or mimic them. As a result of being able to have truly honest relationships I have some close friends whose opinions I seek and value. Today there are people who may not like me and that is ok because today I respect myself and it shows in my actions. I am comfortable in whom I am today and yet remain open to the change and growth of tomorrow.

# March 26

I am often reminded of the quote, "The only real freedom a human being can ever know is doing what you ought to do because you want to do it."[6] For a long time I disliked hearing this because I wasn't ready to want it—for or from myself. I was used to a pattern of defiance and opposition to what others told me. Another saying that rankled me was, "To thy own self be

---

[6] ibid. P. 554.

true." Being in recovery meant I wasn't able to lie to myself anymore. The wonderful veil of denial about my addiction had been pierced by early recovery and I was caught in a sort of no man's land; half in and half out. Slowly I realized that while the judge surely wanted me to behave a certain way—and was willing to force me to do it—the people in recovery were simply saying, "Hey, this is what works for us." They hoped I would "get it" but it was ok if I didn't. They didn't need me and weren't interested in forcing me into anything. Over time I've slowly learned how to be true to myself and what it means for me to want to do what I ought to do. It is an insight that is based on the relationship with my Higher Power. Rather than seeing it as something I am forced to be in compliance with I now see it as a gift. It is a liberating feeling to be free from the bondage of addiction and the constant struggle with others that came with it. Now that my will is properly aligned I can use my own judgment about how I live my life in a way that keeps my natural desires in balance. I am no longer oppressed by the opinions of others and am relieved from my own undeniable failings as I tried to figure out what "I" should do. My relationship with a Higher Power offers me a "life compass" and I know how to use it. I am free to at last really enjoy simply being me.

# March 27

The old saying that it is better to have loved and lost than to never have loved at all may always be a tough pill to swallow when dealing with the cutting pain of lost love. Sometimes it is the simplest facts, the stark undeniable truths of life, that I struggle the most with seeing and accepting. These lessons have been the milepost markers of my own maturation and growth in recovery. I have learned that having love in life is so much more than what my experience in addiction had usually been—an unhealthy framework of a love affair that wasn't based on complete honesty, respect, and faithfulness. One evening while having dinner with friends I reflected on it being the anniversary of my mother's death. She may be gone from this world but her love remains. It was present in the love I felt from the men around the dinner table. It reminds me of the truth I have found in recovery that life is love and to shut myself out from it is simply the old selfish behavior of addiction. The love that is life is inescapable and unavoidable. Even in my darkest days of the crushing isolation of addiction, when my love instinct was hijacked by the disease, I was unable to keep the idea and presence of real love out. Others loved and cared about me more than I did. However, it has taken living in recovery to learn how to retrieve it. My old thinking framed love as some heroic ideal found only in a single relationship. My experience has been that the ability to successfully love others first required me to accept love in all parts of my life—especially, and most importantly, for myself. Addiction was the master that taught me how to ignore, forget, and ultimately lose my love of self. Today it is so different. I try to be open to love in all parts of life and be mature and honest with myself, accepting the lesson that love in life is never permanently linked to only one experience. That it is like the air that is always there for me to breathe. That like life itself, it comes, it exists, and then it is over. Acceptance about my inability to control life comes in many forms. Growth in recovery shows me how to be a part of the love of life—on life's terms not mine. I spent way too much time on the sidelines of my life afraid to risk the vulnerability of honestly exposing my love. Today my life is messy, alive, and open to love.

# March 28

It is hard for me to overstate the importance of self-care in my recovery. Learning to take care of myself has been more complicated than I thought it would be. Notions of being healthy, eating well and exercising are simple ideas but the emotional, spiritual, and social parts of self-care have been more difficult. In recovery I became more settled in life and yet I was still very hard on myself. As I learned more about being kind and caring to others I realized how badly I punished and thought about myself. In working on this I asked myself a simple question. Am I willing to treat myself like I would another person who I was trying to help? It was obvious that I needed to make some serious changes in how I viewed and treated myself. At times I was my own worst enemy. I realized I had many stories, untruths, old ideas, and patterns of thinking that weren't healthy or based in reality. It was a self-defeating fantasy that was part of the script of my addictive behavior and life. As the saying in recovery goes, "bring the body and the mind will follow" and my mind was lagging behind. Acceptance of my own imperfections and failings began with being kind and gentle to me so I could start healing emotionally. I learned I could only find peace and forgiveness through open honest relations with others. That self-forgiveness can never be found alone—only through gently and carefully sharing myself with others. I some ways had stopped using physically but not mentally. My spiritual healing and growth began once I stopped constantly stomping it out with my own old thinking. It was just as hard, perhaps harder, to quit my stinking thinking as it was to quit drinking. I learned that these old ideas and beliefs were mostly just sideways ego and puffery anyway, always extreme and inflated. God forbid I should just be a normal regular guy instead of someone "special and unique." Then I might have to be ok with life and let go of my suffering and self-abuse. Today I am ok with being ok. I am not so special or unique. I am just another middle aged guy trying to muddle along through life and stay out of my own way. I'm willing to give myself a helping hand instead of pointing a finger and yelling at the mirror of my mind.

# March 29

The junction of three distinct elemental forces—the reasoning side of my mind, the powerful instinctual desires of my animal man, and the guiding hand of my Higher Power (my conscience)—was the site of a long and nasty conflict during my years in addiction. Sobriety and recovery brought a sort of uneasy truce that was full of argument, dissent, rancor, and angry frustration between these three areas of my thinking. At times I felt like I was crazy with some sort of split-personality disorder. It took time and some long drawn out and painful battles before things settled down. All three elements are perfectly capable of a well-balanced coexistence and finding that balance was a sign of a healthy maturity that had eluded me for years. It took me a long while to grow up and not be so childishly driven by my petulant instincts or whatever great idea arrived at any particular moment. Just because I want something doesn't mean I should have it or that I need it or that it must all happen right now. Discovery of my underlying morals and values and then learning to live by them is hard work that provides a stability of identity that acts as an anchor against my impulsiveness. It is a tether in difficult and confusing times. Today, by comparison, life is fairly easy sailing. I am able to allow the three parts to work together and enrich my daily life. There are still some honest mistakes and occasional "border disputes" but these events usually provide good lessons and opportunities for growth. There is no substitute for experience in life, but today's life experiences have become valuable learning tools rather than a source of self-destruction. The feeling of being able to trust my emotions and follow my instincts is so wonderfully freeing and exciting. I can live life without fear and express myself in a healthy way. Understanding who I am today allows me to engage with the hopes, dreams, ideas, fears and aspirations of tomorrow without them overpowering me.

# March 30

In early recovery I used to joke that, yes, I still had a heart, and that it was like a hard little dried up raisin that rattled inside an old rusty Altoid can in my chest. Years of living in the harsh reality of addiction had sapped my joy for life and desensitized me to just how insane and painful my daily living really was. For many months recovery was very difficult as I sat confronted by the truth of what I had become. But I did see that there was hope. I saw that like many others around me I too could recover. The promise of being "happy, joyous and free" seemed laughably for off and not very likely for a guy like me—a guy with my kind of problems. When I look back now I can clearly see the truth of the statement that, "The mind that got you here is not the mind that will fix you." In time, by trusting the process and by doing the work, my mind changed as I continued to stay sober physically, mentally, and emotionally. I realize today that not one of the many claims and promises I heard and doubted in the beginning has been unavailable to me. It has simply been a matter of having the faith, patience, and courage to stay the course and do the work. Some things came quickly and others slowly but enough has happened for me so far that I no longer have doubts about the process. My heart has grown healthy again and the rusty old Altoid can is long gone. My life is not all rainbows and skittles but I am content. I am generally very happy today—especially when compared to how I was when I arrived in recovery. I am free from addiction and my selfish insanity. I regularly experience joy directly in my own life and indirectly as I share my life with others. Just as I saw that others had recovered so too have I. The parts of me that I thought were lost forever have returned along with new growth and understandings. However, it took a truly honest effort on my part, and the help of many others, to find my inner self again. I learned that it was never really lost—I was. When I unblocked my path, like survivor rescued from a disaster, I climbed eagerly out into the "sunlight of the spirit."[7]

# March 31

It has been difficult for me to learn how to share with other people what is really going on inside rather than simply just talking about myself. The expression, "I'm not much, but I'm all I think about" plays into the challenge of learning to share my feelings and experiences deeply versus just talking about myself. The mental confusion of active addiction isolated my thinking and cut me off from the healing process of connecting deeply with others. Sharing about my actual experiences and results in life, the good, bad, beautiful and ugly, the incomplete, confusing and unclear outcomes, and the process of how they occurred, creates personal authenticity and a helpful healing connection with others. Simply talking about myself isn't as useful and has little value. It often has an opposite effect with others. I can feel and see the difference if I pay attention to how others respond and engage

[7] ibid. P. 66.

with me. The real benefit of recovery resides not in the "drunkalog" of my story but in sharing the particulars of the lessons of change and growth that occur for me over time. Having close honest relationships with others brings me into the "we" of life. It is in this space that a real interpersonal value is created by the sharing of my actual life events and experiences, my doubts, fears, and hopes, not my opinions and postulations. This is a long way from the "one-upping" storytelling and ego driven bravado of the "don't let anyone in because I'm a tough guy," world of male addiction that precluded any sharing of my inner doubts or fears. In addiction I couldn't share these things because they were too hard to look at. My denial refused to allow me. Today I can have the courage to be open and honest with myself and others. I can share what I find and doing so makes my life much easier, richer, fuller, and more meaningful.

# April

"It takes courage to grow up and become who you really are."
— E.E. Cummings

"Confront the dark parts of yourself, and work to banish them with illumination and forgiveness. Your willingness to wrestle with your demons will cause your angels to sing."
— August Wilson

"Courage doesn't always roar. Sometimes courage is the little voice at the end of the day that says I'll try again tomorrow."
— Mary Anne Radmacher

# April 1

Recovery is a process that occurs one day at a time. A single day is the unit of measure we focus on. And so I often think about the notion of living in the moments of today and what that means. Am I fully experiencing life through opening myself to the way it brings the day to me rather than trying to force my day upon it? This thinking links up to another idea I have learned to be more aware of in recovery—the question of how I show up in the lives of others. During the day am I thinking about how I affect others? How would I be able to know? Am I fooling myself by not paying attention closely to the response of others? Am I willing to hear and accept that their truth is real for them? Often I have lived life understanding myself based only on my intentions rather than the actual results of my actions. Today I get to choose how I act in life and in order to do so I must pay attention to my part in it—to the reality of how I show up in the lives of others—as well as my reaction to the world of today that is taking place around me. It is the only way I can begin to find the truth of seeing if I actually am the man I like to think I am. In addiction my thinking was full of illusion, delusion, confusion and denial. The truth of reality was hard to find. In recovery, I've learned that truth and reality is only found by sharing my thoughts, ideas, and experiences with others. When I live in the mindfulness of the moment I can allow myself the time to observe and participate more fully in the shared reality of life—the reality that exists outside of my own thinking. It allows me to see who I am and how my action of living fits into the world around me. What things within me am I bringing to the world and how can I be a part of rather than apart from? The truth of my life isn't confirmed in the isolation of my unshared and untested thinking—it is found in the review of who I am as seen through the eye of the world around me.

# April 2

Learning to be receptive and open to spirituality was a non-trivial task for me. It was impossible to just decide that, starting today, I will be a spiritual person—although I did try such an approach more than once. The change in my own personal spirituality, my connection with God and the universe, occurred as a result of other actions. Similar to losing weight or having more empathy and compassion, it occurs when I do certain other things. Rather like what Victor Frankl said about happiness, "it cannot be pursued, it must ensue,"[8] so it is with my connection to a spiritual life. What I've learned is that I am the only one who can close myself off from the world around me. The crushing isolation of addiction shut me off completely from any meaningful connection to the world around me. That was clear. Understanding the more subtle ways I prevent progress in recovery has been harder. The world of "me"—my problems, my suffering and injustices, my fears and worries and my anger or resentment—all at times block me from the spirituality of life. Today I am open to receiving what is right in front of me. The friendship of others, the natural world, the history of mankind that I am a part of and a child's curious smile are all some of the many ways I can connect with life. They are opportunities that if I'm willing to participate with result in a genuine feeling of spirituality and connection that is so much bigger than my own little world. In order to connect with the world that is around me I must remain open to it. I must live with my eyes and heart open, facing the world, and be ready to connect with it.

# April 3

The ideas of hope, faith, and trust are closely linked for me. When situations in life are not going well there are often people or events, things I can learn or see, that will give me hope. The challenge is being able to sustain that hope once I've found it. In recovery I quickly saw that the program had worked for other people like me who had also been caught in the trap of addiction. After a while I started to believe that I too could recover. I began to dabble with recovery and wasn't very successful. I struggled with problems of honesty and trust and was confused and disheartened. I was afraid of failing and of not being good enough. I questioned if a Higher Power would work for me—if I was truly eligible—and so I wouldn't fully and honestly commit myself to one. Truly beginning the process of recovery required that I trust a Higher Power. Faith has provided the ability to sustain that trust and to keep it alive and stay true to it even when things aren't going well. At times when I feel unconvinced and perhaps don't fully believe, faith enables me to continue forward in spite of what may be happening. At first my faith was frail but over time I was given examples, real experiences in my own life which showed that when I weathered the storm of today I would return again to the calm sunshine of tomorrow. Again and again I have been shown, clearly and memorably, that when I stay the course and hold fast to my morals and values God takes care of me. These examples have strengthened my faith. They have shown me the truth of my eligibility and place in life and that I am good enough, imperfect yet worthy, to be a part of the love of others. Today I know and

---

8 *Frankl, Viktor E. Man's Search for Meaning. Boston: Beacon Press, 2006. P. 162.*

trust that one of the things that ensure my participation in a full life is faith in the validity of hope.

# April 4

Today I am a part of a life that recognizes the presence of spirituality, of a Higher Power that is present not only in my life but also in the world around me. I can see its connection to us all and observe its power expressed in both the physical and thinking world through people, animals, and nature. I can see people who are closed off from it, lonely, angry, defeated and despairing. I can also see people who don't have much to cheer about in their lives who are peaceful and content. People who, despite their struggles, enjoy life because they have accessed something that can never be taken away—their choice to find and participate in the spiritual side of life. The common existence of some sort of spiritual experience as a core element of humankind is rarely disputed. Always it seems, throughout time, humans have sought and found it. Truth is always a social construct of consensus, a feature of language trying to name something. Spirituality has many names, ideas, and beliefs attached to it that people use to describe their participation with it. My own understanding continues to grow and change, but it is always centered in the notion that I am a human who is no longer a slave to addiction and shut out from living a human life. Just as I don't have to know how to cook to enjoy a great meal, I don't have to fully understand the mysteries of life to be able to enjoy and participate in them. My life in recovery increasingly shows me that each day is a reflection of what I bring into it. If I bring anger, I find anger. If I bring love, I find love. Like a radio I must be turned on and tuned in to the station I want to hear in life. I am of course also affected by what others bring into the world around me and navigating these connections is at the heart of my human experience. By accepting my humanity I open the door to participation in the spiritual side of my daily life.

# April 5

In recovery much of my progress has centered on the ability to deal with feelings and emotions. Learning about anger has been one of the most profoundly difficult and yet ultimately rewarding tasks. I have had to educate myself about the underlying sources of my anger and the subtle ways it shows itself in my daily life. For many years I would quickly get extremely angry and wonder why it was so sudden and strong. Sometimes it was because I'd been keeping something pent up inside until it exploded. Understanding how my unresolved anger affects my daily life in small ways that shape who I am and how I relate with others has been helpful. In my relationships with others I did a poor job of understanding the true sources of my anger. Rather than expressing it and finding resolution I would endure it like a bitter grudge. I would use it as a reason to justify my own selfish actions. While it is easy to express anger at a stranger when driving in traffic, for many years I held onto a lot of unexpressed anger that was directed inward and like a failing toxic waste dump it leaked out affecting others around me. Unexpressed pain, fear, and anger that breed resentment are a key focus of the work of recovery. Resolving anger in a healthy way through examination and expression helps me understand it properly and address the root causes. Often I can find patterns of behavior, old habits and ideas that create situations or circumstances that validate my existing anger and fuel my passive aggressive actions. Ultimately for me today, like most strong emotions in my life, the most important part of dealing with anger is talking to a trusted friend about what is going on. It is easy to talk about anger in terms of the external, what the "other" person or situation did "to" me, but the real value and growth comes in discussing my part and what action I should take to express and resolve it. My goal is to get rid of anger rather than feed and sustain it, dutifully suffer it, or suppress and use it as a justification. I must continue to improve my ability to let go of anger in order to remain spiritually content and peaceful.

# April 6

One of the most interesting and difficult yet fun and rewarding parts of recovery has been the process of self-discovery. It is largely a result of the steps and a continued commitment to increasing my conscious contact with a Higher Power. When I first started in recovery the simple goals of sobriety and some relief from the consequences of addiction was about all my mind could grasp. After being sober a while and doing some step work I began to see and accept that who I believed I was could change. That in fact it already was changing. The lessons about letting go of old ideas and accepting new ways of thinking were becoming less directed to my view of the world around me and more about the person within me. It was daunting, even a bit scary, to be willing to change. It has taken some time to fully grasp the big picture of what truly occurs for me and others as a result of doing the work of recovery. It is truly a miracle and at the heart of it the most rewarding and calming thing of all is the self-discovery of what it means to be comfortable with an understanding of what kind of man my Higher Power wants me to be. The "Promises" that I hear read so often in meetings are signposts on the journey to the truth of my own personal growth and discovery.[9] They mark a cycle of points on a path that guides me in a direction rather than a specific destination. Overcoming my fear of not being good enough—and the hubris of the stories and beliefs that I created to hide that fear—was a vital beginning that opened the door to begin my journey. The raw material of the solution I need has always been within me and my connection to God helps me find it. I continue to search for it each day, as best I can, in order to sustain my recovery. I still don't know exactly where I'm going but I am happy with my journey. The experience of how my life has improved provides me a faith that always carries me forward when I chose to rely upon it.

# April 7

The experience of being able to effectively deal with the problems I face in life rather than run from them is one of the hallmarks of recovery. In addiction, life seemed to be a constant battle of some sort or another that usually seemed epic and unfair by my skewed thinking. These frequently self-inflicted problems were framed as a fantastic struggle that I needed to overcome. My solutions usually involved a quick or tricky "fix" along with the ever present "help" of alcohol or drugs. After managing to scrape through another debacle or crisis I'd have a sort of perverse pride in my toughness and ability to survive. I rarely learned any real lesson from the experience and most often would quickly move right into the next scene in the painful drama that was my life. It was a repetitious "groundhog day" cycle of struggle and suffering. In recovery I have a much healthier approach that generates outcomes that provide me with real self-esteem born of lessons learned and progress made that is tangible and lasting. The comparisons between the two realities demonstrate the efficacy of my new way of living. I have proper and trusted friends who know me. Their experience and support help and guide me through the inevitable pitfalls and confusions of life. They help me get up and move on when I fall and remind me that we all share these human imperfections and foibles that cause us problems in life. They help me face life's unexpected and random events that confront me. In time I have gained increased faith in my ability to live life on life's terms due to my past successes. I can look back and say "I made it through that sober so I can make it through this sober" and then I do. This process has rid me of a juvenile and entitled expectation of a perfectly "fair" life and

[9] *Alcoholics Anonymous : The Story of How Many Thousands of Men and Women Have Recovered from Alcoholism*. 4th ed. New York City: Alcoholics Anonymous World Services, 2001. P. 83-84.

its accompanying self-pitying self-suffering "why me" response. It has allowed me to behave like a man with integrity and strength of character who is responsible and capable. A man who is trustworthy and confident enough to accept the help I need to navigate with grace and dignity through the storms of life.

# April 8

I have found that the heart of recovery lies in creating a powerful and useful connection to the spiritual side of our humanness. Human societies throughout all of time have made use of a spiritually based relationship to something greater than our own individual selves. Recovery is a completely secular device. The global success of recovery shows that there is no wrong way to have a Higher Power. What matters is that I am not my own Higher Power. Human ideas of God vary greatly and I've had many different experiences with other people's version of what God is and sometimes what they think it should mean for me. What I've learned in recovery is that in addiction I was spiritually starving to death. My spirit was poisoned and dying slowly and steadily. My thinking was so distorted and delusional I could not begin to grasp any true sense of meaningful spirituality. In recovery I began to experience how spirituality is different from religion. Today I see my personal experience with my religion as a group expression that inherently enables an inclusion and exclusion of specificity. My own spirituality is a personal experience and is not mutually exclusive with anything or anyone else's ideas or beliefs. My big question in recovery—the magical moment that enabled it—was not so much what kind of spiritual food I would choose but only that I would eat it. Until I quit hesitating and resisting a Higher Power I made little meaningful progress in recovery. Until I became hungry enough, starving and desperate enough, to try some new food in my life I continued to starve and suffer. Rather like a petulant child who cries out, "you can't make me eat vegetables," when I at last tried them I soon came to like them. Similarly with spirituality, until I was willing to really give it a try I had no hope of real recovery. The biggest and immediate benefit for me was personal honesty. Having a Higher Power finally allowed me to begin having some real honesty inside myself, and when I did that, suddenly recovery began to work in a meaningful and deep way for me. As my delusional thinking cleared I realized that I had always been spiritual in some way and that I have always known God.

# April 9

When I think about where I'd like to be in the future it often tests my ability to accept that where and what I am today is enough. My goals when I first entered recovery were fairly basic and simple. Years of active addiction had darkened my life and reduced my worldview. In time, recovery has enabled me to change and make progress in my life in ways that I would never have thought possible when I first arrived. Some days it is easy to be encouraged (as well I should) and it has become ok for me to have new hopes and an uplifting vision for my future. Other days I may despair that I will never reach my goals as they seem so far away. I want it all now. I want to "make it happen" and if I can't I then struggle with self-esteem and question my eligibility, personal value and manhood. These old patterns of thinking are always ready to appear—they may be old but they are not gone. I remind myself that ALL the progress I have made so far occurred one day at a time and entirely within the framework of recovery. I know this is true because nothing was progressing in the right direction in my life before recovery. All I had then was crushing isolation, the pain of loneliness, and failure as I flailed uselessly in my efforts to achieve anything of true value. Today the valid and honest relationships I have with other people and God help me take the small steps each day that create real progress and change. I don't hold too tightly to specific ideas about what the future will bring, as in a sense, those details are above my pay grade. I do know that I'm moving in a good direction and that I will be ok. It is a bit like Christmas. I know there will be gifts but am never really sure exactly what they will be. So today I remain focused on doing the next right thing and let God be in charge of as much as I can. When I try too hard to force my plans onto the future I mostly just unsettle my present and usually sell myself short because it seems that God's plans for me are always better than my own.

# April 10

The chaotic unmanageability of my life preceded and followed my active addiction. In some ways drugs and alcohol were a solution to it. The problem was that although drugs and alcohol provided relief, it was only a temporary relief, one that also usually increased the amount of insanity in my life. My tolerance for unmanageability and the consequences of my behavior grew as my life reached new lows. My ability to make any sensible order of it all shrunk as fast as the chaos grew. Recovery allowed me to stop that cycle and begin to see the truth about myself. I grappled for a long time to truly understand the context and real value that an understanding of my powerlessness provided. At first it simply meant I was weak and broken. Then I saw how it was more related to my own power to choose how I live life. In time, the understanding of my human powerlessness in life has become a comfortable daily reminder of the simple truth and understanding of my place in the world. It provides acceptance of a mature view of the reality of what each day, and my life, can mean—and what change I can, or can't, try to achieve. Today, my patterns of behavior and ways of acting on assumptions and beliefs about life often suddenly reveal themselves in new ways to me. I sigh and shake my head as my Higher Power "takes me to school" and I learn a new lesson about myself. Growth then takes place that allows some difficulty or problem to become reframed in a new way that helps my life become easier and more content. Continued change is available to me each day as I learn more about myself and grow my life skills. It is enabled only through an acceptance of my own powerlessness and humility. If I already know everything, I can't learn anything new. Today I enjoy the sometimes painful process of learning new things, and I gain an increased serenity and confidence from the better understanding of life it brings.

# April 11

I was so lost and low in life when first in recovery. I clearly remember my struggle to understand and implement the idea and structure of having morals and values in my daily life. Today I have a sadness and softness I feel for myself as I realize just how broken and confused I was. It was so hard for me to get my head around what it all meant because in some core and basic ways I had never fully developed any true values or morals prior to my life of alcohol and drug addiction. I could vaguely understand what they were but couldn't connect them to who I was. Addiction had stripped me bare of honesty. There were few rules or morals I wouldn't break and I didn't care or value what that meant for me or others. The expression, "If you don't stand for something you'll fall for anything," was pointed inwards and I was my own worst enemy. The shame of my actions fueled a repeating cycle and downward spiral that lowered my self-esteem and worth. In recovery I came to realize that if I don't take myself seriously enough to care about who I am and what I stand for than certainly no one else will. If I continue to pursue the lower things in life I cannot achieve the higher things. It took time to learn how to rebuild and connect with morals and values in my life—to understand what kind of man I wanted to be and to remain true to those ideals. My life got better as my standards of behavior rose and I began to hold fast to morals and values about who I am today and how those beliefs shape my actions. The self-honesty of being accountable to my own standards of living was a part of the maturation process I had missed in youth. The idea that I can "get away with it" is useless when I become a grown up in charge of my own life. Today I enjoy a real freedom and happiness from simply doing what I know I ought to do. My morals and values guide me. I can look in the mirror and be ok with the man I see there. Today I know who I am and what I stand for.

# April 12

The healing effects of living in recovery have clearly changed my life. When I look back from where I am today there are three clear periods that contrast dramatically. The first is the painful hopelessness of active addiction and the chaotic mess of my life before I got sober. The mental, social, spiritual, and profound physical effects of addiction were devastating. They had a horrid impact on my sense of self and distorted my view of reality. Once I became sober there was a second period that marked the absence of constant suffering. There was less confusion and I was better able to see how damaged I was. The fog had cleared and I was confronted with the challenges of recovery—at which I balked. The hard work of recovery was daunting and full of fear for me. For a while I was willing to delude myself that the absence of active addiction was the same as the presence of recovery. This second period lasted until the pain of being a broken person gave me the courage to accept the healing that working the steps of recovery promised. The third period has opened the door to a life that is meaningful and content. I continue to be amazed at the healing effect of recovery and the way it has led to personal growth. I never knew that there was so much more to life. My previous understanding was limited and unexplored. Today, life is always present and available to me, expressed in the deeper connection and sense of belonging I have in all that goes on around me. The world that was always right there, but hidden and out of reach, has opened up to me and it engages me in a variety of ways. It is like my life is a radio and through working the steps and being active in recovery I finally found the station selection. Now there are many ways I can tune into the healing and growth that participating in life offers. The work of becoming healthy has shown me how healing is the vital element of beginning a journey of spiritual growth. Without healing there is no sustainable growth, only stagnation and wasted effort that fails to take root and create true value or meaning.

# April 13

The distance between the willingness to accept the change that is possible through recovery and the complete surrender that it requires was difficult ground for me to cover. It has meant a profound change for me. Surrender was something that I inherently resisted and I still have a knee-jerk male reaction to the connotations and images associated with the word. In many ways entering recovery felt as though I had lost a battle and was now being held captive. I had to reframe my thinking into an understanding that I was joining the winning side and not being imprisoned. Perhaps it was more like I was being traded to a winning team. I had to stop wearing my old uniform, forget my old play book, and start anew. It was hard to leave my old life, ideas, thinking and beliefs behind. I clung to a belief that I needed them and wouldn't survive without them. I seemed to be stuck in a no-man's land refusing to let go of my dogma about "who I am." One day I realized that my old life will always be available to me if I want it back and that the truth of my hesitation was a fear that I wouldn't be good enough for the new life. This fear had prevented me from making a true and fundamental attempt at change. I knew I didn't want my old life back so I finally surrendered and fully committed to new way of life—to the winning team. From that moment my life began to change in ways that still amaze me. I have become comfortable with the understanding that there are many more lessons coming for me and I am open to them. I hold my faith in God tightly and my beliefs about what I think I know loosely. There has been more surrender since then and each time I have less fear as I grow from the often painful lessons because I know it is a process that works for me.

# April 14

The idea that life is about the journey rather than the destination never held much sway with me while in active addiction. I was always willing to sacrifice today and be supremely focused on some temporary reward. Addiction drove a hyper-focus on certain desires and all else faded into the background. Despite the illusions of my thinking—there was no plan or destination of any merit. The truth of life's value being found in the journey seems very true to me now. In hindsight the fact is that I chose to focus solely on the destination of my addiction and clearly lost all connection to a valuable and meaningful life. Today, the idea of slowing down and taking time to enjoy the simple moments of pleasure in each day connects with me. I am no longer in a big rush. I want to enjoy the life that is available for me and that is only ever experienced in the now. Before it was like I was sacrificing all of the "todays" for some imaginary time in the future that never came. The ability to live in the moment, one day at a time, has created a powerful change in how I think about my life. In addiction I never wanted to go to go to bed. I always felt like I was missing out on something or needed more—that today hadn't been enough. I now look forward to going to bed because I found what I needed in the day and am keen to enjoy another one. I sleep well because the day wasn't wasted and it had meaning. I try to live the simple basic moments of each day in a way that has a value and provides a purpose I can connect with. I have added to the world around me somehow, enjoyed my part in it, and enjoyed being me. There is a comfort and acceptance that comes from knowing my place in my own life and the recognition that my life is a small but valuable part of the world. Today I am better able to grasp the value of each person's day within the context of the past, present, and future of the human experience. Throughout all history our life journeys have always taken place one day at a time.

# April 15

Living life in a wholehearted way has been one of the great challenges for me in recovery. My heart wasn't in my life when I arrived. Addiction had replaced my normal heartfelt desires and replaced them with cold, selfish and uncaring need. I'd lost any love for myself and without it went all true love for others. It took a long time to learn how to use and rely on the powerful truth I find in my heart instead of the easily confused technical reasoning of my soggy and polluted mind. Years of ignoring things that I knew in my heart drove a great loss of faith in God, life and me. The painful truth and reality of being unable to stop knowingly doing things that I knew I shouldn't do was at the center of the spiritual illness that ailed me. Reviving and then relying upon the powerful resource of my heart meant I had to become honest with myself and address my spiritual vacuum. Learning how to do the right thing and be faithful to what I know in my heart has taken both time and God's help. Learning how to recognize and avoid the traps of my distorted thinking took the help of friends. Having real friends meant opening my heart to caring about others and accepting the imperfect nature of us all. The importance of having heart in life is echoed throughout time and runs true in the many sayings we hear so often, "His heart was in the right place" or "we had a heart to heart" or "the effort was half-hearted," the list goes on. Clearly living life without heart was part of my problem and opening my heart has been central to my solution. It has been a difficult and at times painful process, but so is life. Having an open heart allows me to experience and live the "all" of life, good and bad, happy and sad. It is a vital part of my humanness and today it is the part that validates and authenticates the truly meaningful and purposeful connections in my life. I can "think" about life all I want but until I put my heart into it I'm not really living it.

# April 16

My journey in recovery has been largely framed by self-discovery and personal growth. Before I got into recovery my worldview became increasingly narrow as my addiction worsened. I became further isolated and focused on the very narrow, dark, and insane path of meeting my own selfish needs. Thoughts about "who I was" and the time or desire for soul searching self-discovery were long gone. In rare moments of sober insight I knew what I was and that I was horribly broken. Accepting my full participation in recovery has meant welcoming this journey of learning more about who I am as well as experiencing change and growth. It has meant being willing to expand my understanding of who I am and what that means. At first I tried to jam new ideas and thinking into the old me and, of course, they didn't fit or work. It took courage to grow and change and to enlarge my view of who I was. It was difficult to accept that I could and would change in ways that I didn't know or understand at the time. This growth continues as I work to overcome the natural boundaries of who I think I am. Guided by faith and an understanding of my Higher Power this path leads me toward the man that I want to become. This process has shown me that I must be willing to challenge my beliefs and understandings about life and accept that there will always be change as I become more knowledgeable about myself. I can't continue to cling to a fixed idea about who I am or I will preclude the progress that is a vital part of the spiritual growth demanded by recovery. For many great thinkers throughout the ages learning what it is to be human is the ultimate purpose and the true meaning of life. Being open minded about my own personal growth and having the courage to pursue it is one of the great gifts that recovery makes available to me. It links me closely to the idea that life is lived always in the reflection and thoughtfulness of my actions of today rather than my beliefs and ideas about yesterday.

# April 17

Being "a part of" life is such an interesting and deep idea for me today. The main way it is expressed is through my interaction with other people. In the AA "Big Book" it talks about how the alcoholic "will know loneliness such as few do."[10] For me, the crushing isolation of addiction increasingly

---

[10] ibid. P. 152.

separated me from the world and left me "apart from." This separation was present in many ways such as work, community and nature, but was most evident in the destroyed relations with other people, especially those who had been close to me. In recovery I've learned how to reconnect with and accept other people into my life, and to allow myself to become part of their life. At times this two-way street has been a hard and frightening path to walk. Allowing people into my life and letting them truly see and get to know the real me forces me to accept truths about who I am. Allowing myself to become a part of other people's lives comes with a certain responsibility empathy and compassion that requires willingness and honesty. It is only through actively participating in relationships with others that I can truly become "a part of" life. Recovery has shown me that ultimately the human condition requires us to live fully through a shared experience with others. The false ideal of being "the strong man alone against the world" is another one of the childish fallacies that fueled my addiction. All around me, the strength, courage and humble perseverance of human life is pervasive and persuasive. When I connect and share my life with other people the experience is powerful and uplifting. It demonstrates and validates the truth of my place, my eligibility and value, in the world around me. The struggle of human life isolates me when I suffer it alone but it frees me when I see it in others and share my own. It allows me to take my place as "a part of" in the world of other lives all around me.

# April 18

Addiction provided an illusory sense of control that was compelling and it easily drew me under its spell. I deluded myself that I could control my use, and through it my world. I was large and in charge right up to point when it would all crash apart. Reality and truth would suddenly emerge as I once again faced the wreckage I'd created and its stark consequences. It was always easier to run back to the bottle for relief rather than face the hard facts and change my behavior. When I tried to change—which wasn't often—I was unable to and those good intentions and promises were fleeting. In recovery I've learned how to rely on a Higher Power for help. I found a power, other than myself, that could help me solve my problems. It took me a little while, a few failed attempts, to learn how to allow this new power to work for me by truly accepting it and then getting out of the way. Honesty, hope, and faith marked the beginning and bit by bit I came to see how my desire to control life, and its outcomes, was naive and childishly foolish. My hubris had no basis in reality. Working the steps of recovery helped me understand a new relationship with the world and I became better able to let go of the illusion that I could control life—and the delusion that I actually was. It has certainly taken faith, but also practice and experience, to see how this new approach works. Learning to "let go and let God" isn't easy at the best of times and I still need the help of my friends when times are hard in life. Recognizing my controlling nature, my efforts to exert my will into the world around me, is a skill that I will always be working to improve because the benefits are so clear. Almost all my problems are centered in actions based on the misguided thinking that my way is how things should be for others and the subsequent attempts to make it so. The reality I must remember is that I struggle to properly control even my own actions. Getting myself in order is a big enough task—never mind trying to get the rest of the world to act a certain way. When I do the work of taking care of my side of the street I can relax and take it easy knowing its ok to leave the rest up to God. Almost always his outcomes seem better than what I could have planned. And though they aren't always the way I'd hoped or thought they might be, so far, I'm always taken care of.

# April 19

In recovery, acceptance of the validity of imperfection has been an important idea for me. I think in some ways an addictive life is a great example of the insanity of a desire to only find value in an absolute outcome while being trapped in a very rigid belief system. I spent years of wasted effort painfully and unsuccessfully trying to recapture some idealized notion of perfection that didn't exist. My life seemed framed by futile efforts that could never be fully achieved, like trying to recreate just the right buzz or finding the total relief of some illusory peace and escape. Sex was another way of trying to reach this elusive goal of perfect satisfaction that I was somehow entitled to or would be measured by. Sometimes there were intense moments of contentment but they were always fleeting and in hindsight always vaguely false and inadequate. In recovery the goals and targets for my life, my morals and values, help guide me on a path where progress and outcomes aren't measured in absolutes. Seeking spiritual progress not perfection reminds me that the value, the goal, is to walk the path—not wear a halo while winning a gold medal and despising any lesser result.[11] The work of the twelve steps helps me understand the role of humility with respect to my expectations of myself and others. The idea of holding everyone to perfect standards is a delusional fantasy that my addictive mind uses to stymie my recovery. Of course that fact is that none of us are perfect and we all make mistakes every day. Pursuit of a goal that

---

[11] ibid. P. 60.

can never be perfectly attained is a great example of the virtue of living "the good life."[12] In some ways, claiming perfection as the only true value makes life impossible and perhaps, like cynicism, is merely the refuge of the lazy. Seeking perfection as the only result of value is the perfect way to ensure no one, myself or others, will ever be "good enough"—so why bother at all? Often it is the choice of the best path, not a perfect one that I must make in my day. Clearly the meaning and purpose in my life is found in the art of the actions I take each day and how those choices reflect my morals and values.

# April 20

Often my thinking and expectations about life can be unrealistic and out of touch with the reality of daily living. My years of substance abuse started at an early age and postponed and distorted the normal maturation process of young adulthood. When I arrived in recovery many of my ways of thinking were still quite youthful and not fully developed. They didn't work very well in the real world. Addiction also had a tendency to drive my thinking toward an excessive focus on the external, which exacerbated my inability to find internal solutions to my problems. I'm often keen to focus on what others are doing and see them as the source of my problems. I would hold people to mythical and unrealistic standards of behavior which perpetuated the problem in a self-fulfilling way. In general, the same was true with my basic worldview—creating constant feelings of irritation, and angry dissatisfaction, as people and life always seemed to let me down. Recovery has helped me better understand how the reality of life is always a source of confusion and difficulty when it collides with my often childishly oversimplified ideas of what life should be and how others should act. Recovery has provided my thinking with an internal focus and a more realistic view of other people and life that is mature, and compassionate. The sayings in recovery about "not judging my insides by someone else's outsides" and "if I'm not the problem there is no solution" slowly began to make sense as I realized that life is always very complicated. I have to do the work on myself, for myself, to become better at life by increasing my emotional maturity. I have learned to recognize and let go of my childish expectations of what the world and its people should be. I have been able to grow up and accept that the world isn't going to change just for me—I must change for it.

---

[12] Plato. *The Trial and Death of Socrates : Euthyphro, Apology, Crito, Death Scene from Phaedo*. 2nd ed. Indianapolis: Hackett Pub., 1986. P. 48.

# April 21

Early on in recovery I remember being quite overwhelmed by the idea of having a spiritual experience of any kind. The entire notion just seemed rather out of reach for me. I truly was a long way from that sort of capacity and part of my apprehension was that I didn't fully understand what it all really meant. Initially I saw a spiritual awakening as something I would somehow magically achieve one day rather than as a process that would slowly bring results in small ways. To make progress I had to quit trying to figure out exactly what a spiritual experience would be for me and just start moving in that direction. I did that in part by learning to understand and define what kind of man I wanted to be and then trying to do the work to become that man. At first it was very hard for me to stay on track—even with some of the simple ideas like not lying or avoiding behavior that wasn't aligned with where I was trying to go morally. Many times I was trying so hard to be in charge of myself that I struggled to allow and accept my Higher Powers help. Somewhere along the way I began to realize I was doing things in a new way and life was becoming easier and more automatic. I began to see the small signs of spiritual awakening that were taking place. I realized that I am always in charge of, and responsible for, my actions in life. I make the decisions and choices that define who and what I am—but increasingly they more closely follow the guidelines of my Higher Power. This is the great freedom that arrives when I align my will properly and remove myself from the struggle of fighting life instead of going with it. The automatic ease and comfort that became part of my daily living has continued to open the door to an increased spiritual consciousness. These awakenings are steadily gathering for me into an experience that I can rely on like any other experience in life such as a skilled trade or a path well-travelled. Life has largely become easy to do well and brings great satisfaction. It is mostly comfortable and I am usually quite content. Having some small degree of daily spiritual contact has over time created a spiritual experience that allows me to better accept and enjoy my place in life.

# April 22

I clearly remember at age fifteen the first time that someone told me I was "burning the candle at both ends." I'd never heard the expression before and wasn't sure how I felt about it being applied to me—but I could see their point. That is what I was doing and it seemed exciting and clever, the prerogative of youth perhaps, but in the back of my mind I was concerned about my candle running out too soon. That perhaps I was off track and foolishly misusing or wasting my life. Of course at age fifteen I didn't give it too much thought and quickly chose to live large now and that I'd figure out these deeper questions later. After all, I was having too much fun to stop now. The postponement of these sorts of important questions about how I choose to live my life was ultimately central to my later addiction. Looking back now I can see how I was trying, even then, to fit more, more, more, into each day. I was frantically pursuing more than normal, more than my share, and I could rarely get enough. My life was all sizzle and no steak and it became a meaningless maze of chasing things that brought nothing of lasting value. Recovery has shown me the valuable pleasure of a simple day done well. It has shown me how to live carefully and with a purposeful meaning that allows each day to contribute to something larger. "Slow and steady wins the race" was another one of those sayings that I dismissed without ever fully understanding and today I am glad to have been able to find the truth it contains. My addictive mind still wants to make things happen childishly fast. Now! Now! But the experience of recovery has shown me that the self-esteem and integrity of a good life is only built slowly and deliberately. Each day has small lessons and gifts of spiritual understanding that are available to me if I slow down enough to receive them. Today as I look back on the dramatic changes that recovery has brought into my life I can see that it all happened in part because I learned how to live one good day at a time.

# April 23

Learning how to be a friend to myself has been a hard task to accomplish and often seems incomplete. I remember in very early recovery being absorbed by the question of self-forgiveness and being unable to get the answer I needed or a solution that resolved the question in a meaningful way. People would say things like, "If your Higher Power forgives you then shouldn't you?" Nothing seemed to really fit and I was often stuck in a sort of weird combination of self-pity, loathing, hate and despair that didn't feel quite right either. It was all very odd and uncomfortable. At root it kept me in a place of feeling like I wasn't good enough or was perhaps ineligible for success in recovery. Today, after working the steps those feelings are largely gone because I better understand the prideful futility of seeking a self-forgiveness that doesn't exist. I can't really point to any magic moment or one thing that brought the change. It has been a gradual change. I have learned acceptance and tolerance of my disease and what it means to be in recovery. I have patience and openness with the imperfections of God's world as it is expressed in others and me. I can accept that I am not the judge, jury, or hangman for the actions of others—and most importantly, for my own addictive past. Letting go of the powerful desire to punish or forgive myself has been a central part of letting God be in charge and relying upon a Higher Power. My job today, having done the steps and remaining active in recovery, is to live my life well and let my Higher Power be in charge. I realize today that my selfish self-centeredness and desire to control life was a big part of these feelings of guilt. It was another way for me to remain in charge and not, "let go and let God." Accepting life on life's terms has allowed me to accept my past and be free of its dark pall. Living in recovery has shown me how to be a friend to others and, most crucially, to myself. Because love is always a two way street that flows openly and connects two parties together I couldn't really love others until I could love myself—even just a little. It has been a good example of the truth in recovery that time takes time and that by staying the course more is revealed. Freedom from those old feelings is another example of the amazing gifts that continue to arrive in recovery.

# April 24

It is easy for me to at times get overly caught up in worrying about the framework of the big picture of my life. Clearly it is important to think ahead and to have goals and plans but my addictive mind has a tricky time with maintaining the boundary between sensible planning and future-tripping. Suddenly I find myself feeling upset or hyper-concerned about how my future has been screwed by my past. Or that my "todays" aren't good enough and that I should be doing more—achieving more (usually more and rarely less!). I wonder and then worry about what is going to happen as my thinking quickly shifts into desperate concerns about how I can control or force a certain outcome into my life. Suddenly I am in charge of life and trying to act as the director again which is something that I know doesn't work well for me. It is during this shift in thinking that I lose sight of my own powerlessness and faith in a Higher Power. I then find myself making poor choices based on self. The lessons of recovery help me re-center my thinking and keep me focused on how I live today. I can then accept that I have no true grasp of exactly who or what I may be one or ten years from now. I can't predict what skills I will have or lessons I will have learned. However, I do know that today there are many great changes that have taken place that make me a much different person than I was a short time ago. I could never have predicted the kind of "today" I have now from where I was back then. My only true choice is to add value to my life within the framework of today and trust that my "tomorrows" will continue to unfold just as they are supposed to—just as God plans for me. In my own plans I usually sell myself short by overestimating what can happen in the short term and underestimating what can happen in the long term. Learning to find meaningful action and value in the "today" of life—by being spiritually aware and accepting of the chance to live that exists right now—frees me from the oppressive obsession and unhelpful worry of the past or future.

# April 25

The idea that there is spirituality in the world that is always present and available for me to connect with took some time to understand and become a reality for me. At first it was more of an unknown and far away concept that I had rarely experienced. When I arrived in recovery my own spirit was downtrodden and barren, rather like an old radio that barely turned on and didn't really play anything but noisy fuzz. It took time to do the work to recharge my batteries and tune into the spiritual side of life. The darkness of my addictive world had become all I knew. I remember trying to recall if there was ever a time I'd really been happy in life. The doom and gloom was woeful and my selfish mindset was full of pitiful suffering and victimhood that locked my feelings of worthlessness in place. Accepting and then learning how to see and engage with a more spiritual way of life has been a wonderful and interesting journey. At one time I for ten weeks kept a "sight and sense" journal where I would write a descriptive sentence or two each day on things I saw in the natural world that I connected with spiritually. Perhaps a bird fluttering around a building corner and landing nearby or the sounds of the trains through the morning fog as the sun rose. By paying attention to the world around me in a formal way I increased my ability to positively connect with a sort of spiritual vibe, a charitable healthy feeling that allows me to find a stronger participation with my Higher Power through the natural world. It makes the world around me more pleasant, meaningful, and kind. There is little doubt that the natural world has always been a rejuvenating resource for the spirit of mankind. The intersection of the animal part of ourselves with our more spiritual and thinking side has always been a zone of discovery and as humans we are confronted with the reality of abstract thought that our gift of reason provides. While we may indeed be somehow separate from the animal world, in many ways we are still inherently and powerfully connected to, and a part of, the spiritual wonder of the natural world.

# April 26

When I began to travel the road of recovery I was confronted with themes of my powerlessness over addiction and selfish self-centeredness. Both of which seemed oddly obvious yet easily denied. My defects of character deftly switched gears from one set of addictions to another as I moved away from alcohol and drugs but retained my compulsive thinking and addictive behaviors that evidenced themselves in a variety of other ways. I laughed when I first heard someone say, "I'm not much, but I'm all I think about," because it rang so true for me. Ironically enough I didn't realize then just how true and deeply rooted my problems really were or how profoundly they affected me. It took years to slowly find my way to the root causes and conditions of my addiction and then truly confront my character defects rather than continuing to exchange one flavor of symptoms for another more subtle sort. An important aspect of the art of recovery that I've learned centers in my increased ability to deal with counterintuitive truths and paradoxes. Many years in active addition had left me very lost in life and I certainly wasn't on a winning streak when I arrived in recovery. Yet my ego and denial were so distorted I could still think I was on top of the world instead of in the gutter. This insane ability to delude myself about what was really going in in my life diminished as sobriety led me back to reality. The work in recovery has helped me get well. I'm less selfish and am no longer mired in a constant battle to meet my own needs. I am able to participate in real friendships and relationships with others that are meaningful and rewarding in lasting and healthy ways. As always, it's a work in progress but I, and others, can see the change and growth that recovery and a reliance on God have provided. Over time I have been able to recreate my life by recognizing unhealthy beliefs and selfish patterns of behavior and then replacing them with healthy ideas and actions that are centered in a worldview in which I am a part of—rather than my part in a world I'm apart from.

# April 27

The truth I have found in the value of persisting in the building of friendships has been shown clearly to me over the years. One of the first great casualties of my youthful beginnings in addiction was the ability to build and maintain healthy, trusting, and reliable relationships. My childhood had some bumps in the road that didn't help my relationship skills and then substance abuse became the trusted friend that was always there for me. Prior to recovery, I had few people I called friends and most of them were mere acquaintances with a shared mutual bond of meeting the selfish needs of our addiction. I really didn't learn how to be a friend or how to allow myself to have a friend in the full meaning of the experience until I was sober and in recovery for a while. The process of the steps, of being a sponsor to others, and of participating in the ongoing activities of the broader fellowship has allowed me to connect meaning and experience to sayings like, "to have a friend one must be a friend." It has allowed me to gain an understanding of the value of having acceptance of my own faults and the faults of others. By learning more about who I am and how my values and morals shape my boundaries—as well guide my actions—a framework has evolved that I can work within to build and sustain meaningful and deep friendships. Perhaps the hardest part has been being willing to keep trying and not walk away when things become challenging or difficult. It has been only through sustained effort over a long period of time that a reliable trust has emerged to create the safe and honest place for true friendship to exist. Today I am lucky to have many friends. While some very close, and other less so, they are all founded in a long term reliability and honesty that persists through our shared challenges with each other and in life. They show me clearly and vitally that I am not alone or unknown. Today I stand with others who know me and help me as I help them and our shared truth provides an anchor in our lives.

# April 28

The question, "Do you want to be right or do you want to be happy?" forces me to confront and consider deeply my desire to be in control of others and the illusion that I am. My need to be right, to control life, became a liability that had devastating results. I used to believe in my thinking about my drinking that, "This time will be different," despite all the evidence to the contrary. The mistaken belief that I was right caused many severe consequences and nearly killed me more than once. In recovery I learned that honesty was indeed at the center of any progress and that I had been wrong about a lot of things. I found strength in humility and saw that the need to be right all the time is a weakness. I learned to focus not on the actions of others but instead on the question of what was right in my own thoughts and actions. Sometimes, I may in fact be right about the questions facing someone else in life. However, I am never right to try and impose my will on them—and all I am likely to get for my effort is frustration and unhappiness. Thinking I know what is right for others is usually my way of trying to control them. It gives me an irritating and valueless bone to chew on that distracts me from seeing my own faults. I become restless and discontent which drives my addictive behavior. There is an endless supply of other people's faults and problems for me to be upset about so it becomes like an addiction itself. Often it points to something going on with me that I'm avoiding looking at. Recovery has given me the insight and strength it takes to face these truths about myself. It has shown me the futility of distracting myself by trying to control the lives of others. The reminder that, "If I'm not the problem there is no solution," is another truth that has taken time and practice to learn well. Today, I'm less worried about the enticing attractions of delving into other people's lives. I stay on my side of life's street and try to stay focused on the rigorous self-honesty I need to keep it clean.

# April 29

A steady and constant theme of recovery for me is one of personal growth and self-discovery as a result of continuing efforts to increase my spiritual contact with God. Progress in this area occurs as I explore a deeper understanding of who I am. The simple truth for me is that if effective progress is to be sustained there are often unavoidable and significant lessons found only by going through painful personal growth. I had painful experiences in my life before I started drinking and a great many more during my years in addiction. That these experiences shape me and impact my daily living is a fact I can't ignore. In active addiction my anger would randomly explode and often hurt people in grave ways. At other times the pain was a potent subject for my obsession that would drive depression and self-pity as I perfected a dark, dangerous and brooding persona that I consoled with alcohol, drugs, women, etc. After a while it wasn't clear which was driving which. Was the pain the reason I used—or a storyline I relied upon to justify my use? The pain in my life distorted and skewed my thinking and actions for years. In recovery, self-discovery and healing confronts my past and reconciles it. Living my life as an active participant in the lives of others with whom I share my truth and fear allows me to see, heal, and be free of my painful past. I am learning to let go of the myths and false beliefs that I clung to so tightly in addiction and integrated into my personality. Through the help of others I find the true me. It can't happen on my own because the mind that is broken can rarely see its own faults. Honest relationships with others provide a mirror of experience in which I can begin to see who I really am without the distortions, mistakes and misbeliefs of my own thinking. The idea that I am never mistaken is laughable and so it is important to aim that insight at my understanding of who I think I am if I sincerely want to experience growth and change in my life. The honesty and open mindedness of recovery allows me to accept myself and others and not be a relentless victim who cherishes the mistakes and pain in my life.

# April 30

The idea that no one else "makes me do things" because of how I feel about their actions has been critical to my recovery. As a grown man, I alone am responsible for how I choose to act regardless of the behavior of others. In recovery this idea seemed alien and unreasonable at first. Clearly these people I met in recovery had never spent any time with the kind of people that I had! After a while I began to understand what they meant. I think that learning how to react differently to my cravings helped me see their point. I learned that rather than immediately reacting to the desire to drink or use I could instead allow myself to choose how I responded to those feelings. The same process became true for other things that triggered my feelings and emotional responses. Learning to be in touch with my feelings and to understand and experience them without allowing them to force an unreasoned reaction had been a powerful lesson that helps me live more effectively. Today I see how much room for change still exists within the framework of how I understand and participate in life. The results are dramatic as I continue to be released from controlling behaviors and thinking that I wasn't aware of before. The story of Plato's cave reminds me that personal growth and discovery requires open-mindedness and courage to change beliefs that are so deeply held. Being better able to avoid unreasoned and emotional responses to life allows me to work on correcting the false thinking behind them. It helps release me from the bondage of my selfish self-centeredness that wants to put all of life into some sort of personalized context that makes everything about me. The steady train of misbeliefs and false perceptions that I can create and react to has taken years to begin to grasp and understand. Today I am better able to stop and choose how I react to difficult emotional situations. Life is more peaceful and content when I am thoughtful about how I choose to act rather than responding childishly to life's agitations and difficulties.

# May

"I prefer to be true to myself, even at the hazard of incurring the ridicule of others, rather than to be false, and to incur my own abhorrence."
— Frederick Douglass

"A quiet conscience makes one strong!"
— Anne Frank

"Nothing is at last sacred but the integrity of your own mind."
— Ralph Waldo Emerson

# May 1

The spiritual awakening that is at the heart of my recovery is a remarkable and magical event to witness and participate in. Sometimes in early recovery I would groan at many of the clichés I would hear. However the simple facts of my life, and the lives of many others I know in recovery, are inescapable. The truth and value of our spiritual growth, progress, and contentment are unavoidable and undeniable. My life today is so very different and completely changed. A big turning point was when I was able to see the first small changes in my life and really embrace the concept of recovery—to take the small first steps of living in a more spiritual way while leaving the cynical skepticism of my jaded worldview behind. Today my path of spiritual awakening finds many ways of expressing itself. I enjoy a spiritual and inspiring connection with nature. I see Mount Rainier and often ponder the many other human lives that have gone before me here in the Northwest who for thousands of years have also paused to enjoy and marvel at its majesty on a clear bright day. At times with a group of friends I am able to randomly and unexpectedly share from my heart a spiritual connection that is a gift of the sort of truth, honesty, and integrity that nothing in addiction could ever offer. As the cliché goes, "You don't know what you don't know," and I certainly had no idea how different and rewarding life would continue to become when I opened the door to a spiritual awakening. The remarkable and at times startling truth is that it keeps getting better—reminding and encouraging me to sustain the simple daily needs of my recovery. Every day, to some degree, I work diligently to remain connected to a sense of spirituality. I work to find new ways to explore that connection through nature, prayer, reading, physical activity and my interactions with other people. I have seen how easily I can drift away from a sense of gratitude. I have learned that my spiritual awakening can falter and ebb if I don't work each day to grow and maintain it by taking meaningful action into the world around me.

# May 2

Ironically, it has been true that is has taken time for me to understand how to be ok with the fact that some lessons in recovery simply take a long time to understand. In recovery there has been a lot to learn about codependency, enmeshment, and the art of having good boundaries with other people. It seems to be one of those parts of life that will always bring more to learn. For me, some of the most practical lessons have been in the area of personal boundaries that provide a sort of safety net for life. I have had to read about the subject, talk about it with others, discuss our experiences, and then practice my own skills. It is critical and beneficial knowledge for my recovery. Learning the ability to have healthy boundaries first required an understanding and acceptance of the ways that I didn't have them by discovering examples of how their absence impacted my life. While it is vital that I don't keep secrets (becoming my own Higher Power) it is also vital that I share myself in ways that are prudent and preserve the renewal of my self-esteem and dignity. Poor boundaries have at times been the result of my own blind and unknown self-deprecation, grandiosity, and self-abuse. Over or under-sharing has been a way of manipulating people by driving them away or drawing them closer and of unconsciously trying to control life around me. At meetings in recovery we share in a general way about our experiences in order to help others. It is in the discussions with my sponsor or other trusted friends that I can safely explore the specific details of my experiences in ways that are appropriate for me and others. Over time I've learned how easy it has been for me to behave selfishly using the veil of helping others to hide my own neediness, ego, and excess—or to become drawn into the drama of others that is none of my business. Having and maintaining good boundaries allows me to share myself in the right amount, in the right way, for the right reasons, and with the right people. It generates and sustains a feeling of stability, integrity, and safety in my life and protects me from being overly enmeshed in the lives of others.

## May 3

At first I was frustrated in many ways by the process of recovery. It seemed overly complicated and confusing with absurd approaches and ideas that felt contradictory and counter-intuitive. When I look back it is easy for me to see why I felt that way. On arrival in recovery my mental state was pretty grim. Years of alcohol and drug abuse had diminished my capabilities in ways that weren't at all clear to me and the damage took some time to begin to heal. In addiction, my warped motives reframed my thinking in ways that were unhealthy and often anything but honest. Also, the simple fact (that even today I often still like to forget) is that at times living life and sharing it with other people can be absolutely complicated. My addictive mind wants to find simple and consistent solutions—similar to the easy oblivion of intoxication—and I struggle with the complicated, unyielding, and incomplete realities of life. The passion and paradox of the human condition is one of desires and designs all taking place within a framework of imperfect motives, flawed communications, and misunderstandings. The wonderful and engaging differences between us all also represent the exciting opportunity and richness of participation. Honesty was the element that allowed me to start my journey in recovery and it remains a clear goal that I practice imperfectly. A subtle irony is that often the most confusing and difficult place for me to be honest is within my own thinking. This means that I often seem to learn lessons a bit later than I would like. Understanding my underlying motives and the ways in which they affect my beliefs and viewpoints in life provides insight that always reveals more truths, some very hard to accept, as I continue to grow in recovery. The process of self-discovery allows me to see how my truth and honesty is not an abstract value. It can be more like the weather than an answer to a math problem. It is more of a creed and belief system that runs like a river with many aspects and elements that are always moving and changing—requiring that I always pay close attention to its course.

# May 4

Recovery has taught me many lessons that are by nature unfinished. Often they are more of an introduction to ideas, concepts and themes of understanding that then begin to evolve and grow in meaning and value. There are many subjects that one could study for a lifetime and only scratch the surface of—and most surely personal growth and understanding of what it means to be human is one of them. I am reminded of the longer view when people share at birthday meetings and they attribute long periods of recovery to simply doing life one day at a time. Sometimes my excessive focus on the problems of today can make it hard for me to also maintain a sense of the long term view. Keeping sight of the longer perspective makes the wins and losses of each individual day less critical and all consuming. My addiction framed each day with a sense of critical importance that was unreasonable. The struggle of addiction gave my world a false end-of-the-world type urgency and the outcome of each little event was excessively exaggerated. Having a longer term understanding of life and a faith in my Higher Power brings acceptance about the results of each day and detaches from them an overly emphasized meaning. Recovery has shown me how to experience difficult things while being able to keep a reasonable distance from them. A bad day today will not last forever and I don't have to wear it like it is a permanent cloak of doom. I can detach unreasonable meaning from it and let it run its course. Learning how proper boundaries work within my own thinking and interactions with others means that I can understand when to detach myself from obsessive over-involvement with certain situations. It is a feature of perspective that acknowledges a longer view of my life's journey. It enables a realistic understanding that there will be good times as well as hard times and some wins, losses, and draws as life unfolds. My entire relationship with another person is never framed solely on the results of just one situation. My entire life or my place in the world is never framed solely on the results of just one day.

# May 5

The idea that I can control the world around me seems inherently flawed and yet is so easy for me to grab ahold of. Every day offers me the chance to participate in a vivid and wide range of possibility and potential that at times seems overwhelming. The feeling of powerlessness is unavoidable in life and so how I choose to live with it becomes a vital question that is at the core of my addictive behaviors. Recovery has shown me how accepting my powerlessness can be a very freeing and liberating experience. It is a huge relief to simply focus on the simple tasks that are within my control and leave the rest up to my Higher Power. Over time I've grown to enjoy a fuller and more meaningful sense of the acceptance and meaning of life on life's terms. There are many things in life that I sometimes would like to control. I want to make things happen and have my way with the world. Addiction repeatedly punished me for such thinking and recovery has shown me its folly. I can't control life, nor can I negotiate with God for the specific things my desires seek. Perhaps it is a fear of an unknown future beyond my control that drives the addictive desire to pursue unhealthy actions that provide an illusory sense of control. I must instead pray for the help I need to do the things I'm supposed to do each day and have faith that the rest of life will play out the way it is meant to. God's plan for me has always been, without exception, better than my own childish efforts to control the world around me. Faith in the work of my Higher Power is a fundamental part of being able to make progress in recovery. I participate openly in life today and try to keep my side of the street in order. The rich embrace of life awaits me and is only available in daily increments. Today I am able to greet it knowing that it will be composed from the wide range of all of life's experiences in ways that I can never control.

# May 6

There is an old saying that goes something like, "If my only tool is a hammer then all my problems become nails." In addiction I only had only one solution and all of life became reframed into it. I rarely questioned my beliefs because any sort of self-examination was likely to pierce my alcoholic denial and expose the depressing truth and sad reality of my addictive behavior. Recovery has increasingly opened the door to a larger tool kit of solutions that in turn allow me to address a wider range of experiences. It expands my awareness of what is really going on inside—feelings, emotions, morals and values. It increases my understanding of who I am and how I relate to the world around me. Doing the work to become more aware of myself allows me to then be more insightful about how things take place in my life and to better see my part in them. In addiction my selfish self-centeredness closed me off from any self-awareness and replaced it with denial. Today I am more aware and understanding of my own strengths and weaknesses. I am more accepting of my imperfections and open minded about new ways of thinking. I am fully aware when things aren't going well and rather than sitting in denial I am able to do something meaningful that may provide change and growth in my life. When I think I know everything already it is hard to learn anything new—and so I must remain open minded about what I think I already know if I am to learn new things. When I accept and embrace an attitude that there is always more to learn I become more aware of the lessons, often subtle ones, which surround me each day. Today I enjoy walking with my head up, seeing the world around me and engaging with it. There is a lot for me to be thankful for today and I am keenly aware of how lucky I am to no longer be zombified by addiction. Over time my confidence and reliance on my own intuition has grown as I increasingly deepen my relationship with a Higher Power. This spiritual awakening helps guide me and I often find myself naturally handling difficult situations with an ease and grace that surprisingly comes almost effortlessly.

# May 7

It is interesting and helpful to consider the role of language in my relationships with others. I have learned a lot of new ideas and gained insight that was the result of learning the language of recovery. Individual words can have many meanings. Their combinations and the context of how they are used, both correctly and incorrectly, add to their meaning. Understanding that language is interpretive and subjective—that ideas attach to words differently for everyone—is a powerful reminder of the complexity of communication. The challenge of healthy communications starts with my own clear understanding of what it is I am thinking, how I am trying to say it, and my ability to confirm that it is received as intended. Often what I think I am saying is not always what someone else is hearing! Experts say that much of language and communication is visual. Sometimes my body language clashes with my words and my underlying honesty. Saying one thing while meaning another and then hoping whoever is listening picks up on it is rarely useful. It is nearly always unhelpful for me—leading to resentment, irritation or bitterness. I've heard that in recovery we should learn how to say what we mean, mean what we say, and not say it mean. Good guidelines for anyone I should think. When I first arrived in recovery my speaking often relied on a wishy washy roundabout style that I used to hide or candy coat ugly truths about myself and my actions. My words fooled me more than anyone else. Recovery has allowed me to understand who I am and what is going on with me a lot more clearly and as a result I can express myself more directly and simply. I have nothing to hide and can share myself carefully and honestly. It allows me to be a better listener and more thoughtful, considerate, and clear with others. It is always hard to not let my words fly out unfiltered before thinking them through. I try to be respectful to my own ideas and thoughts, as well as those who would hear them, by thinking about what I say before I speak. It is a common courtesy that wasn't very common for me before I found sobriety. Today I can pay attention to, and value much more, all of my communications with others.

# May 8

I can often get weary of all the effort that is at times required to remain open-minded and willing in recovery. It isn't easy to reflect on the past and then reframe my feelings and emotions in order to see them in a more generous and general way—especially those parts of my life that were difficult and had a powerful effect. However, like most of the hard work in recovery there is a value to be found in the process. Coming to terms and making peace with my past improves my experience in life today. The realization that my parents, given their own shortcomings and problems, generally did the best they were able to in raising me is a helpful one. I can reflect on how well I have done as a parent or friend and realize that none of us are perfect. Being generous and accepting about how I view history by focusing on the whole picture rather than just the worst parts helps me understand the frailties of humanity. My parents had faults that I can latch onto and so did their parents before them, and so on and so on, highlighting the futility of any attempt to place perfect blame. Ultimately, my life is about my choices and my decisions. Accepting and forgiving others for their human faults allows me to move on with my life and be free from the grip of my past. Today I don't have to constantly rail about the past or repeatedly re-live it in the framework of today. I leave it where it belongs and focus on my actions and attitudes—the where and how of choosing to lead and live my life. I do of course find a benefit in reviewing the near past and understanding it in the larger context of ongoing human life. I can then make use of that general perspective in my life today. It allows me to understand my family relations as they are and see the folly of an expectation of perfection. And to accept the brokenness that is a part of us all. Understanding my own faults and having personal integrity and self-identity gives me safe boundaries that protect me from the brokenness of others without having to exclude them from my life.

# May 9

It took a while for me to become able to find some quiet time each day and connect spiritually with life. At first in recovery even just a few quiet moments could seem oddly uncomfortable and my mind would quickly turn to a list of things in life that were pressing on me that day. I remember how difficult the questions of daily life were. My life was very chaotic and my thinking was quite confused. I felt this daily sense of urgency against the backdrop of a need to make progress toward my goals. Taking a few moments to step away from the daily scramble was often hard and a bit painful because I would just dwell on the past or worry about the future. Today when I think about the time I spend praying and meditating in quiet reflection, or while just taking a break, it is clear to me how much it helps my life become easier. Taking a few minutes here and there each day to quietly relax, settles my thinking and reminds me of the bigger picture of my life. It reconnects me to the vital insight that life only ever exists in the now of each day. The spiritual connection to being "a part of" is the vital piece that anchors the rest of my life in real meaning. In addiction, loneliness and isolation was unavoidably a part of who I was and today it has been replaced by a sharing and participation with the larger world around me. That horrid and constant maniacal sense of futile urgency and unfulfilling hopelessness is long gone. There is an easy comfort and roominess in my life today that has space for those refreshing and inspiring moments that fire my spiritual connection. I can allow the quiet moments that contain perspectives of peaceful contemplation instead of being dominated by pending tasks or fears about transitory needs. Each of these reflective moments brings another small slice of the longer life view that is there each day for me. In time those little slices have added up into a powerful spiritual awakening that solidly roots my peacefulness and buffers it from the hectic and needy day to day clamor of life.

# May 10

It has taken some time for me to learn how to be comfortable with being ok with being ok. I am reminded of those moments at the end of some period of struggle, a close call or achieving a difficult goal, and having that sort of "ok—what now?" feeling that was odd and deflating. I often suddenly felt a bit lost or purposeless. I think much of my life before addiction, and certainly during it, was framed in the constant pursuit of something. A nagging and searching effort or mission to achieve something that would validate who I was and prove that I was good enough—that I belonged. I would show the world and force my will upon it by exerting my power and efforts. Often when things didn't work out and my efforts failed there was a feeling of powerlessness that I couldn't accept and I quickly blamed others for my failure. My struggle would immediately continue again as I then moved onto to trying to control the next outcome. I was completely unable to accept myself or my place in life around me simply as it was. Recovery has shown me that my powerlessness is unavoidable and that the only relief from my desire to fight it is to accept it. I now realize that those moments of "what now" and of winning or failing are not a measurement of my self-worth or success in life. Acceptance of my powerlessness allows me to be ok with being ok. I can simply do my best in life and leave the outcome to my Higher Power who guides the direction of my thinking and efforts. I have found a tremendous freedom and liberation from this new perspective that allows me to always be "good enough." By avoiding the things I know I shouldn't do and doing the things I know I should—and by remaining in contact with my Higher Power and friends—I have become very comfortable with my powerlessness over the world around me. Today I understand the power that I do have within my own actions and thinking and I work to exert that power in healthy ways that are guided by the principles and morals I have found through doing the work of recovery.

# May 11

The learning that is a part of recovery never stops. Some days it is exciting and other days it can be tiring and almost dispiriting when another difficult truth or lesson appears. There were many truths that I had often heard described but never considered in truly meaningful ways until spending some time in recovery. At times these sayings or truths seem to contradict one another and yet seem so perfectly true individually. I would ask myself how that can be. Recovery has taught me a lot about the maturity of understanding and open-mindedness that allows for making better sense of the world and my life's part in it. It is ok for many things to be true and at times contradict one another because there is always more than any one person's understanding of truth. The experience of life is fluid and what is true in one moment may not be in another. The nature of the world and the people in it is always changing and the context of my situation in it requires daily decoding. Having acceptance of this understanding helps me go with the flow rather than attempting to control and capture single moments of circumstance which I then try to sustain and maintain. Thank God I don't actually have such power or control because I made a real mess of my life when I thought I did. Today I get to practice learning, understanding, and being open to the new ideas and thinking that are in front of me. I can then try to find the parts that work for me in my life today—saving the rest for another time when they may make more sense or have more meaning. There is no snapshot of perfection or point of arrival that marks the completion of my journey. Plenty of experiences in life have shown me this truth. The exciting new car is within weeks just another car and the job I seek that will make my life perfect soon becomes just another job, and so on. The truly lasting lessons are those that create values within me that guide my thinking about how I choose to accept and enjoy the day that is here today.

# May 12

The true value and full experience of friendship is something I am still exploring and my understanding of what it means grows as I age. Prior to recovery, and certainly in active addiction, friendships were more often like business relationships that centered on what we could do for each other. They were partnerships that were mutually advantageous, formed for the purpose of advancing our own desires and satisfying needs. The framework of support was that of camaraderie which brought closeness and bonding in some ways but left out the vulnerability and honesty of a true friendship. When problems arose I was quick to cut bait and move on. In recovery I've learned a critical truth—that I can't live fully without real and meaningful friendships based in honesty and compassion. In education there is a great value found in participating in study groups rather than learning solely on our own. The understanding and experience of recovery as a "we" program has meant becoming willing and able to go deeper than superficial friendships. I must build close relationships with friends that create an expanded and shared life experience for us both. This shared space is where I can learn about myself through a fuller experience of humanity with someone else. I desperately need the help of other people who know me because their thinking and insight provide a point of reference that is outside of me. Just as no sailor can ever find his ship's course without using an external point of reference, so it is for me in life. When life's storms arrive and my view is clouded or misguided it is the deep friendships with others that save the day. Life is much easier and fuller for me when I develop friendships that show me things I would never have seen on my own. I rarely had the honesty, humility, or willingness to overcome the fear and vulnerability of being truly close to my friends until recovery showed me that it was only through these strong relationships with others that I can fully participate in life.

## May 13

In recovery we are told that resentment is the number one cause of relapse. That it is a critical element within our efforts to recover. My experience has shown me many clear examples of how this is certainly true. Over time my understanding of how resentment shows up in my life has grown and I've become better able to recognize the multitude of subtle ways it influences me. Expressions like, "If I'm not the problem there is no solution," used to irritate me because I felt strongly that my problems were often centered in the actions of others. Today the lessons I've learned serve as a critical reminder that only I am responsible for how I chose to respond to my feelings. That it is solely up to me to address my thoughts—and that no one else can. When I demand that the actions of others be responsible for my relief in life then generally I am screwed. In the past I have spent much time being worked up and angry about the actions, or inactions, of others. When I become agitated and controlling in the lives of others I unavoidably suffer. I create demands and expectations and flail emotionally with judgement, righteous indignation and bombastic rhetoric. I can chew on these perceived injustices like a dog on a bone, condemning the actions of others and inversely inflating my own sense of injury. I have come to realize that in life there is a never ending supply of these bones to chew on. I can always find fault in others. Today, these thoughts have become a laughably stark reminder of my desire to control life and my penchant to remain stuck in familiar unhealthy patterns of thinking and behavior—a comfortable ability to create my own misery that coddles and cuddles my "poor me" victimhood. Over time I've broken free from the grip of this sort of thinking but it can easily reappear. Today I am better able to recognize it, examine the truth of what is really going on, and do the adult and healthy work of finding ways to let go of my resentments. I can talk to friends, choose some action I will take, and move on. I am fully responsible for my own feelings and my own freedom to resolve them.

## May 14

The understanding that my physical self is unavoidably linked to my spiritual self is an important reminder of the various ways I can be conscious of how well the connection to my Higher Power is doing. My recovery is based on a daily reprieve that is contingent on my ability to sustain a fit spiritual condition and so it's important that I'm able to recognize when I'm perhaps drifting away from that fitness. I have often heard it said that self-care is our primary task in recovery and it takes many forms for me today. Having a commitment to physical well-being in terms of my diet and exercise is one part, but also how much rest I get and what activities I pursue can have an indirect impact upon my spiritual fitness. Simply taking the dog for a quick walk changes my outlook and provides a moment to connect with the natural world around me. Getting some fresh air and stretching my legs connects me to a more basic animal part of myself. I have found that my mental, spiritual, physical, and social selves are close companions—when one suffers they all do. In recovery I've learned that I live my life only in today and that there are no shortcuts that avoid this truth. I have a commitment to doing what I know I ought to and surely taking care of my physical needs is undeniably an important part of the self-care that my Higher Power encourages. Having a focus on maintaining the health of all areas of my life allows me to notice when I'm out of balance. By being in tune with my physical self I can notice the signals that alert me to problems in other parts of my life. I can ask if I am hungry, tired, or stressed about something? Do I need a break, some meditation or exercise? Have I been eating well and taking care of myself? Being aware of and addressing my physical needs helps keep my mental and spiritual health in balance. The disease of addiction centers in my mind yet also manifests in physical ways. Full recovery must address the entire range of the complex human system that includes the spiritual, physical, mental, and social parts of my life.

# May 15

There is a part of me that always wants to win. It can be a very strong feeling and at times will quickly consume my thinking. As a child I used winning as one of the ways to value myself in life. Competition is of course an important part of our social structure, but like so many parts of life as an addict I typically carry things to extremes. If a little is good, more must be better and I take one part of an idea and chase it so hard that I miss the other more subtle parts of it. For many years the result of this outlook led me to frame the world into a zero sum game. In all things there must be winners, losers, and no remainder—no other option. America particularly enshrines the framework of winner/loser in its cultural dialog, with the most popular sports eschewing the option of a draw. When I approach life with this thinking everything becomes a battle. So much of our cultural narrative about what it is to be a man centers on this sort of thinking and the result is a very limited set of options. In recovery I am reminded that life is rarely exists in black and white absolutes. If my only approach is from a perspective of battle than I will often be in fights that I can only lose. Of course addiction is a perfect example of a battle that I could never win. The cultural place of alcohol created by a system of pervasive marketing that tries to place it as a core part of being a man, a symbol of our virility and success, as a reward and entitlement for having won, is of course a bunch of rubbish. Recovery allows me to see through the crass manipulations of consumerism and understand the more profound and important values and meanings of life. By learning to cease fighting and go with the flow an entirely new and fascinating world opens up for me. Suddenly the subtleties and nuances of a more meaningful life display themselves. I become more spiritually able to be a part of how life unfolds around me instead of trying to control it and fight over my share of a very limited prize. I have become part of a much larger reward. When I am constantly battling over the individual trees I can never get into a position to see the forest.

# May 16

In recovery I've learned that in many ways the ability to trust is closely linked to the principle of faith that undergirds the third step. Like many men, both in the program and in out, trusting others can be a hard thing for me. Experiences from my childhood and life in general dented my ability to trust. In active addiction that trust was further weakened as I grew to view all people with wariness and suspicion. It seemed that in life whenever I trusted I would ultimately get burned. Despite this apprehension, and usually because of my poor judgments and decision-making based on selfishness, my trust was often misplaced. This then perpetuated the myth of an untrustworthy world. Ultimately as my addiction and failed efforts to control my behavior grew it got to the point that I couldn't even trust myself. The total annihilation of any ability to trust was then complete and I was living in a world that was truly bleak and harsh. Even the relationships of those closest to me contained little or no trust on either side. I found that in a world with no trust there can be no faith. There was a complete hopelessness and terrible loneliness as I struggled to find any sort of lasting contact with reality. In recovery I was exposed to the truth of seeing people who had been as sick as I was and had recovered. I couldn't understand how it had worked for them or if it would really work for me. I was asked to have faith that if I followed the path of recovery I too would recover. The only way forward was to trust that it would also work for me. I had to become willing to believe that doing things I didn't understand or think made sense would lead to recovery. Slowly but surely I started to rebuild a capacity to trust and was able to begin to grasp a true faith in a Higher Power. Today I have faith that as long as I keep walking in the right direction on the path of recovery my Higher Power will continue to take care of me and perhaps most importantly—that my spiritual connection to life, and a comfortable and rewarding place within it, will continue to expand.

## May 17

There is an obstinate, illogical, defiant and unreasonable part of me that often seems to want to fight the pressure to change. It usually comes out when I feel vaguely threatened or criticized. Often it doesn't really seem to matter what the suggestion or request is—my natural disposition is to personalize it and then resist it. It is a sort of belligerent trait of insolence that is rarely based in any rational thought. I know I am being unreasonable and that what I am resisting really isn't that big a deal but it is still very hard to let go of the inclination to oppose it. Learning how to understand this defect of character and to recognize how it manifests itself on a pretty much daily basis has taken some time and work. In recovery I am less likely to be subject to the completely insane and illogical results of this natural defiance but it is still something that I find myself having to work through. When my life is going smoothly and things just seem to be working easily I realize that I am in tune with my Higher Power and that my will is aligned properly. When I am doing what I ought to be doing things work out easily. When things are a battle, when I'm struggling and fighting life, usually my will is maladjusted. I am fighting my Higher Power. It is hard to see the problem when I am stuck in the middle of it—my emotions and angry defiance block me. I realize I am overreacting and behaving excessively but just can't seem to let go of whatever it is that is upsetting me. It has taken practice and the experiences of feeling foolish later when I calm down to teach me the skill of thinking more reasonably in the moment. I have found that prayer and meditation help to release me from myself. Talking about it with someone else often helps me gain the insight needed to see my self-imposed disorder. To become unstuck, I must step away for a while and regain perspective. Then I am able to adjust my thinking to a more reasonable state. Today when I am agitated I realize that it never hurts to simply take a little time-out and connect with the bigger picture of a spiritual connection to life.

## May 18

The old saying about "taking time to stop and smell the roses" was something I didn't take very seriously when I was younger. I was far too busy with my own plans and activities. I had things to do, places to go and people to see! This sort of excessive self-involvement is another example of how my efforts to control life blocked me from its enjoyment. In addition, this attitude reached new levels as I become willing to trade all of life around me in order to feed my selfish addictions. The realization that I was behaving in ways that were not healthy, were anti-social and hurtful to others, brought a vague uneasiness as ideas about "karma" and notions of God's punishment weighed on me. I would quickly create justifications and reassurances about my own cleverness and ability to beat the system. The good and bad in life became the results of my own actions as I deluded myself about the true powerlessness and lack of control I have in life. Recovery has taught me to understand that present in each day is an opportunity to live well. The spiritual element of the world is always available to me. There are easy and comfortable moments and blessings to be found all around me when I chose to be free of my own obsessive thinking and take the time to participate more fully in life. I realize that the good and bad things in my life aren't the punishments of karmic justice or the rewards of my own super-powers. Yes, while I must certainly take responsibility for my own actions and the consequences of my choices, I mustn't delude myself into thinking I'm in charge of things that can never be controlled. The spiritual part of the world goes on all around me. It is unconcerned with my personal situation but always willing to allow me to be a part of the good and peaceful moments it provides. In this way I can always take a break from the needy selfishness that magnifies my wants and problems and instead remind myself of how insignificant they really are in the bigger picture of the spiritual world all around me.

## May 19

The deep changes that take place in recovery are interesting and clear when I consider how differently I approach life today. Today I have found a way to consistently find contentment in my daily life. It is so different than how it used to be. I remember being younger and hearing men tell me that I should save a small percentage of each paycheck and slowly over time I would have enough money saved to perhaps buy a car or a home. I always thought, "Not me, I will find a way to get rich fast so no need to save slowly." I thought I was too smart for that sort of slow and steady approach to life. This idea that somehow I was different and that the rules didn't apply to me joined nicely with my ideas of excitement and selfish reward in life.

This exceptionalism drove thinking that said, "I deserve more, I want it now and I can make it happen." The idea that pursuit of material things through my conquest of life would bring me happiness was ineffective. Ultimately, in a sadly ironic twist of fate, my inability to control life and force my will upon it did lead me to the one thing I could briefly control in life—my escape from it. This escape in turn took control of me as I became powerless in addiction. Recovery has shown me how to find meaning in my life through a spiritual approach. Today the purposeful content of my actions contribute to the world around me and provide meaning that is valuable and lasting rather than fleeting excitements and hollow attainments. It is this meaning that creates the contentment in my life today. Having the spiritual recovery of working the steps, the human value of honest friendships, and the dignity of being of service to others allows me to accept my past and enjoy my present. It give me confidence in the plan my Higher Power has for my future. My spiritual capital has been created slowly, like the advice of saving a little every day, and in time it has added up to something larger than I could ever have imagined. I have learned how to find meaningful activity in my life that provides a simple and profound contentment.

# May 20

A person's search for truth has many names and forms but all seem to center on a theme of spiritual growth. I can sometimes feel lost for words to describe what I feel is going on with me because it is often not completely clear. Language is always imprecise to some degree, interpreted by each person's own understanding of the words they choose to use and so the search for truth seems very personal to me. It must first occur at level below that of words—in the "heart and soul" of my being. The art of self-examination requires me to find quiet times of introspection that allow my inner voice to be heard. The modern world of persistent and hectic "interrupt driven" communication with its endless stream of parsed interaction with others can block me from deep interaction with myself. In the insanity of active addiction all contact with my spiritual side was blocked and my inner voice was hidden, rejected and ignored. Today, my selfish willfulness can still block me from doing what I know is right or ignoring the feelings inside that something I'm doing is wrong. Life in recovery is clear about the importance of prayer and meditation. It allows me the quiet time to find and receive a better understanding of who I am and what is going on with my inner self. As I've practiced and worked at becoming closer with my own spirituality it has enabled me to cut through the socialized wrapping of what I think the world around me wants my truth to be. It provides the truth of my own feelings and a path to my core beliefs and values. The search for the truth and wisdom to understand who I am and the ability to hear the language of my own truth centers on my spiritual journey and the quieting of my mind in order to hear the messages from within. They help me know when I am on track and provide the quiet comfort of serenity and purpose. Through the process I become wiser about who I am and where I stand with my Higher Power and my place within the world around me.

# May 21

The ability to gain understanding and acceptance of who I am is one of the great benefits of recovery. As children the point of reference with which we judge ourselves is mostly external and our identity is linked to the opinions and values of others. For me however, the normal teenage struggle of trying to develop my own sense of personhood remained unresolved as I careened into addiction. I never grew skilled at examining my feelings and I avoided the hard work of self-discovery that normally co-locates those external points of reference with internal ones. As a result, my life became framed in that cliché of one who doesn't stand for something and then falls for anything. My idea of who I was shifted based on the beliefs of those around me and became subverted by addiction Recovery has shown me that the natural and inescapable loneliness of being human cannot be avoided by merging my identity with others. Instead of my identity being framed in an effort to become part of a truth that resides in other people I can instead rely on the truth that resides within me. I must go through the maturation process and develop my own identity. I am the only one who can do this work that takes place in my mind, heart and soul. Knowing who I am and having moral behavior that supports my values and beliefs allows me to have integrity of self and a connection with a Higher Power. Finally accepting this truth instead of avoiding it with addiction allows me to understand that I alone am responsible for who I am and that the process of self-discovery is what truly enables me to be "a part of" the world around me. One of the most interesting parts of this process is how it becomes expressed in my evolving interests and passions in life. Today I am able to follow my own interests and hobbies in ways that are independent of the opinions of others. Who I am isn't framed or constrained by an external belief and so I can experiment, grow, and find all sorts of ways to express my participation in life, be it fishing, music or perhaps even visiting an art gallery.

# May 22

One of the great liberties of human life is our freedom to think and express our own ideas. When I share my thoughts and ideas I publish parts of myself in a way that helps me learn more about who I am. It is a practical way of developing a spiritual connection that overcomes the fear and shame that tells me I'm not good enough—ineligible and valueless with nothing to contribute. Sharing with others validates my own unique identity and place in the world. To some degree we all grow up facing the tyranny of the majority—the pressure to conform and fit in and accept the cultural norms and beliefs that surround us. Religion, consumerism, manliness, education and the all-important work ethic promise to help us "get ahead" and do well in life by conforming to the beliefs of others. While there is much good in some of these things, the relentless pressure to conform can stifle my own thinking and preclude the self-discovery and experimentation needed to figure out my own ideas and beliefs. For me, the fear of not being good enough and of not fitting in was combined with a rebelliousness that found a perfect solution in alcohol. Ironically enough, in addiction I became subject to a whole new twisted and deformed set of cultural values and norms that were even more tyrannical. Addiction left no room for questioning or discovery, only the base savage need to consume at any cost that increasingly eroded my humanity and personhood. The word recovery itself is insightful when considering the path to renewal it provides. The focus isn't to recover all that I lost, but instead I recover from the effect of addiction that precluded an ability to find my own true identity and beliefs. I get the chance to answer questions about who I really am, what I stand for, and what I think about life's meaning and my place in it. I have gained the confidence to transcend the fear of society and its demand for a mindless conformity of "being right" as I explore my own answers to questions of God and humanity. It has given me the ability to express those ideas within the friendships that make them real. By being heard I can at last become "a part of" and enjoy some true integrity of self rather than simply parroting what I think the world wants me to say and think.

# May 23

A friend of mine often jokes that if someone wants to really know how he's doing they should ask his wife because she is perhaps likely to provide a more accurate answer. The crux of self-discovery and learning who I am in life is one of the main themes of recovery as I face the inherent loneliness of my own humanness and the character building of personal growth. Learning who I am makes my relationship with a Higher Power both possible and increasingly effective. One of the truths I have found along the way is that the ability to be intimate, honest, and caring develops slowly as I build a relationship with myself and others. To create a long lasting bridge between two people there must be strong foundations on each side from which we build outwards towards a middle ground. Nowhere is this truth more evident than in my relationships with women. The old and unhealthy false clichés about manhood kept me in denial and prevented any progress. Fear of not being good enough and a lack of experience and understanding of intimacy with myself precluded me from finding it with others. I easily confused and substituted sexual lust and emotions for meaningful love and closeness. I suffered a crippling inability to share my own feelings and thoughts, partly because I struggled to allow someone that close to me, but mostly because I simply didn't know them myself. My relationships were shallow, co-dependent and transitory. They were more like the relationships with my favorite bartenders that could change on a whim. Recovery has helped me begin to learn the language, the skills and the craft of personal growth and human closeness with others that is vital in an intimate loving relationship. Overcoming the profound lack of understanding of my fear, and the ultimate acceptance of it as an always present part of any relationship, breaks through the denial that keeps me always vaguely isolated and lonely in the company of others and allows me to explore a bond that is solid, stable and trustworthy in my intimate relationships today.

# May 24

The interlinked relationship between honesty, denial, responsibility, and accountability is often hard for me to understand precisely. Like many parts of recovery, time takes time and the process reveals more as I become experienced and better able to interpret my feelings and emotions. While the cliché about the "layers of the onion" is an overused one there is a certain usefulness to the image because each layer can only be revealed, and truly observed, after the previous one has been removed. Often-times life events take place that directly relate to a level of personal understanding that I haven't discovered yet, making it hard for me to accept or see my part in some situation or problem. The process of being accountable for my actions in life and ensuring that I don't avoid or ignore the problems I create—often by being overly focused on other people's actions—helps me build integrity about who I am. It helps me find my place in the world and define proper boundaries about what is, and what is not, my business. Attending to the business of keeping my side of the street clean in life means admitting my mistakes and resolving the problems I create. The process can provide a deeper self-understanding. It gives me a level of self-esteem and confidence that allows me to have an open-mindedness and acceptance about my own mistakes, faults and failings. It offers a practical and effective way to face and overcome both my fear of not being good enough and the denial of my shortcomings. By investigating and admitting my faults and mistakes I am invoking honesty and integrity in clear and meaningful ways that help me become a better man. Similar to many themes of recovery, it is this process of self-examination that provides a way for me to turn what have been weaknesses and defects into insightful strengths that improve my life and increase my usefulness to others. Today I see the benefit of facing my faults and admitting my mistakes so that I can truly learn the lessons they offer.

# May 25

The process of a spiritual "house cleaning" allows me to become much healthier in several ways. By sharing my faults and mistakes with another person my insides become more closely aligned with my outsides. The "who I am" to the world around me is no longer in conflict and denial with the "who I am" on the inside. This process of "coming clean" with another man and then having the commitment to recovery needed to continue keeping my spiritual house in order allows me to become more comfortable with accepting and confessing my own faults and shortcomings. I am learning how to use this process as a regular and frequent part of how I stay in tune with the world around me. I can find relief regularly and easily instead of grinding through the overwhelmingly difficult and painful results of situations that have built up over months—festering inside me until they can't be contained or are discovered. The honest conversations with others and admission of failings or personal struggles also allows me an insight to the process of spiritual growth itself. I am reminded of how it is, and always will be, an ongoing part of my walk along life's path using the principles of recovery. It shows me another way to find freedom from the peculiarity of the bondage of self that traps me with an excessive concern with the faults of others. It helps maintain the shift to personal responsibility that replaces my tendency to blame others for my problems. Recovery has shown me that I become free by confessing my own faults rather than the faults of others. My own tree of spirituality grows taller and straighter as I seek my own growth instead of twisted and bent from peering and judging at the actions of others. Lastly, sharing my failings frees me from the burden and weight of the guilt and shame of my faults and the keeping of secrets that traps me in the past and future. I can walk lightly; open to the world around me, participating fully in the now of each day.

# May 26

The lack of any realistic vision for my future and a complete absence of faith and hope was a hallmark of my life in addiction. All I was concerned about was the immediate future, how I was going to get through the next day or two. Plans or ideas any longer than that were always unrealistic and invalid because even in the fog of addiction they didn't bear scrutiny. I knew it was just talk that wasn't rooted in any sort of meaningful reality. Even then, in subtle underlying ways, I knew that there was no real future in what I was doing but my denial kept that truth at bay. The removal of an imagination of a future that had any connection to truth was a big part of the hopelessness of my addiction. I was resigned to the ongoing downward descent of my life into an ever worse condition that I unconsciously accepted. Recovery slowly returned the ability to imagine a future for myself in meaningful ways. At first it was small things, a tiny spark of hope that there was something. Although it was hard to see what it might turn into or if it could be sustained. Over time that hope grew, and as my progress in recovery continued to bring improvements to my world, emotionally, spiritually, mentally and socially, I began to have faith that my hopes were valid. It slowly became possible for me to imagine a new future for myself and recovery provided the tools and support I needed to pursue it. Being sober for a while has allowed me to see the path I have walked already. I've come a long way by simply approaching life one day at time and I see the truth of the results it brings. I've learned that my own ability to dream and imagine what my life will become is a valuable way of encouraging my progress. Sometimes it works out just as I'd imagined but usually there is more. I most often underestimate what the future can hold in the longer term. The process of following my dreams enlarges them as the reality of my progress opens new horizons of thinking and experience. Life has become a journey that helps me understand the joy of each day and its vital contribution to my future—and my past.

# May 27

In human life it is often said that the gift of reason is what separates us from the animals. The ability to use logic and language allows us to see the course of our life, to plot our future and learn from the collective experience and expertise of the past. It allows us to make choices and gives us free will. Unlike the animal kingdom, the world of man is also uniquely aware of our own mortality and as a result I am easily led away from the satisfaction and enjoyment of today by the worries and concerns of what will happen tomorrow. Fear can overcome my faith and drive efforts to shape and control a future that hasn't arrived yet. Many of our actions in life will hold meaning long after we are gone—in buildings, books and culture, or in the memory of my family and friends. This ability to act into history can perhaps create a God like desire to determine the outcome of my own life. It can easily allow me to lose sight of my truly basic animal nature and reality. Addiction was an experience that prevented me from learning and understanding my own true powerlessness in the world. It had the opposite effect by giving me at first the illusion and then the delusion of control. It allowed me to avoid and deny the acceptance of the ultimate symbol of my own powerlessness—my ultimate mortality. The self-centric modern world loves to highlight conversations about personal legacy and grandiose symbolic achievements. In recovery I've learned to reframe my life in the now of living that takes place each day. It has shown me how living well and helping others today will create meaningful change and goodwill that contributes to tomorrow. In recovery, I often hear people speak about how we stand today on the shoulders of those who have gone before us. I try to not give away today in the worry, fear, or attempt to control a tomorrow that is not yet formed and has not yet arrived. My life continues to improve in recovery as I trust in God and keep it simple each day while working on the things that are in front of me. As my sponsor often reminds me, sometimes the next right thing to do is the dishes.

# May 28

Becoming and remaining open minded has not always been easy for me. Learning how to loosen the death grip of control I have on life is an ongoing and subtle battle. In many ways, becoming involved with drugs and alcohol at an early age left me somewhat of a grown child. I held onto an almost childish thinking about right and wrong and how things are "supposed to be" along with a tenacious belief in the validity of what "I knew" to be true. My worldview was often very black and white with little room for subtlety, variance, or the "grey areas" of a more mature and reasonable understanding of life. My approach was unreasonable and petulantly childish at times, lacking the mature insight and appreciation of the complexities and imperfections of human nature. Recovery has shown me that it is not a "one size fits all" world. The ability for each of us to have our own understanding of a Higher Power is an example of how there are often many correct answers to the same question. It highlights the fallacy of approaching life with a framework that says there is only one right way and that your ideas have to be wrong in order for mine to remain right. Seeing that choices that are different than my own are not a threat opens the door to an ability for me to be safe while being wrong. Only then was I able to see that I'm only true to myself when I choose to follow my own path to my own truth. I no longer need to adopt and defend a truth that some else has forged—one that I've not fully authenticated and understood through my own thinking and beliefs. The search for my own morals and values, and using them to evaluate in a flexible accepting way what I see in others, allows me to be open to new ideas that can expand my worldview and underlying beliefs. I am no longer closed minded and forced to be stuck in a pattern of thinking that may not be suitable for the man I am becoming. The process of being open-minded and examining my beliefs more fully allows me to be more confident of who I am and what I believe in today.

# May 29

Learning to have a relationship with a Higher Power began with my willingness to do two things each day. The first was becoming honest about my actions and efforts. The second was being willing to kneel and pray—saying "help" and "thank you"—even for just a moment or two each morning. These two things were catalysts in allowing me to finally become a part of recovery and opened the door to change in my life. When I arrived in recovery I, like many new arrivals, struggled with rigorous honesty. At first in recovery I regularly lied to myself and others about important things making it difficult to have a meaningful relationship with God. As I tried to stay sober it became clear that I could have no valid or helpful relationship with a Higher Power unless I became honest. While I could ask for help (and I'm certain that God did look out for me when I was in active addiction), in order for recovery to actually work I had to be willing to do my part. Just as I can't find love by hoping someone else's ability to love will create my own, I can't expect God's spirituality to somehow strike me like a lightning bolt and render me changed. I had to learn to be honest with myself about who I was, what my actions were, and most importantly, make an honest effort to change. I had to stop doing things I knew I shouldn't. I had to learn that I can't listen to God when I'm busy asking for what "I" want. I am often unclear as to exactly what God's will is for me—but I have a long list of things I know that aren't. Early in recovery I made a decision to build a relationship with a Higher Power. Over the following months and years that relationship has become stronger and my knowledge of what it means to be honest, to have hope, faith, courage, integrity, and a small degree of humility—all within a framework of spirituality—has grown accordingly. In order to become "a part of" I had to do the work, the same work that those in recovery before me have done.

## May 30

The human ability to review my past experiences and continue to learn from them long afterwards is a powerful force in my recovery and spiritual growth. In so many ways I am inherently and inescapably propelled in my actions and thinking today by the experiences of my past. In addiction my view of life became very grim, short, and shallow. It was darkly focused on the survival of each day and the desire to avoid any review of who I had become and what I was doing each day. Recovery allows me to learn more about who I am today through a better understanding and re-framing of my thinking, beliefs, and how I relate to my past experiences. Some of my most difficult and painful memories are of events that I wanted to forget and pretend never happened. Those same events have now become valuable in their ability to be useful to others in recovery. Standing water often stagnates. It requires a river of new water to flow through it to remain fresh—and so it is with my experiences in life. The stagnation of addiction nearly killed me but today I am able to bring new experiences and new ways of thinking and understanding into my life. As I learn more about myself I am able to look back at my past experiences and see the undeniable truth of personal growth that has occurred for me in recovery. This helps me in the "now" of today by providing me with the understanding that I don't have to have a complete grasp of today's lessons. I just need to keep moving along and trust that in time more will be revealed—provided I am willing to continue to do the work of review and self-examination. Each day is another chance to be a part of the life that is around me. To be open to finding new pieces of insight that may add to and expand my understanding of the lessons of my past. I can never change the truth of my past but I can always increase my own understanding of its meaning, purpose, effect on me, and its potential value.

## May 31

In recovery I have faced some unpleasant truths about myself and my past. I have learned how to try to live life on life's terms and not avoid or escape from the painful struggles of life through addictive behavior. I have come to accept that the full richness of life provides a wide range of experiences, some of which are painful and difficult. Tragedy, anguish, grief and loss are ultimately unavoidable in life. The experience of miserable suffering and pain is a part of life and recovery offers me the opportunity to go through it sober with the support of others. Many things in life cannot be fixed, changed or repaired—they simply are. They often serve as stark reminders of my own powerlessness in life. The great truths of life and death are humbling and they help me understand the simple value of my own existence. In recovery I have learned how to be a part of the "we" that is life. I can share in other people's suffering without having to try to cure, relieve, or abate it. The expression of compassion and simply standing with someone in their pain demonstrates a fuller connectedness with life and the importance of my freedom from the isolation and bondage of addiction. It is often an uncomfortable and difficult experience and recovery has shown me how to participate fully in these movements. They are powerful and partly remain with me long after they are over. Today I have friends who are with me through thick and thin, who understand and accept the storms we face in life. Regardless of how the problems came to be—my friends are there to help me weather them. I too am able to be a support to others in their most difficult times and calmly accept and experience it with them. There is a profound love of each other's shared core humanity that I feel in these experiences. It reminds me that I am human, and always a part of a larger shared world with others. Today in recovery I need never stand alone.

# June

"A grudging willingness to admit error does not suffice; you have to cultivate a taste for it."
— Aaron Haspel

"I knew if I stayed where I was, nothing would get better; nothing would change. If I wanted to ease the pain, I had to try something different."
— Sharon E. Rainey

"The willingness to grow is the essence of all spiritual development."
— Bill W.

# JUNE 1

The reality of having had a spiritual awakening is a constant force that acts in many ways to keep my mind in a good place. It is an ever present reminder of what my life is like today because of the choice to take my place in recovery. In a way it is a steady confirmation and affirmation that I am on the correct path in my life journey. Addiction blocked any kind of spiritual connectedness to the world around me and in recovery I can still at times become blocked. I sometimes allow fear to overcome my commitment to faith. It is easy for me to confuse the healthy self-reliance of my own thinking (that occurs when it is aligned with my Higher Power) with that of the selfish fearful mindset that occurs when I am trying to be in charge and control. Over time it has become easier to recognize and correct my course when this happens. Until I experienced a prolonged reality of living on a spiritual basis I used to disdainfully discard such a notion. Today, having experienced it as others said I would if I followed their path in recovery, it is easy to see when I am blocked from the "sunlight of the spirit."[13] I quickly notice when I become unable to enjoy the simple signs of nature around me, am intolerant and dismissive of others, or overly frustrated, restless and discontent. Today I am rarely controlled by my fear of the unknown. Sometimes it takes a while to re-gather my calm and certainly not all days are easy. However, I am better able to accept that a part of the struggle of life in recovery is the work of staying on a spiritual path. It is the critical element in sustaining successful recovery. Always I find that the cause of my problem is not that the world around me has fundamentally changed—it is I who has allowed my thinking to drift away from the spiritual world that surrounds me. Often I must open myself to it again through a renewed commitment to prayer and meditation or by helping others. The fantastic gift of experiencing a spiritual awakening allows me to face life in an entirely new way that continues to become more rewarding.

# JUNE 2

There is little doubt about the addictive qualities and feelings that are a part of falling in love. The art of building a romantic relationship with another person can be life's greatest challenge for many people. It is perhaps especially so for the co-dependent addict. Over the years I have

---

[13] *Alcoholics Anonymous : The Story of How Many Thousands of Men and Women Have Recovered from Alcoholism*. 4th ed. New York City: Alcoholics Anonymous World Services, 2001. P. 66.

learned many lessons about healthy boundaries from my relationships—the enmeshment that occurs from a lack of personal boundaries, the bad motives hidden under good ones, and the many levels of personal honesty that I continue explore. Of course in addiction my relationships were largely shallow and dishonest, driven by my physical needs and a desire to attain some fantasy image of a bond about which I knew or understood very little. Active addiction precluded any sort of meaningful and honest relationship. In recovery, I've learned how to have more honesty in relationships with both my partner and most critically with myself. The tools of recovery provide an ability to better see who I really am and to become honest and familiar with my own feelings and needs. It has opened an entirely new understanding of what it means to be in love. In the past I have used women as a way to try and fill gaps in my own personal development, uncomfortably trying to participate in some kind of "union" of two people into one. Recovery has shown me how codependency can mask my own undeveloped personality. I have had to learn how to become a more emotionally mature and developed person so that I can have healthy relations with others while properly maintaining my own personal integrity as an individual. I have had to learn how to be healthy and whole with myself before I could be successful in an intimate loving relationship with another person. In addiction, I often claimed to love someone else without the understanding of love that first comes from being able to love one's own self. Similar to how in recovery we can't give away what we don't have, the same has been true for me with love. Until I could learn how to love myself in a caring and meaningful way I remained unable to do so authentically with another person.

# JUNE 3

Finding meaning and purpose to our existence is one of life's greatest and most difficult spiritual questions. For me, when the idealistic dreams of my youth were confronted with some of the harsh realities of life, alcoholism diverted my search for any sort of spiritual meaning or purpose in life. I found meaning in partying and extremes. Slow and steady was for "regular people" and I wanted to be on the fast track to life. Ultimately that approach didn't work out very well for me as my addiction took its predictable path. I lost myself in a mystifying morass of moral malfeasance that left me spiritually corrupted and empty. My inability to find any sort of individual meaning in life seemed to preclude me from authentic participation in a satisfying life shared with others. The further away from society I drifted the more I sought out great plans and quick solutions that would suddenly solve my problems. Unfortunately in life, history shows us that there are few "on-demand" instantly available solutions to achieving sustained spiritual growth.

I have found that the process of recovery has occurred slowly and steadily, an ever increasing capacity that I can add to by doing small things well each day. Finding meaning and significance in the simple routine of living has become my greatest reward in life. Recovery has shown me the futility of spending today focused on tomorrow or yesterday. It has only been through the slow and steady accumulation of each worthwhile day of living well that I have managed to change my past. Today I can look back in life and find satisfaction with how I am living. I can clearly see how those many days, most of them on their own quite plain and ordinary, have added up to something meaningful. This truth reminds me to slow down and enjoy the often humdrum tedious parts of my day. It has allowed me to find meaning in the simple things that in themselves perhaps have little value but as part of the larger picture they become important—similar perhaps to how my individual spirituality becomes an important part of a greater human possibility.

# JUNE 4

Often it is easy for me to feel connected to my Higher Power when things are going well and my spirits are high. It is much harder to maintain that positivity and reliance when I'm down in the dumps. The lesson of HALT— asking myself if I am hungry, angry, lonely or tired helps me realize that my own self care is always an important element of recovery and that I am responsible for taking the action required to maintain it. However, sometimes feeling out of sorts is just how it is for me. I've learned the importance of accepting that some days are simply difficult and rather than getting worked up about what is going on and becoming obsessed with finding out what the problem is that "I" need to fix, or determining exactly what is "wrong', I can instead realize that I may not have the answer myself. I can choose to let go and let God. Ultimately it is up to me to take action and sometimes that action is to rely on my faith in a Higher Power. Of course once I have the bit between my teeth so to speak and am chewing on the problem like a dog with a bone it can be extra hard to simply let go. Faith allows me to see past the darkness of a particular moment in time and to pull back my view into a larger frame and remind myself of the facts about my recovery. Over the years I continue to move along the path of recovery, sometimes quickly, sometimes slowly, sometimes in the bright sunlight and other times in the dark rainy dreariness of a difficult day. When I am in a low spot I can look at the bigger picture and remember that this too shall pass. I become better able to quit fighting it and just let go. I'll often find relief within a few hours or days and in a week or two am rarely able to even remember what the problem was. It is important for me to remember that today I am not alone—ever. I always have the relationship with my Higher Power to rely on. In some ways this understanding of the absolute and constant relief from the crushing loneliness of addiction that my Higher Power offers is perhaps the greatest source of gratitude for me today.

# JUNE 5

The ability to accept change in my life has been one of the hallmarks of my recovery. The ultimate symbol of futility was the unwillingness to change that sustained my continued addiction as I held onto ideas and modes of thinking that were clearly failing me horribly. Fear of change and the unknown of a different future, the idea of losing what I had even though it was awful, kept me in a "groundhog day" cycle of pain and despair. Recovery offered me a mechanism and structure with which to pursue a spiritual awakening that required a major shift in how I looked at myself and my beliefs—who I was and how I related to the world around me. It provided a pathway on which I was able to allow these changes to occur by invoking a spiritual relationship with a Higher Power. I am no longer able to justify my actions and beliefs by simply saying things like, "Well that's just how I am." I am compelled to exert personal responsibility to examine and consider how my actions shape my experience in life. Despite the lessons of personal growth and change that I have found in recovery it is still easy to find myself in a rut of sorts, resting on my spiritual laurels as it were. I must remember to see the world around me with an open mind and fresh perspective. The undeniable truth of the nature of life is that it is always a process. The constant framework of life and death is present in all things around us. Nothing stays the same forever and to fight against the inevitable changes that take place in my life is childish. Not only am I more mature physically but hopefully I am also mentally and spiritually older in ways that enable greater wisdom. In addiction I spent my days foolishly trying to hold onto to some sort of magically false ideal or vaporous moment of intoxicative bliss. In recovery I can embrace change. Having faith and hope provides the courage to walk through new phases of my life calmly with an acceptance that, like the rest of the world around me, I am "a part of" life, right where I'm supposed to be, no longer in denial and fighting a battle destined to end in failure but instead gracefully enjoying a journey that continually evolves.

# JUNE 6

In recovery we often speak of progress and there can be little progress without change. One of the most fundamental effects of recovery has been a re-creation of the way I think about myself on a day to day basis. The "truth" of who I am and my understanding of how I view myself and my place in the world has shifted profoundly from the perspective and reality I arrived with. Not long ago, a friend in recovery who has known me for many years mentioned that "how I speak" has changed. Language at its core is very subjective. The words I use have a specific connotation and meaning that is the mechanism of how my truth is shared. How I express myself, the words I choose to use, provide a context and meaning that creates a larger picture than just the words. This image that results from how I choose to express my thinking can have a profound impact on how I see myself. It is an effect that is deeper than my spoken words. My very thoughts are mostly formed with unspoken words and so my thinking becomes constructed within the framework of the words I choose. My life in addiction was a downward slide that became ugly, grim, and desperate. I didn't drink my way into a higher social status or a more uplifting and spiritual setting—it was of course the very opposite. I ended up in low places with people who had also lost their way and often their health and minds as well. Today I don't curse as much. I avoid words that are angry or self-defeating. The language I chose to use both internally and externally is a part of the non-physical and spiritual world I try to connect with and live in. In addiction I was in some pretty horrible places both physically and mentally. While in recovery I have made progress. My world has dramatically changed and along the way my language and thinking have changed—together—because perhaps that is only way it can happen. The responsibility of taking action within the framework of my own recovery is always present and it often arrives in the choices I make in both my thinking and action.

# JUNE 7

For many years I was convinced of my ability to avoid the mundane requirements of taking the "normal" route in life. I wasn't willing to conform to the responsibilities and duties of society that most others complied with. I felt superior to the average person and that while in some ways the rules may apply to me, I could certainly find my own smarter and faster path to success. I had this idea that I could somehow avoid the hard work, the detailed daily slog of life, and instead just "wing it." While I did have some success with that approach I was often woefully unprepared and lacking in the deeper skills necessary for any sort of sustainable success in life. Fleeting moments of victory that seemed to vindicate my approach soon disappeared as life continued to repeatedly defeat me until I was unavoidably confronted with the simple fact that I was broken inside and deeply flawed spiritually. This wasn't a news flash. Instead it was more like an unspoken truth that I had always known. For years it had lurked around a dark corner of my innermost self, a shadowy voice of doubt, inadequacy, and fear that I was desperate to avoid. Over time my fear and avoidance combined with addiction to distort me into someone I barely knew. My unwillingness to deal with my spiritual malady almost killed me more than once over the years until at last I became entirely willing to go through the painful process of facing my fears and shortcomings. There was no shortcut around this ultimate challenge of discovering who I really was in order to reconcile my past with my present. Recovery provides a single solution that offers the steps as a way to free oneself from the past and enter a new life. It worked for me as it has worked for millions of others, but only when I finally became entirely willing. What I have learned is that for years I was trying to find a shortcut to life that doesn't exist and that in recovery each of us must take our own lengthy and often difficult path to a sustainable spiritual awakening.

# JUNE 8

There was a truly deceptive element to my life when I was in active addiction. Looking back, it reminds me of those experiments in which the subject and environment is controlled, perhaps like on those "hidden camera" type TV shows where the person is misled and doesn't really know what is going on—their actions are largely predetermined although they don't realize it. Everyone else knows what is going to happen next except them. For them it is real, emotional, and appears unbelievable but yet authentic. Then suddenly the truth emerges and they shake their heads in relieved disbelief. Living life in recovery has in many ways been a similar experience except that the moments of truth and insight continue to arrive as I increase my own self-discovery through lessons that build upon each other. The lessons I learn today could not have occurred without the lessons I learned last month, or year ago. There are obvious examples of this change in my life when I see how much I am able to truly enjoy the positive things in life today—the celebrations, other people, the arts and music. I am able to be present for these things and experience them fully. I recall attending a church recital and listening to organ music that was written 400 years ago and I was able to lose myself in the sound, the texture, and the melody as I thought about all the generations before me that have enjoyed the same music. Being able to fully experience the moment, to participate in the richness of life around me, is a gift of recovery that is available each day as a result of a connection to a Higher Power and a willingness to choose where I place my daily focus. Just as there will always be a wide range of negative things in life for me to focus on there are also many positive things and it is my responsibility to decide which world I want to spend most of my time in. Just as witnessing the joy and relief of recovery is unavoidable when I attend recovery meetings, so it is with the community of life and the world of nature that is all around me.

# JUNE 9

Learning how to have healthy relationships has been a vital element of my new life in recovery. I have learned how to have deeper, honest and more meaningful friendships rather than the superficial and non-trusting ones before in my life. Learning how to be honest with myself has opened the door to honesty with others and I have also found that the same has been true with love. I never was able to comfortably love myself wholly until finding the honesty and integrity that recovery has brought into my life. Nowhere has this change been more dramatic and powerful than in the ability to understand and participate in loving relationships with others. In addiction my relationships weren't very healthy. There was little trust or honesty and my idea of what love should be was juvenile and immature. Commitment, tolerance, compassion, patience, and responsibility were often absent and without them my relationships were transactional and begrudging. I held up a frame of some idealized love rhetoric and expected a person to fit into it rather than discovering and learning to love the person in front of me. Today I am able to commit fully and honestly to my relationships, be they acquaintances, co-workers, colleagues, friends or romantic in nature. In my closer relations I am able to have faith and trust in a Higher Power that allows me to grapple with unavoidable and difficult emotions and vulnerability in new ways that are not so enmeshed and codependent. I am not trying to save, fix, or unite with someone else to make myself whole in order find a love or status that I seek. Instead of using another person as a way to repair or improve my unsatisfied life I am able to show up as a person who is whole and loving—arriving from a space of contentment and willing to share my life openly with another. Developing an ability to form a true relationship with another person has required much more than rhetoric or knowledge. It continues to be a process of patience, tolerance, open-mindedness, forgiveness and compassion in which I grow as a person as I connect more deeply with others.

# JUNE 10

My sponsor is fond of reminding people that the first word of the twelve steps of recovery is "We" and that it is a program that can't be done entirely alone. When I arrived in recovery I had no honest or healthy relationships with anyone at all, least of all myself. The people I had been close to were also struggling with addiction and so there was no firm ground around me on which I could stand and gather myself. I had to leave that world behind and move to a world that in many ways I knew very little about. In recovery I found a place to begin to learn how to live a sober life and build honest relationships. That slow and difficult process started with my sponsor and the other men who were part of our group. By spending time with them I was able to see how others in recovery lived their lives and what it meant to a part of the "we" of life. I had to let go of the pop culture messaging of being a rock or an island as some sort of ideal of self-reliance that is so often promoted as an insight or guide into what being a "real man" is all about. In recovery I continue to learn that the truth of manhood is found in my ability to be open with others. I am learning how to accept help in order to take care of my own business so that I can be an example to others of how recovery works. Today I have many close friends and we share what is really going on in our lives. It is a blessing to have the closeness, love, and support that these men offer me and I am able to make much better choices through a shared understanding of life around me. We learn from each other as we progress through the unavoidable challenges and difficulties of our recovery and continue to improve our ability to live life on life's terms. The poisonous effects of addiction skewed my thinking and altered the very chemistry of my mind in profound ways that became entrenched and enculturated over many years. Just as it took a long time to reach my bottom in addiction, the path of recovery is a long steady journey I could not have followed alone. The guidance and example of those who have gone before me continues to show me the way today. I must remain in regular contact with my friends in recovery to ensure I am still growing spiritually and benefiting from their insight and experience.

# JUNE 11

When I first arrived in recovery I remember being so muddled and confused. Counselors at treatment discussed things that I thought shouldn't have been so painfully difficult to grasp. I struggled with even most basic concepts and questions about myself and my behavior. My inability to think critically was disheartening and in many ways I was a complete stranger to myself. For many months I struggled greatly to connect with an understanding of my own values and morals. At first it was a hard question to engage with at all, but as I worked on it I realized that the difficulty lay in my own lack of self-understanding and insight. I wasn't able to connect to these concepts because I'd never really connected them to me—to who I was. This gap made it very hard to make any progress. Also, one of the clearly unavoidable consequences of sobriety was that the guilt and shame of my actions in addiction were starkly revealed. The distortion of my thinking, natural instincts, and desires caused by addiction had made any sort of effective self-examination profoundly distant and unclear. It was a terrible combination of a clearly present and painful problem with a foggy and difficult to grasp solution. What little understanding I did have of a value system most often centered on materialistic and external comparative measurements—how much money I had, clever escapes and deals I had done, women I had been with and the extraordinary stories of insane exploits and "drunkalogs." Recovery has helped me become more aware of who I want to be and how to value my own actions meaningfully against a more realistic and valid internal reference. The value I place on my moral beliefs and understandings like personal honesty, compassion, and fairness is the baseline of how I determine my identity today. My self-esteem and worth are generated and maintained through my actions each day rather than my possessions or my past. The ability to look at who I am and be happy with what I see is a gift. It occurs as a result of the choices I make about how I live my life through healthy personal interests, service, having honest relationships with others, working the steps, and maintaining an active conscious contact with my Higher Power.

# JUNE 12

I remember seeing a small fruit tree in a garden at the side of a house that had been trained to grow into a spiral shape. It was very creative and decorative but also somehow sadly misshapen and malformed. I started drinking alcoholically at a young age and in some ways addiction caused me to grow up crooked and malformed, rather like that tree. In addiction I never was able to do the hard work of looking at myself and finding my own truths or to face the facts of my past and take true ownership and responsibility for who and what I really was or what I actually stood for. However I was good at forming a temporary truth about myself for any situation that occurred. I could re-define my past or my beliefs the same way I could choose my clothes. I would pick whatever "truth" I wanted about who I was based on what I thought any particular situation needed. Depending on what story I was telling my personal truth was shaped accordingly. The real me was someone I didn't know. When I sobered up and began trying to change my life I struggled for a long while because I remained largely unwilling to face the difficult and uncomfortable work of self-discovery. In some ways it was easier to say, "That's just the way I am," and avoid the often very painful and wrenching requirements of spiritual growth. Fortunately I am not a twisted tree trunk, unable to reform myself, and recovery has helped me learn more about who I have been, who I am today, and who I am trying to be tomorrow. It has taught me how to find myself and choose my own path forward while breaking free from my old ideas and belief systems that defined and limited my thinking about who I am. It is amazing how a simple and small beginning—a willingness to let go of the beliefs that prevented a truly deep and meaningful self-examination— has led to an incredible journey of personal growth and discovery. Even though I am just a simple individual, I have found an ocean of explorative opportunity within myself. Today, instead of the fear and worry about what others are thinking and doing, I am able to know what I am thinking and believe in. I follow a path guided by a security of faith and spiritual belonging rather than the isolated longing and fearful worries of addictive thinking.

# JUNE 13

It was hard to get past the cycle of shame that became an ingrained part of my life in addiction. The guilt of my actions were so oppressive that the only relief I could find was a temporary one provided by the continued daily escape of inebriation that continued to make things even worse. Each day would be a repeat of the previous one, a bizarre and tragic sort of repetition that kept me trapped by the negative forces of active addiction. The relentless burden of shame and guilt eroded my ability to sustain any sort of self-worth or esteem. When I at last sobered up things seemed even bleaker as I was confronted with a clearer view of what had happened in my life. In early sobriety the wreckage of active addiction lay around me as though I was sitting alone in the remains of a bombed-out city of disaster. As I slowly put my life back together and moved further away from those days I was still haunted by my past. Many of the problems took years to overcome and some may never be fully repaired. The challenge was to find a way to become able to build a new life without remaining trapped by my old one. Recovery has shown me that I can reframe my understanding of the past and in turn rebuild my own personal esteem and self-worth. When I look back at some parts of my life I cannot be proud of who I was or how my actions impacted others, however, I can look at who I am today and know that I remain willing to repair my past. As I start each day I can look in the mirror and know that yesterday I lived well. With each day in recovery my past slowly becomes more balanced. I have learned that life will always include happiness and sadness, successes and failures, and I am better able to be content in life regardless of the inevitable ups and downs. I can experience them without creating punishing meanings about them that aren't valid—no longer defining myself as a person by my past actions. In addiction my life was defined in extremes of highs and lows while today it is smoother and easier. This helps me to let go of the negatives that come my way and not see them as symbols or harbingers of a personal failure. Instead, I can see the many good parts of who I am and how I live my life today that provide self-esteem and gratitude.

# JUNE 14

Today I am very grateful for my sobriety and am experiencing things in my life that in those last years of addiction I would have never have imagined possible. Back then the idea that the pitifully incomprehensible demoralization and abject suffering of many years in addiction would have some value was an idea that would have been hard to imagine or understand. Those final years were so full of chaos and insanity that it is truly quite amazing I survived them. My sponsor suggested that not only had my Higher Power been looking out for me during those times but also that God had a plan for my future—that there was a reason I had survived and made it to recovery while many of those I was with at the time didn't. The idea that there is a purpose to all I had been through and that there was a value to be found in it all was hard to believe, and yet there I was. In the years that have followed since I found the world of recovery I have experienced the truth of that message of finding value in my past. It presents itself each day as I am able to be a part of life in a way that adds value to the world around me. By simply staying sober and showing up I have learned how to be directly and indirectly available to others in ways that are helpful and meaningful. Finding meaning in my daily life has shown me that the strength I have inside that allowed me to survive has a useful and needed purpose. My Higher Power has a plan for me and while I may not know the details of what that plan will be, knowledge of its existence connects the strength inside me to a greater meaning in my life. The understanding, truth and experiences of recovery offer me a hope and faith for the future that is deeply rooted and profoundly comforting. The deep acceptance of living life on life's terms and relying on God loosens my grip on the selfish and self-absorbed need to constantly control, correct and judge the world around me. It allows the difficult parts of my life to occur and run their course naturally. This powerful faith derived from overcoming the incredibly painful and difficult problems of addiction has relieved me of the constant and often subtle fear in my life that took so many forms as it drove ridiculous behaviors and insecurities. Today there is a calm peacefulness that resides within me unlike anything I have ever known before.

# JUNE 15

It is interesting how profoundly my understanding of what it means to be a man has changed in recovery. Over the years the relationship with my father was often troubled and difficult, particularly when I was in the downward spiral of active addiction. Recovery has given me the chance to rebuild that relationship as well as the ones with my own sons. As I've grown closer with my father I have learned how to become a better son and a better father through the love and tolerance of understanding our shared imperfections and humanness. What also stands out in my mind is the larger picture of how being a man, a son, and ultimately a father is part of the longer journey of humankind. I am linked to a fundamental spiritual connection that I share with the men who have come before me and those who will come after me. I am a small part of a very long line of men, with each of us having a chance to shape the world around us in a positive or negative way. Understanding my place in the cycle of life, the opportunity that is my chance to be the man I'm supposed to be, is a perspective that has real meaning for me today. I am able to understand how important my life is in small and large ways to the many people who are part of the world around me. From family to work and from friends to strangers, how I show up in the world is a reflection of my efforts to be a man doing my part as a human in the world around me—and in that way perhaps all men are connected as sons and fathers, followers and guides, learners and teachers with the other men around us. This basic connection with the male part of my place within the natural cycles of life seems to include an unavoidable and hardwired sense of duty and place that active addiction cut me off from. That disconnection from my place in the world was experienced in subtle yet core ways that weren't clear to me until the process of recovery connected me through forgiveness and love to these larger themes of family, society, and human social structure. These things in turn offered me a way to reconcile the conflict, longing, pain and joy of the closest and important personal relations that are at the heart of my identity and family experience.

# JUNE 16

There is a lot of focus in recovery around the ways in which acceptance of life on life's terms becomes a tool for living. In active addiction my understanding of what was real was off-kilter and often wildly incorrect. I tended to exaggerate things, to personalize them and seek meanings that weren't really present. If things went very well, then it was because I was great. If they went badly then it was because I was awful. Recovery has helped me find a more mature perspective that places life's events into a framework of understanding that is realistic. I am no longer so obsessively self-absorbed and self-centric in my thinking. The world does not revolve around me and my actions don't have some sort of cosmic effect, as though I am the personal conductor of life's karmic force. Instead, I have learned to do my best each day and accept the ups and downs of life as they occur without allowing them to take an oversized form within my thinking. The obsession of addiction went well beyond the desire for alcohol or drugs. It became a way of thinking, a key part of my approach to life, and I would constantly make my problems seem much larger than they really were through an obsessive preoccupation with them as I tried to force my will onto the world around me. It seems odd to think back to how I could spend days or weeks upset and worrying about things I had no real control over as I went over and over past events, plotting and planning for some future resolution and a way to get what I wanted. I would spend hours explaining and repeating twisted stories to others as I allowed people, places and things to consume my day—acting as though I could somehow magically change the past. Today I am better able to avoid the unrealistic personalization of events in my life and see how we all face things that go right and wrong regardless of our own actions and efforts. Frustrations and mistakes no longer take on a meaning that I foolishly extend into a symbol of some of sort of star-crossed fate that is going to define my life forever. Learning how to let go and let God and to simply try again until I get it right has brought a great freedom that allows me to always have space in my day for the good things that are present rather than allowing the negative to consume me.

# JUNE 17

The crushing isolation and loneliness of addiction is a powerful fact that in some ways became clearer for me in recovery than it was in addiction. My drinking days were confusing, with a lot of delusion about what was really going on. I wasn't able to think clearly and even in those rare moments of relative sobriety it was disturbing and uncomfortable to realize that my mind wasn't well. I remember the vague and persistent feelings of fear and doom, and my need to quickly turn away from the raw truth of my hopelessness and desperation. In early recovery I remember hearing people say that the mind that got me there wasn't the mind that would fix me. There was a sober hopelessness and loneliness that was so overpowering and scalding but I could see that others who had been like me had recovered. I became able to have a faint spark of hope that recovery might also work for me. Looking back I can see how my addiction ultimately centered on an effort to fit in and be a part of the world that I was apart from. Recovery has shown me how to be ok with myself enough to allow others to begin get to know me. Slowly I have learned how to be a friend to others and as a result they have become friends to me. I have learned how to take hold of the hope of early recovery and through the work of the steps make it a part of my life. With that hope has come many changes and discoveries about who I am and how I view the world. I realize today that I can never properly judge the outer limits of hope by setting my own expectations on life. Already recovery has given me more than I could possibly have imagined when I began the journey, and so today I can better grasp the infinite nature of possibility that is at the core of hope. I have come to have acceptance and comfort in the truth of my belonging and a belief in my worth and value as a part of the world around me. I belong. I am a part of. Today I ride the wave of hope that has flowed through mankind in all the generations that have come before me and remain a small yet equally valid part of the hope that will remain when I am gone.

# JUNE 18

It is important for me to remember that the honesty of the first step is centered on my own actions and thinking and not the actions of others. I consciously chose to drink and use drugs. I chose to do so even though I knew that the choice would in all likelihood have grave consequences—a reality that I in turn chose to minimize and deny. In active addiction my thinking was often externally focused on the actions of others which provided an endless array of "reasons" why my life was full of problems. I could always find other people to blame in order to avoid looking at how my how my own actions and choices were destroying my life. The mental obsession of addiction was most profound for me when my thinking was befuddled with alcohol or drugs but the truth is that in recovery I must continue to consciously work with my Higher Power to direct my thinking in ways that free me from the bondage of selfishness and self-centeredness. Nowhere is this more evident than in my inclination to obsess and find fault with the actions of others. Like a dog with a bone I can chew on a perceived slight or failing for hours, then store it away in order to return to it later, refusing to let it go, even protecting and hiding it if need be. Today I understand that I am responsible for my own choices, inside and out. I'm a grown man and I get to choose what things I think about and how I direct my feelings. The ongoing process of recovery has helped me become better at laughing at my own imperfections and offers me a way to overcome these defects of character so that I am no longer imprisoned by my own skewed thinking. I am able to recognize when my thinking is distorted and falling into old patterns of anger and judgement, and then stop. The reality of learning how to cease fighting life has become easier with time and experience. Today I take responsibility for my choices and no longer have to obsess about others to avoid honestly facing the facts about myself. I have no one else to blame for how my life is today other than the man I see in the mirror each morning. The simple and unavoidable truth of my life in recovery is that how I choose to live today determines how I feel about the man I see tomorrow morning.

# JUNE 19

The fact that life isn't fair can be irritatingly demonstrated to me with unfortunate regularity. Dealing with that unfairness requires a mature understanding of the general proposition of my acceptance of life on life's terms. I can recall that having a twisted sense of "right and wrong" was a big part of my life in addiction. Because I was often doing things that I knew were against any kind of moral code or values I often lived with persistent feelings of fear and apprehension that never completely left me. The guilt and shame of my actions were linked to a foreboding and always present sense of impending dread that was connected to the idea that I should, and probably would, get what I deserve—punishment of some sort. Also tied to this thinking was an idea that I could rebalance my accounts, that if I did some good things it would somehow make up for the bad. However, my inability to cease doing things that I knew were wrong made nonsense of that idea. While the idea of "Karma" is popular, it resides in the general and never the specific. The glaring truth was that I was insane to think I had any control over such things, or that life was really able to be controlled, or that there was some fated harbinger of justice out to get me. All this thinking did was to ensure that I avoided responsibility and was able to justify my own selfish self-centered actions. Recovery has slowly shown me how to be ok with living each day well and not believing that the world revolves around my actions or thinking. The only control I have is over my choices each day. If I make good ones I can add another good day into the bigger picture that becomes my life. While I can bring some element of restorative justice to my life by living well, the currency of my good actions today can never be payment for my bad actions of tomorrow. Today I see that life on life's terms brings a full range of experiences, good, bad and average for us all and that my connectedness as a human to the world around me stems solely from how willing I am sustain my faith in the value of my decision to live in a spiritual and kind way to myself, others, and the greater world around me. While sadness and pain are always a part of life, I need never again suffer in the crushing isolation and spiritual loneliness that arrives with the madness of addiction.

# JUNE 20

Hope springs eternal. One of the most magical parts of my journey in recovery has been the re-creation of hope in my life. Thinking about it brings a smile to my face as I realize just how important and fundamental hope has become in my daily life. It is like a familiar reliable friend in whom my trust is never misplaced. In addiction I become mired in a devastating hopelessness that was disheartening and separated me from any meaning in my life. There seemed to be a general darkening of my world as it grew smaller and consumed by a soul and spirit crushing isolation. I lost any ability to see a future for myself that was of any value or purpose. It is remarkable when I think back to just how desolate my life view was. I can see how the path of addiction truly is one of hopelessness and that without recovery I was doomed to live in dread and despair. At the time, I felt there was no way out. Today I see how profoundly mistaken I was. Given the fullness and richness of my life today, how was it possible that life could have appeared so bleak? I think that the loss of hope was perhaps one of the gravest results of the searing mental confusion of active addiction. In recovery I slowly was able to see that other people who were undeniably similar to me had found a way to recover and their example provided a rekindling of the fire of hope in my life. The broader lesson that has been shown to me over the space of a few years is that hope has no boundaries—it has no limits or borders and isn't tied to things or particulars. Today hope is like air or time for me, a simple and basic part of life that can surely be relied upon. It is a trusted resource that allows me to understand that there is always more in life for me to discover and learn, to participate in, to experience and grow from. There is an element of the cycle of change in my life that only hope allows to proceed. Faith in the hope of my Higher Power's plan for my place in life links me to the spiritual world and a relationship with God. I can see each day as a small part of a greater story and my life as a small part of a greater purpose—both of which are simply parts of a much larger image that I am free to participate in today.

# JUNE 21

I have heard it said that only addiction can bring the gift of recovery. A simple truth of my life is that there have been tremendous highs and lows over a wide variety of experiences and lifestyles. At times it seems as though I have lived several lives, each very distinct and different. Living with my own self as the center of the universe during the insane roller coaster of active addiction I experienced intense moments of delusional intoxication and dreamlike feelings of power and control followed by great lows of isolation, loneliness, and hopelessness. When I was living as though I was my own God I was deluded and trapped by the mental obsession of addiction. I could not see or connect to anything other than a distorted and twisted facsimile of myself and my perceived entitlements in life. I shallowly pursued a hedonistic gratification that disconnected me from the spirit of human life. The fundamental gift of recovery has been the ability to find a spiritual power greater than myself that can solve my problems in ways that are healthy and sustainable. I have found an ability to have faith in my place in a world that allows me to greet each day with active participation and contribution. It took me quite a while to develop and enjoy the comfort and acceptance of a spiritual awakening in my life and to then integrate the experience into my daily living and thinking. I must care for it through prayer, meditation, and action on a daily basis in order to sustain it. Living my life centered in the day that is here now frees me from trying to rewrite the past or control the future. I find meaning and purpose by being a useful and helpful part of what is in front of me today and being mindful of the experience of living that is always found in the now of life. The next right thing is never in the past or the future; it is always in the now of each moment. When I live in the moment, engaged and open to the experience, I can find meaning and purpose that allows me to be connected to my own life as it is shared with others. The gift of my participation with the spiritual world connects my life to meaning and purpose. It is like the natural world, the sun and the moon, reliably available each day should I chose to connect with them.

# JUNE 22

Over the years in recovery I continue to explore and learn more about what kind of man I am trying to become. It is a journey that remains difficult because while I am much happier with who I am today, having accomplished many changes in my behaviors and understanding of self, much of the obvious work has been done and so today's challenges are not as numerous. However they are often more subtle and difficult. As is so often the case in recovery, I have learned that a flawed understanding of the problem can hinder my pursuit of the solution and leaves me asking the wrong questions. For many years before recovery I had been seeking solutions to problems that I didn't fully understand. The question of manhood is a prime example. I wasn't able to be the man I wanted to be because I didn't understand the underlying question of what it was that I was trying to become. My ideas and thoughts about what it meant to be a man were trivial, one dimensional and trite, bits and pieces of conversational tidbits, movie scenes and consumeristic marketing that were meaningless an unconnected to any moral philosophies or the values that underpinned them. I had to learn what it means to be a man by observing others and examining myself in order to discover what kind of man I wanted to be. It was a process that was all about who I was on the inside in tandem with how I behaved on the outside. It demanded open and trusting relationships with other men in which I could share, explore, and create self-integrity. It has required that I develop a serious thoughtfulness and accountability to my own values and morals that are in turn demonstrated in my actions. I have had to live and share my life with other men in order to see what works for them and for me. It was frustrating at first because the solution was not what I thought it would be. It was ambiguous and more complicated and difficult than I expected because there is no one size fits all answer to these deep questions of my own personal identity. It continues to be a process of some artistry and skillful creation that takes time, energy, practice and effort. Today it is easier because I am more experienced and am part of a group of men on a lifelong spiritual journey who together share their experience of what it means to be man.

# JUNE 23

Self-delusion is a tricky business, and its results continue to be a hallmark of my disease. I still discover things about me that I have for years taken as truths—as fixed beliefs—that when confronted by honesty and examination turn out to be misguided, inaccurate, and often just plain wrong. Many times in active addiction I was confronted by the disturbing and painful consequences of my disease and I refused to see that I had a problem. As things progressed I could no longer avoid the truth of these things but I chose instead to simply ignore them and attempt to place blame with others to protect and enable my continued addiction. Plenty of people told me that I had a problem but until I was able to become truly willing to leave my old life behind I wasn't able to grab onto the new life promised by recovery. It was only then, when I fully conceded to myself that I was the problem, that I was able to begin to see just how blinded by addiction I had become. When I look back at when I first arrived in recovery I can chuckle as I recall the sincere and deep skepticism with which I greeted a counselor's comment, "If you don't break the law you won't get arrested." What? Shocking news! I clearly remember the confused and deluded process of my foggy mind actually finding it hard to believe him and being both confused and alarmed as I realized the truth of his words. I was confronted by the delusion of my mental state slowly being pierced by such a simple truth. Delusions about who I was, and stories I've told myself so many times that they had become true, all worked to conceal the truth from me. Over the course of many years, fear of not being good enough, of being inadequate, of failure, shame, or appearing weak drove my creation of a vast mess of muddled storylines about who and what I was. Working through the steps in recovery has allowed me to grow up enough to begin the journey towards a life without self-delusion. The slow process of unwinding and untangling the truth from the false of my thinking and an increasing ability to allow my truth to not only be exposed but also shared allows the real me to be enough. Acceptance of my disease allowed me to find the path toward an honest and comforting acceptance of myself.

# JUNE 24

One of the most confusing things for me to tackle in early recovery was the problem of shame, and a perceived inability to forgive myself. I clung to the comfortably uncomfortable shroud of my past deeds and bemoaned my fated inability to find any sense of self-forgiveness. My muddled mind and the playbook for the game of life that I had used in active addiction left me lost and confused. I was confronted with the undeniable fact that my understanding of what my life was—who I was and what I thought was really going on—had all suddenly come into question. For years a self-propelling endless and worsening cycle of mayhem had continued as I drank to escape my feelings and then created more wreckage as I drank. My underlying problems, the causes and conditions of my situation became buried deeper, farther away and hidden, as I struggled to understand the insanity of my current problems. Self-loathing and shame ground me down into a man I barely recognized at times. In recovery I slowly learned that it was through love that I would be able to break free of that cycle. It was the love of others and the success of stringing those first sober days and weeks together that opened the door to a new life that centered on a spiritual, loving, and caring approach. As I began to care and find love for others I also became uncomfortable with learning to love myself and was confronted with my lack of self-worth and sense of shame. I discovered that forgiveness is something that can never really exist in the singular—it must always occur between two people—and so my fascination and obsession with some panacea of self-forgiveness was really just another symptom of my self-centered egomania that makes the entire world about me alone. Self-forgiveness was an illusory means to an end, a false dichotomy that hid an inability to truly face and let go of unsustainable justifications for my shameful past behaviors. It was a problem I could only transcend through getting right with God and the world around me. I could then truly accept that I am forgiven and share in the love that other people have for me. I become free of the shame and my old past by beginning to create a new history of esteem by living well each day. Instead of being trapped by my past in the inaction of a life without a spiritual connection, I found a new life that sustains and guides me.

# JUNE 25

Without doubt, one of the most irritating and annoying things I would run into during my first months of recovery were those sheets of paper that listed different kinds of "feelings." Often they would have a round face next to each word that attempted to display the feeling, just in case I'd forgotten what the words happy, angry, tired or sad might mean. The goal was to determine my own feelings and as a process it was slightly more uncomfortable than running into a friend at the bar whose wife I'd just slept with. In addiction, feelings were uncomfortable and debilitating. I drank to avoid them. In recovery I've been able to learn and practice how to deal with my feelings in healthy and rational ways. They are an unavoidable part of life and either I deal with them in a healthy manner or not—and the not dealing with them didn't work out well for me. So today I try to be in touch with my feelings and allow them to be part of my daily experience without being senselessly driven into reactions by them. While I often still find them powerfully disturbing and difficult, I have learned that I no longer have to avoid them. In the past they were often painful and so my reaction was to simply avoid, flee, deny or divert them through some sort of counter-feeling that I could control—like anger. Slowly, I have been able to learn how to experience my feelings without freaking out and attributing crazy ideas or thinking to them. There are a wide range of feelings that I can now participate in because I have a spiritual understanding and faith that assures me I have nothing to fear. It is a brave new world that is still uncomfortable, but connecting with my feelings is a critical and rewarding part of being a responsible adult. Recovery has provided me a broader framework of participation in life that allows me to experience the full range of emotions and feelings that a healthy human encounters while remaining cognizant of the bigger picture of life and my place within it. As a result I can observe my feelings without becoming a hostage to them, and in turn begin to exert some control and management. I am no longer the petulant child driven by base animal instinct and instead can be an observant and thinking adult who brings perspective and rational thought to my emotional experiences.

# JUNE 26

The idea that personal recovery is centered on the maintenance of a fit spiritual condition remains truer than ever for me. It is interesting how the degree to which I have become better able to participate in a spiritual relationship with a Higher Power is tightly linked to my ability to be in touch with myself, my own feelings, my actions and personal truthfulness. People often "unplug" from the hectic world of daily world life and take time to "plug-in" to another activity in order to rejuvenate. A walk, hike, group meeting, church, journaling or reading a book are all examples of refreshing experiences that can reconnect me with my own internal equilibrium and balance, and ultimately with my spiritual connection to the world around me. In addiction, all contact with the spiritual world was lost in a fog of self-inflicted delusion, selfishness, and painful isolation. In recovery, each day I must ensure that my contact with God is present—that I am in touch with the humanity of my spiritual world in order to survive and thrive in the material world. It seems that in the process of recovery, from the very beginning of sobriety, it was important that I made an honest dual effort to get right with myself and with God. One would not work without the other. The challenge moving forward is to sustain the clarity of purpose and gratitude that helps keep me in tune with a spiritual solution that provides me a Higher Power I can rely upon to help me in life. Just as I must get dressed each morning, so too must I establish contact with my Higher Power lest I go forth into the day naked. Just as there is no right or wrong language for humans to speak, the only wrong answer is to have no language at all. There are times when I can get blocked from my Higher Power because I am not fully heartfelt or honest. My part in the relationship is to be fully willing and honest with myself about my troubles, to share with myself and others what is really going on inside. I have friends I trust. I can pray, counsel, pray. The power never goes out in God's world. The lights are always on and so if my spiritual lights are dim I must work on myself to reconnect properly because, as they say, if I'm not the problem there is no solution.

# JUNE 27

The ability to take pleasure in the simple moments of everyday life is one of the greatest gifts I have been given in recovery. It is such a contrast from my days in addiction when there was little or nothing about the average moment that satisfied me. I was trapped in a constant state of uncomfortable displeasure unless I was able to be drunk or high. As much as I craved the effect of intoxication I also was equally enthralled by the capacity to do so. The fear of running out and not being able to get loaded drove a constant struggle for more that when overcome brought a feeling of relief and control that I had what I needed—it was almost as satisfying as the intoxication itself. Facing life sober was at first painful and hard. It has been a slow road of learning to be patient with myself and recognizing the progress that I have made rather than lamenting what I don't have yet. It has been a slow but steady transition to place where I can enjoy ordinary life for its simple self. What used to be a short list of false pleasures that ultimately yielded nothing but pain and suffering has today been replaced by a growing list of pleasures that are meaningful and lasting. Once I got past the emotional instability of early recovery and began to have a spiritual awakening, the rich and varied experience of being connected to my human nature, of sharing life with other people, while not always fun and enjoyable, became interesting, challenging, and ultimately very rewarding. This awakening allows me to enjoy activities and moments that are a natural part of each day. What I have learned is that there is an element of portability to those majestic moments, the great natural highs, that when I first became sober offered examples of how life can offer great pleasure. I can find the same reverence and mystery of life in simple daily events that occur all around me. I must choose to seek them, just as recovery directs me to seek a relationship with a Higher Power. When I look for the simple messages of the good life they are always right there in front of me, easily available when I choose to humble myself and see them as the reflections of the great mysteries of life that they are a part of.

# JUNE 28

The reality of powerlessness and lack of control in life was one of the most difficult things for me to understand and accept in recovery. I could perhaps more easily see and accept how I was powerless over drugs and alcohol because upon any realistic sober reflection I had to admit that I had no control and was powerless once I started drinking or using. I had repeatedly fooled myself into thinking that somehow this time would be different and that I would be able to avoid another humiliating defeat at the hands of addiction. Of course it was a fight that I ultimately I never won, and so the admission of powerlessness over alcohol or drugs wasn't too difficult to grasp. However, the idea that I also had no real control over the world around me was harder to accept. The ingrained ideas of manhood that our culture installs about being in charge of one's life and making things happen is hard to overcome. However, its unavoidable hollowness rang true as I often was just as uncomfortable with my successes as I was with my failures. In fact I was often more uncomfortable because just as it was hard to admit my own self as the cause of my failures it was even harder to claim that my successes were solely of my own making—there was a hollowness to my claims of success. Today, there seems to be an unavoidable element of general happenstance to life in which the genius and grace of my Higher Power resides. I must remain humble and right-sized as I acknowledge its role in the outcomes of my life. And so I must divorce myself from this illusion of control that creates a delusion of a prideful personal power and importance in my life. I have found release from this trap of trying to achieve control in life by learning how to live each day to the best of my ability with motives that are in line with an understanding of my Higher Powers will. Some days I have more ability than others. As long as I am doing my honest best then I can have acceptance around the results, be they good or bad, mundane or surprising. When I bring myself honestly and sincerely to life I am able to live with the results no matter what they are because I am not in control of the outcome. The outcomes are the job of my Higher Power.

# JUNE 29

When I arrived in recovery I struggled greatly with feelings and emotions. They seemed to be such powerful reflections of my own self-image and were often disturbing and disconcerting. They were part of the "story" I told myself that I used to define my expectations of who I was and how I behaved. How I viewed anger was one of the scariest examples and I sometimes wondered if I would ever be able to fully recover. During my drinking days there were many times when my anger was absolutely out of control. Things would build up and then I would sometimes explode over the smallest things. Knowing what was going on didn't stop it and in fact only seemed to work to somehow perversely justify my behavior. In yet another example of deferred and denied responsibility I would claim that was "just how I was." Recovery allowed me the chance to sober up, to clear my mind and thinking so that I could get past the delusion and insanity and begin to decipher and decode what was really going on inside me. Learning how to understand, express, and reconcile the anger about my past allowed me to begin to learn how to deal with the anger of the present. In recovery I have become better at being in touch with my feelings and dealing with them in healthy mature ways. Anger is an unavoidable normal human experience that is ok for me to participate in once I learn how to do so in a sensible way. In fact it is often a most useful tool for helping me uncover new depths of personal discovery that I am unable to reach normally. Getting riled up about something often seems to break free and disrupt my patterns of thinking, my beliefs and ideas about myself and life, so that I can in turn reevaluate and examine myself in a new light. As with other feelings and emotions, ultimately I am in charge of how I think and feel so I must learn how to examine, understand, and express my anger in healthy meaningful ways and then move on. I am no longer afraid of, or controlled by, my feelings of anger and can instead view my agitations and disturbances as being symptomatic of deeper causes and conditions that represent opportunities for growth and personal development. It is a process of self-discovery that often strengthens and deepens my relationship with a Higher Power.

# JUNE 30

It has been my experience that in life there are few wrong ways to be positive and upbeat—but a hundred wrong ways to be dour and negative. I've heard it said that in life we find what we bring. I know that in addiction I was bringing chaos and selfishness to the world and that is what I most often found in others. It is not possible (as the song suggests) to always look on the bright side of life, but I think it is a good goal. Each day the reactions of the people I interact with offer a reflection of how I am showing up in their lives. We all know people who seem to be stuck in a funk of "bummer-hassle-downer" all the time. They are a drag, and bring everyone around them down. How miserable it must be to live each day in a self-created dark cloud. Today is the only place my life is actually lived and I alone shape and control my actions and attitude within it. Recovery has shown me how to worry less about the past or future. I can instead work to accept and enjoy my imperfect life as it is today. In order to do that I must make the decision to be positive about the problems I encounter and quickly shift into the process of solutions and outcomes rather than dwelling in difficulty, negativity and suffering. While I mustn't be naive and foolishly deny that problems exist, my ability to think critically should be a starting point in the process of solutions rather than a place of wilting resigned comfort and disdainful malaise. It takes little effort or skill to find faults in life and my disease of addiction plays to this fact, wanting to ferment a restless and irritable discontent while offering a solution of escape and denial through intoxication that always ultimately worsens and deepens my problems. Recovery has shown me how to find a solution to my problems through a reliance on a Higher Power that it is enabled by my own actions and choices. I can note the problems in life without becoming a hostage to them, and increasingly my ability to add value to life, to be useful and helpful in finding solutions, has been increased. It is amazing how different my experience with the world around me is when I approach it positively rather than negatively. It allows me to access and enhance the positive spirituality of human life that is all around each of us.

# July

"Humility is realm of a humble heart."
— Lailah Gifty Akita

"True humility is not thinking less of yourself; it is thinking of yourself less."
— C.S. Lewis

"If pain doesn't lead to humility, you have wasted your suffering."
— Katerina Stoykova Klemer

# JULY 1

The importance and value of taking meaningful action is one of the most useful things I've learned in recovery. Often I know that there are things I can and should do that would be helpful to my current situation and yet I chose to avoid them and instead remain stuck in the problem. This classic trait of addiction is difficult to overcome. In addiction my life was a series of traumatic events that each seemed to be of themselves singularly life defining. My whole world would center on whatever the latest drama was, as though it was a unique and special event. My inability to see the continuum of chaos that was going on prevented me from being able to place those events into a proper context and understanding. The myopic worldview of life being entirely framed by the problems of each day shielded me from any insight or ability to see the bigger picture of how insanely unmanageable my life had become. Addiction was ahistorical—keeping me fully immersed solely in the demanding grind of meeting my daily needs. This pattern of thinking carries with me into recovery as I still tend to over-emphasize the problems of today. When that happens I lose perspective of the bigger picture of life and my place within it. I forget that the problem most likely isn't as big or important as I make it out to be. My alcoholic defiance keeps me stuck fighting longer than I should—enlarging my frustrations and shrinking my sense of order. Often the best thing I can do is take a break from the problem. I can visit a friend, go for a walk, or tackle another regular task that is part of the everyday cycle of my life. By participating in the regular parts of my life I am reconnected to the larger picture of who I am and how I play a part in my life. I regain insight and see my problems for the temporary setbacks or forks in the road that that they are—as simply part of the journey rather than the end of it. The old advice to take a break from our problems so that new answers and ideas emerge is true and I must remember to let go and let God—sooner rather than later. Life is easier that way. The willingness to take the meaningful action, that I know will help me in life, opens up the opportunity to improve my world beyond the scope of a single day or event.

# JULY 2

The path of personal growth and understanding that I walk in recovery continues to be both rewarding and difficult. Learning how to take full responsibility for my actions in the world has been a slow and ongoing process. I have a hard time with the boundaries between blame, pity, injustice and the space in between what is my business and what is God's business. In the past, few things were ever my fault and I relied on blame as a mechanism for relieving myself of any personal responsibility for the situations I had created. My alcoholic mind focused on people, places and things that were unfair and I avoided the challenges of solving my problems preferring instead to focus on their causes—as though the process of apportioning blame would somehow fix them. This clouded thinking was very hard to work through. Of course, the reality of life is that I must be at the center of solving my own problems regardless of how they occurred. Learning how to separate the reality of life that brings things that are at times unfair from my ability to create suffering and pity from the responsibility of my own duty to make the best of things, is at times quite tricky. I can easily get stuck feeling woeful and bitter rather than accepting things and getting on with life. This desire to place blame defeats my progress toward solutions and seems to stem from the underlying requirement of denial upon which all addictive behavior is built. Years of denying that I had a problem—or that the consequences of my addiction were related to my own choices and actions—left me unable to accept responsibility in a mature and adult way. Learning to overcome this crippling immaturity and irresponsibility is one the fundamental gifts of my recovery. Most days I must honestly face the realities of my life rather than deny or ignore them and recovery has shown me how to do so in a way that creates meaning and value from my difficulties. It offers a reminder that I am powerless over the world around me and that I can only control myself. And so, in order to make progress and be content I once again find myself at the place of understanding that if I'm not the problem there is no solution. Only I can take the action that is needed for me to be a healthy man in my own life.

# JULY 3

One of the hardest things about accepting change in my life is learning how to let go of situations that continue to baffle me. I want to control and fix them as I force my will upon them. This problem seems centered in an overblown sense of defiance and entitlement—that once I get my mind set on something I somehow automatically must also deserve it. I then move into a space that is inflexible and narrow. Other options fade and I place excessive emphasis on a particular idea or plan. Then when things don't work out I become justified in my anger and desire for retribution, or find misery as I flounder in resentment and irritation. Recovery has helped me decode these complicated inter-linked patterns of behavior and provides me an ongoing framework in which to explore and improve my reactions to them. Freedom from the captivity of addiction began providing relief from the cycle of my own problems and I quickly began to have real change and achievements in my life. In fact, recovery has done so much in my life that it's easy to think all things are possible. This miracle of transformation can delude me in other areas of my life and make dealing with the normal problems, the general success and failures of life, very difficult. Having overcome so much in the journey from addiction to recovery I perhaps feel that I can achieve victory in all things. This is of course not very realistic. It is still easy for me to get hung up on a particular idea or goal and pursue it long after a reasonable person would have said "enough" and have moved on. Like a defiant child demanding things his own way I can become unreasonable and closed off from the world around me. I must remind myself in these situations to rely not on my own will alone but also seek and understand God's will for me. I can reach out to close friends and advisors with an open mind and willingness to gain new perspectives and perhaps be able to really hear and accept things that I don't want to. Learning how to hold on loosely and be gentle with myself continues to take time and a conscious and directed effort.

# JULY 4

When I look back at my youthful days of drinking and drugging there is a laughable irony that I can see today. I can remember wanting to make sure I wasn't a "normie', someone afraid to have fun and take risks, and I was confidently assured in my choice of a lifestyle that was open and free from the constraints and rules of old fashioned society. I didn't want to subject myself to the ideas of living a simple life, doing things slowly, and carefully adhering to restrictive ideas and beliefs. I wanted to be free of the stifling ways of the past. The irony of course is that ultimately I became a prisoner of my own addiction—never wanting to look at myself while busily beating the drums of another person's messages about life. I never learned how to find my own path in life because of the delusion of addiction. I had a lot of rhetorical catch phrases about how to live life—lyrics from songs and slogans from posters—but nothing that really connected in a meaningful way to any true measure of self-discovery or my own values or beliefs. I was trapped in a culture of excess and consumption that fed a self-absorbed need for inebriation and partying. For all my claims of freedom from the clutches of normalcy I became more of a prisoner without even knowing it. There are few incarcerations more profound than one in which we are trapped without even knowing it. Trapped by an addiction that was slowly taking everything I had in life, it kept me deceived and deluded as I willingly sank further into its clutches. In recovery I have found the freedom from the guilt, shame, and hidden issues of my past. Freedom to be able to learn how to like the man I am today and shape how I continue to grow in the future. Freedom to look any man in the eye and be clear about who I am without having to boast, mislead or deceive. I am free from the lies I constantly told myself and others. It has taken hope, faith, courage and willingness to open the door to who I really am and I was afraid of what I would find. Opening that door has allowed me the chance to change, grow, and become free, at first from addiction and alcoholism, and then at last free from the bondage of self.

# JULY 5

Learning how to live life without trying to control the world around me has meant having to rely on an undefined sense of a spiritual connection to a Higher Power that is always hard to fully describe. It links me to a vision of life with a larger purpose and meaning within the world around me. I remember being very confused at the concepts of a Higher Power and spirituality, religion and God. I struggled with a desire and urgent need to have a clear and concise definition of their meanings. Desperate to leave my old world of addiction behind me I wanted to find this spiritual connection that people spoke of—to know what it meant and understand it. It was frustrating to listen to people attempt to describe a spiritual awakening and try to interpret their experience in a way that connected to my own understanding of who I was. Slowly I've begun to understand that in some ways spirituality is perhaps more like my reaction to art or music. It is imprecise and subjective and that even with the same song or picture its meaning may be different each time I experience it. I can perhaps never properly or fully translate my own spiritual experience in words because language is a tool that is too common—it is a lowest denominator of common understanding and the individual spiritual experience is always profoundly unique and special. No matter how many lovely descriptions of another's experience I hear it will always remain something that can't be fully understood until I do it for myself. The meaning and understanding of spiritual events and beliefs in my life also vary. They ebb and flow as I learn how to become more comfortable with the interpretation of feelings that connect my spiritual and intuitive side to the world around me that I now engage with more deeply. The soul of who I am that was denied and blocked in addiction is today free to participate in the whirl of the natural and spiritual world around me. I used to groan internally and feel somewhat frustrated at the term "sunlight of the spirit" when it was read or used in conversation but today I understand and smile because I have learned how to live in the brightness of a spirituality that inspires and guides me each day.[14]

# JULY 6

It is interesting for me to think about the timeless realm of past generations that have gone before me and the relationship between the larger questions of humankind and my own place within this cycle of human life. While certainly a brief and small piece of a much larger puzzle, my life represents a chance to live and be a part of the shared human experience and its immensely long journey. Perhaps the great mystery of human life is that of our shared collective experience—an energy and connection with each other whose limits and fullness may never be fully known or understood. Each of us are given the chance to participate without ever seeing the full past or future of our human story, only our own experience in the lives of those close to us and the stories of the past that combine with our hopes for the future. And yet we absolutely get to live our own story in our own life today. The spiritual knowing that I am a part of something larger than myself that is so timelessly powerful and important gives meaning and purpose to the actions of my life that I take each day. In recovery we all are part of the miracle of changing lives and finding meaning and hope for ourselves and others. Human life seems earmarked by a faithful and hopeful pursuit of an unknown and mysterious future that we are all inevitably a part of now and forever. This unknown aspect of the future drives my acceptance and reliance upon a Higher Power. Ultimately we all have little control over the future, as demonstrated so clearly by the misfortunes that strike even the most powerful and wealthy or kindest and most considerate among us. The spiritual awakening provided by the process of recovery frees me from the trap of ruining my present with fears about the past or future and connects me to something larger than myself. I am never able to define an answer or provide an explanation that fully captures the unknown mystery of the human spirit but I have always known that it exists. Recovery has shown me how to connect with my own spirit so that I can in turn connect with the spiritual aspects of the world around me and understand that I am truly never alone. It matters not how it works or that its science remains unknown. It only matters that it has changed my life.

# JULY 7

[14] ibid. P. 66.

In early recovery all of my problems seemed to come from outside of me. It took a while to own the fact that almost all of my problems today were because of my own actions. Once I stopped drinking it was amazing how those insane problems started to go away. I was able to begin to live life normally again. In recovery I began to learn about the underlying reasons—the causes and conditions—which remained and continued to create problems in my life. Without the alcohol the problems were still there. The consequences just weren't as tragic and out of control. Learning how to understand the personal boundaries that are part of being a mature adult has taken a lot of time and work. Drinking and using at an early age meant I missed out on a lot of the normal and healthy development that leads to a well-adjusted self-actualized person who understands themselves and their own personal integrity. The lack of personal integrity left me lost and unable to navigate and negotiate my own place in the world and combined with the shameful outcomes of my addictive behavior to leave me ill equipped to make good choices in difficult situations. The old adage of one who stands for nothing will fall for anything was reflected in my inability to hold fast to any morals or values as my addiction spiraled further out of control. Recovery offers the structure of the steps as a solution to this personal void and lack of personal spirituality. The process has been one of discovery and development that helped me build my own sense of integrity and value. It has been a long road of learning what it is that I don't know and then being willing to admit those shortcomings. Then I needed to find a deep willingness to become ready to make changes to some of my most core and privileged personal beliefs. The process of true personal growth and development has been one of the hardest and most rewarding parts of recovery. It continues to bring profound changes in how I understand myself and my place in the world around me. Learning who I am as an individual—being able to honestly see and understand what that means—allows me to make choices, the difficult "yes" and "no" decisions, about my life that were never possible before.

# JULY 8

The traditional stereotype of the American male is full of myth and often promotes values that often are out of touch with today's modern world. In recent generations there have been huge changes in the meaning and definition of family, the role of women in society, equality of human and civil rights and an increasing inclusion of all people. All of these changes have dramatically altered what it means to be a man in the modern world. The world of our grandfather's father is in many ways as distant as those of the first settlers in America and yet many of the stereotypes and thought constructs about maleness that persist originated in those days. It is laughable to watch some movies that are scarcely fifty years old and see how much has changed. In addiction the old ways were perfect for my image of a "hard working, hard drinking man" who could conveniently avoid the complexities of a modern world and the importance of developing strong meaningful relationships with family and friends. In recovery it is an ongoing struggle for me to learn how to be emotionally present. When I first arrived it was a battle to simply deal with physical sobriety and notions of emotional sobriety seemed rather distant and confusing. However, the path of recovery leads directly to our underlying causes and conditions that are then cleared away to allow the formation of a foundation of emotional well-being upon which a spiritual awakening can be built. Dealing with my "feelings" and understanding how my addictive mind uses old fashioned ideas and beliefs in order to accommodate and enable my selfishness is an ongoing process of discovery. I have learned to be open-minded about the things I believe and my underlying motives. I am prepared and willing to examine them often as new ideas are presented. Sometimes I change—sometimes I don't—but the process is what ensures that my thinking is current and valid rather than blindly holding onto to ideas and myths that don't serve me well. Today I have the ability to "lean in" to emotional conversations and feelings with myself and others so that I can engage and learn, change and grow, in ways that were cut off from me in the past. I am able to truly connect with people in ways that are honest, meaningful and deep reflections of my own emotional capital.

# JULY 9

The understanding of approaching life from the perspective of managing only "my side of the street" begins with cleaning it up and keeping it clean. The process teaches me about personal responsibility and brings justice, self-esteem and integrity. It also helps me experience and learn how to have proper boundaries with others by offering a framework of understanding that helps me remain focused on my side of the street in life and let others learn to do the same. As a co-dependent person it is very easy for me to want to get all involved with other people's business—particularly their problems. I think it is normal to want to help and care for the ones we love but there are times when I've realized that my own motives are mixed. What really drives me to help another? Is it to show off or validate my own expertise, to appear superior, or "be right?" In addiction I had many of my own problems and being able to focus on the problems of others unconsciously served several functions—none of which were healthy. By focusing on solving the problems of others I was able to take a break from my own, feed my codependent needs, and become over-enmeshed in the lives of others. By attempting to "help" others I was able to demonstrate a sort of control of life into their situation that I was unable to exert into my own. These situations provided an ability to enjoy a positon of perceived superiority that validated the sense of denial around my own life by providing examples of how my lack of ability to deal with problems wasn't perhaps as bad as some other peoples. In recovery I've learned that sometimes the best way to help someone is to let them follow their own path, despite my concerns, and continue to be kind and supportive as they experience their own personal growth and discovery. I have come to believe in the power and truth of the need for each individual to find their own way and learn their own lessons in order to truly overcome their own addiction. This is the process that allowed me to at last take real ownership and responsibility for my own actions and their consequences, to really see "my part" in what was going on around me. It is important that I don't preclude others their chance to make the same discovery by trying to carry their load or solve their problems for them.

# JULY 10

One of the first things I learned about in recovery related to the fundamental relationship and link between fear and faith. I wrote those two words together on the side of my first Big Book to remind me that when I am in fear it is usually because I have abandoned faith and reliance upon my Higher Power. When I am trying to control life and run the show myself I am usually fearful at some base level and afraid that things won't work out well—or in the way I want them to. The idea of replacing fear with faith is fairly simple but learning how to put it into practice regularly, and thoroughly, has taken years of practice. The first stage is recognizing that my actions are being motivated by fear and then understanding in what way I am trying to control an outcome. Ultimately, when I have slipped away from faith and into fear it is because I have lost sight of my ability to trust in the results that my God will provide. Seeing how my faith and ability to trust work together enables me to remain connected to God's plan for me and allows me to step back from my own desire to take charge and force my will into the world around me. A profound lack of trust was one of the greatest defects of character that I arrived with. It has taken a long time to learn how to trust myself and others in a reasonable manner. Today, trust is no longer about an expectation of perfection because I, and others, will always make mistakes and be less than perfect. However, learning to accept that fact as a reality—and that it doesn't mean I cannot trust—has taken a long time. My inability to trust others, and ultimately my Higher Power, is part of what kept me sick for so many years. It is an effective barrier to forming and sustaining strong personal relationships. It is only through faith, the ultimate spiritual expression of trust, that I am able to free myself from the bondage of a thousand forms of fear. To be human is to see owns own personal failings and comfortably accept that there is no perfect trust. Life will always be imperfect as will all the people who live it, but when I remain faithful to my Higher Power and allow God to work in my life I become free from the burdens of self-inflicted fear, worry and hopelessness.

# JULY 11

Having an excess of structure or clinging to rules and guidelines and wanting to make sure that each moment counts for something are all ways that I try to overcome fear through attempting to control how I appear to the world around me. When I first began recovery I needed a lot of structure. It was important that I felt safe and secure about what were the right and wrong things to do. I wanted to know just how many meetings I needed. What type of meetings were "good ones." How fast to work the steps. How to find (and keep) a good sponsor. How to control my recovery so that it would work out just right—just the way "I" wanted. One of the fallacies of attempting to control my life so rigidly is the assumption that I am in charge of its master plan, or that I even know what that might even look like. Recovery has taught me how to have trust and faith in my Higher Power's plan for me. My job is simply to do the best I can each day and find contentment in my life. I don't need to have my entire day plotted and planned out in a furious attempt to make that happen. The goal of recovery is to allow me to achieve a spiritual awakening and experience has shown me that achieving that goal can never be fully mapped out and designed. It is a process of personal growth and development which requires a certain flexibility and variety that allows for spontaneity and the exploration and discovery of the unknown. Many of the most important moments of growth have occurred for me fairly randomly in ways that were unexpected and unanticipated. Those "aha moments" of insight often arrive when I am relaxing and thinking of nothing in particular. And so it is important that I don't always postpone the unstructured and playful parts of living for a future date when the timing is "better." There will always be many important tasks or duties with which to fill my day. Slowly I've been able to realize that play and recreation, meditation, walks, and quiet moments are also equally important parts of each day that create the space needed to stay in touch with the spiritual side of my human nature. The measure of my day's success isn't only what I accomplish in the busy world of life's demands but also the time I spend in the joy and discovery of the enjoyment of simply being human.

# JULY 12

I grew up in Dublin where many of my friends lived in stark poverty. I remember clearly how some of those people were consumed by the negativity of their circumstances while others remained very positive and upbeat. The old grandmothers would say things like, "You are where you're at—and sure you spend your whole life there—so you may as well enjoy it!" The experience remains a reminder to me that regardless of the overall circumstances of my life I can choose to enjoy the day that is in front of me by approaching it with a positive attitude. I can chose to remain hopeful and focused on the good things that are present rather than creating a dreary daily memorialization of the parts of my situation that aren't good. There is a sort of odd power I can find in the sense of control that comes with being negative. By expecting the worst for myself in life and focusing on its unfairness I engage with the certainty of finding the worst in life and shut myself off from the uncertain possibilities of the positive side of life. Understanding the importance of choosing how I feel about my life allows me to avoid the self-indulgent selfishness and perverse comfort that can be found when I choose to be unhappy, miserable and suffer. It takes courage to focus on the positive and remain hopeful rather than passively choosing to sit, uncomfortably comfortable, in the negative. I can instead choose to focus on being open to the day ahead and what it may bring. In recovery there is an expression that reminds us to "stick with the winners" which has little to do with themes of the material world of new cars, great jobs, attractive partners or the accumulation of possessions. The winners in recovery are the people who have found a new life through their own spiritual awakening. The opportunity to share in this treasure of life that is found within us all is always available for me to participate in. However dour my personal circumstances might be there is always a meeting to go to, people to share with, and the natural world of my Higher Power to be a part of. The choice of being positive or negative in life is a reminder that while I can't control the positive things in life I can surely control my own negative downward spiral of addiction and that when I'm charge my life can quickly become a very dark place. When my Higher Power is in charge there is hope and brightness.

# JULY 13

I enjoy reflecting on the significant changes I can see in myself that are a result of recovery. Some are very simple and specific while others are profound and general. Sometimes the "old me" struggles to accept the truth of these things but when I look closely they cannot be denied. The awareness of how much fuller and richly meaningful my life is today often causes me to shake my head a little bit in disbelief. Life today is so very different. In addiction I was closed off and isolated. There was always a lot of talk of living a full life. Stories I told myself and others about things that would happen in the future mixed with the lies about the present to create illusions and delusions that seemed so grand but they were never real or lasting. The reality of life in addiction was that there was little action outside of the grind and demoralization of a worsening darkness of confusion and despair. Goals I set for myself never become anything more than goals and I would find myself noticing how I was stuck in the same place, telling the same old lies, and making the same promises that never came to fruition. Recovery has allowed me to grow in ways I never thought possible. In ways I never valued or believed were options for me. Today I am worthy of, and participate in, honest healthy relationships with others. I am open to pursuits and activities that are so much more than I expected them to ever be. I can look back and see how I have not only set goals but then gone on to accomplish many of them. This ability to be more conscious of my own power in the world, to actually be the man I am meant to be, has taken time to fully realize, accept and trust. At first I wasn't sure that I could sustain this new life but over time I have come to believe and trust the faith in my Higher Power that enables and continues these miraculous changes. My life has gone from a bad black a white movie set on repeat to full color high definition with all kinds of channels and options. I was never aware that life could be so full, rewarding and gracious. This awareness, this spiritual awakening, is something that I cherish and hold close each day. It supersedes my frailties of emotion and selfishness and constantly reminds me of the authenticity of my place in the world.

# JULY 14

The gift of life has a new valuation for me in recovery. It has only been since I have had the chance to live this new life that I am able to really see how far off track I was in my old life. At first in recovery I had quite a lot of bitterness and regret around the many years that were so misguided and poorly spent during active addiction. However, over time I have gained a sense of acceptance that has allowed me to let that go and simply enjoy the time that I have today. I must remember to take the time to reflect on the journey of recovery because it is truly remarkable how much my approach to life has changed. The ability to find purpose and meaning in relationships with others continues to grow and that opportunity seems to be a reflection of my own growth as a person. Increasingly I am able to see how the shift from being internally focused on trying to control life in ways that suit my own needs and demands has shifted to a more useful approach of participating in life around me. This change allows my own life to shine more brightly. The meaning and value of my own life has increased dramatically the more I share life with others and try to live in a way that is spiritually rewarding and fulfilling. One of the great paradoxes of recovery is that I must give it away in order to keep it. This truth is rooted in the idea that I can't give away something that I don't have. Only through the process of working through a program of recovery, of actually doing the hard work with myself, was I able to then begin the joyful work of carrying the message to others and being involved with their recovery. It is this final step that continues to provide a deep and inspiring well-spring of hope and understanding that nourishes and sustains my own spiritual growth. And it is this work that demonstrates the vital role provided by an understanding that change and growth require new behavior and action. The things I have done in the past for my recovery aren't always the things that are needed for me in the future. Each new step on the path of spiritual growth is one that leads me into new places and experiences that I can navigate well because of my past efforts. However, I can only ever find and deepen my understanding of them by today by doing the work that is required today.

# JULY 15

One of the more interesting things I've learned in recovery has to do with truth. The honesty of the first step relates in a powerful way to my own understanding of self. Learning to be honest with myself about the truth of my addiction occurred when I was confronted with the results of my actions upon the world around me. My own sense of self was clearly distorted and inaccurate and I struggled to engage in any sort of soul searching or process that yielded meaningful insights. The confused and lonely attempts of trying to solve my problems with the mind that created them demonstrated the falsity of thinking that comes with isolation and loneliness. The powerful fact is that the truth about who I am is rarely found only through being alone. I need the insight and help of other people who know me to share their opinion and point of view. It is only through honest relationships with others that I have an ability to fully discover and confirm the truth about myself. By opening up to others while participating fully in life I am able to identify and understand the preset notions and false beliefs I create about myself and see through the eyes of others who I really am. Thus the work of self-discovery perhaps somewhat ironically requires the inputs of others. The process allows me to truly discard those false beliefs and ideas about myself and begin to incorporate new understandings about who I am. In many respects the various stories I told myself about who I was were not accurate—I could kind of sense this disconnect but my understanding of the difference was shallow and incomplete. I found that a profound gap existed between the understanding that I am worthy of true friendship and really believing it in a way that allowed it to happen. Often when I did things well and received praise I struggled to accept it because I wasn't truly reconciled properly with a belief in my own eligibility and self-worth. Over time I have learned to fully accept these truths as being valid. It has only been through deep and sustained friendships that my faults, failings, strengths and goodness are validated properly and accurately as the honest reality of who I am is exposed. Today, I continue to find the real truth of who I am largely through my relationships with others.

# JULY 16

For many years my life in addiction was surreal. It was dreamlike—and a very bad one at times. As I look back at those days I realize that a fundamental part of the problem was that I didn't take my life very seriously. I wouldn't have admitted it at the time but the fact remains that my behavior demonstrated clearly that I wasn't taking seriously the valuable gift of life I had been given. I took extraordinary risks that put me and others in jeopardy. And yet, amongst the chaos and insanity of my addiction I still had an expectation that the world should take me seriously—as though I had some unique and special insight about life. I was delusional. At the center of this delusion was the loss of any connection to a greater purpose within the world around me. I had become an outsider to the world, beastly in my primary concern for meeting my own hedonistic desires and needs. Addiction had taken over my sensibility, the understanding and acceptance of my validity and place in relation to others that allowed me to remain connected to life. In the midst of the confusion resided the fateful knowledge of the unspoken truth of my loss of personhood and its ultimate undercurrent of death. An implicit yet unstated awareness of the direction I was headed and its inevitable end result. Despite all my claims of "living large" or enjoying the "high life" I knew that in fact I was dying. The dualism of this reality, the veneer of an outrageous party lifestyle and false freedom of lawlessness could never reconcile with the tragedy of my undeniable downward spiral. In those dark desperate and lonely moments of clarity the dread of my addiction cut past the bravado of my rhetoric and coldly grasped my heart with the clammy hands of doom. In recovery I've learned that until I take my life seriously, valuing how I conduct myself, certainly no one else will—or should. The acceptance of the spiritual reality of my life in the greater scheme of the world helps me place a value on how I live each day. It forces me to review and come to grips with the ultimate question of how I choose to live given that my death is inevitable. It drives me towards an acceptance and understanding of a vitally important truth. I am, in my brief life, an important custodian and participant within the great cycle of humanity and that my contributions, no matter how minor I perceive them to be, truly do matter.

# JULY 17

The question of spiritual growth and development, the transformative capstone of 12 step recovery, required a core change in my thinking and beliefs. For years, specifically in addiction and in general with regard to the modern world, my life was about achieving material goals and performing purposeful tasks, the work of each day. There was a sort of daily performance of creating and adding value, of some sort or another, through actions that demonstrated my ability in the world and my skills at surviving, competing, acquiring possessions, getting ahead or in the case of addiction—getting loaded. This fundamental purposefulness of the modern world that creates value through hard work, the taming of nature and extracting of its resources and the demanding world of industry and commerce drove a framework of meaning and purpose within my life. Ironically this incessant effort to improve my world was always focused on things outside of me rather than things inside me. In all possible ways consumption was king and contemplation was lost. All my energy was spent in the attempt to pursue rather than considering the why of what I was doing. It was secondary to value and tend to my own spiritual growth—my person inside—when all my energy and effort was spent on the external world—my outside person. This framework became distorted into one of total subjugation when my life shifted into addiction. I was quickly unable to do anything other than live life wholly centered on my own selfish needs. Recovery began the path toward a readjustment of how I viewed the world and my place within it. Not only was I able to reconnect to an ability to function within the norms of the community around me, but I began the journey of self-discovery that opened the door to a spiritual awakening that connects my actions in life to the world around me in a new and more fulfilling way. Today I am able to see the monumental importance of asking the bigger questions about who I am, why I want what I want, and how I can find meaningful and lasting contentment from within rather than temporary solutions that distract and disturb me—clouding the real questions that living a spiritually aware life bring. In order to work on me I must take time away from working on the world around me.

# JULY 18

A large part of the spiritual awakening that I feel in recovery centers on compassion and the idea that all humans are part of the world of a loving Higher Power. If the gift of reason and language is what separates us from the animals then perhaps we are all in some way connected in our ability to see God within us and in each other. This contrasts so clearly with the selfish world of addiction in which I lived for so long where I viewed people as a resource to be used. The desire for conquest and control and the willingness to battle for things lead to a constant framework of fighting and a perpetual wariness of others. The dog-eat-dog world and constant themes of competition and winning seemed so central to me before I slid into addiction where those ideas were then expanded into an extraordinary callousness and depravity that regularly launched itself onto those around me. The idea of being welcoming, kind, or valuing an ability to be loving and tolerant were the opposite of the reality of my lifestyle where any sort of graciousness was based on a sub-plot of the spider and the fly. I often joked that yes I was religious because I would "prey" every day. This perspective of seeing others only within a framework of what I could get from them was a hallmark of my addiction. Recovery has slowly offered me a way to change how I view people. The kind and welcoming greetings of people in recovery who in most cases were genuinely interested in how they could help me—without asking for anything in return—was at first unnerving and difficult to accept. Through the process of the steps of recovery I've been able to awaken a spiritual connection with all people around me that resides within our commonality as humans. I often believe that the clearest path to my Higher Powers presence can be found in the person who is right in front of me at any given time. The wonder and gift of human life, the power of reason to choose which actions are ours and the awareness of our own mortality, is visible in all people I encounter regardless of the circumstances of their life. Being spiritually awake allows me to accept and see others with compassion for their humanity regardless of how close or distant our worlds are.

# JULY 19

The journey of learning who I am, and taking my place in the world around me, centers on the relationships with my Higher Power and close friends. As I learn how to share myself with God and others I in turn learn more about myself. I am able to better understand who I am and where my side of life's street begins and ends, what my business is and isn't, and establish better boundaries around my actions and the actions of others. In the past, failure to answer the core question of who I am and what I really stand for created confusing problems and deeply entrenched conditions in my life that caused much pain and suffering. I was in a semi-constant struggle with people and battled places and things. I often found myself caught up in situations that I had inserted myself into in ways that I perhaps thought were examples of being helpful and caring but often was more about hiding bad or selfish motives under seemingly good ones. I repeatedly put myself in a position to get hurt and then bemoaned and railed at the injustice of my suffering while denying my own part in its creation. The combination of sneakily seeking my own needs and an inability to say no lead to overly enmeshed relationships with poor boundaries that helped keep me trapped in the spin cycle of addiction to which I applied some vague and illegitimate sense of meaning, purpose and value. Today I have more clarity about my place in the world and am better able to be firm about who I am, more accurate about what I am and am not entitled to in life, and understand how this plays out in my relationships with others. The work of building a relationship with God has opened the door to a more self-sustaining and fulfilling model of meaning and purpose in my life that directs my actions in ways that bring self-esteem and add lasting value in my relationships. I can be strong in my ability to have proper boundaries with others and be honestly helpful without having to join the crazy parade. My motives are more aligned with the will of my Higher Power. Until I was able to better understand who I was, and accept my eligibility as a fully qualified participant in life, I wasn't able to stand up for myself in meaningful ways that are healthy and useful.

# JULY 20

When I was younger I liked to think of myself as a man of action; purposeful, decisive and confident. I had little time for any of that self-reflection, introspection or namby-pamby navel gazing, self-doubt or sitting around talking about my "feelings." The result was that in many ways I was a shallow, callous, insincere man who ultimately stood for nothing and was largely ineffective because I rarely completed things properly and instead sought shortcuts and trickery as pathways to my achievements. I lacked the personal character to stay the course and was simply making life up as I went along which really meant living life with no plan at all. The results weren't very good. This lack of self-knowledge and failure to develop a strong sense of self, of my own values and beliefs, left me a stranger to myself. I look back and remember how awkward and uncomfortable I often became when I was forced to spend any time at all in reflective or contemplative situations. I was never keen to spend the time to take a good look at myself and when I did it was disheartening and confusing. Being alone was usually a discomforting experience which I avoided because all there really was for me was loneliness and most often it was served with strong feelings of self-pity and shame. I struggled with insecurity and feeling unsure and doubtful which in turn propelled me back to action rather than reflection because doing something was better than sitting around in vaguely fearful discomfort. Recovery affords me the tools and skills to build relationships with myself, my Higher Power and others, that I can use to discover more about who I am. The process of self-discovery has allowed me to transform the experience of being alone so that today I understand and experience the difference between solitude and loneliness. I often hear people talk about the value of, "pray, counsel, pray," in reference to the important task of taking my life seriously. I have learned the truth and understanding that if I don't take the time to listen to myself, then there is little value in having others listen to me. Ultimately I am alone in life with my own thoughts and experience and in order to share those messages with others and learn from them I must first hear my own messages to myself.

# JULY 21

Learning how to "Let go and let God" has been a hard task and the process has been full of fits and starts as well as successes and failures. My desire for perfection, a core symptom of my addictive desire to control and arrange the world around me, is a subtle and dangerous foe that leads me quickly and quietly away from my reliance and acceptance of the will of my Higher Power. When I become overly focused on the idea that I should never, or rarely, make mistakes I restrict my own personal growth. I adopt a stance of controlling intolerance that drives me away from a spiritual outlook and closer to the idea that I should be managing the world around me so that I can ensure the perfect outcomes of my actions. Acceptance of the idea that I must simply do my own personal best to align my will with that of my Higher Power—while leaving the results of my actions up to God—is an easy task when things work out the way I want and much harder when they don't. My years in addiction comprised wave after wave of attempts to force my will on the world that all ended badly. In many ways these repeated failures drove an unreconciled sense of self-infliction and pity that was soul crushing and left me overly sensitive to my own failings and errors. Oh how

I can beat myself up for simply being human—as though in some way I should somehow be better than that. In recovery I have begun to understand the power of a spiritual awakening that allows me to enjoy a more simple and powerless place in the world. It makes room and space in my living and thinking that accepts and welcomes my errors and omissions, my quirky faults and mistakes as I move forward in life learning and growing. I have learned that the real goal for me today is to avoid doing the things that I know I shouldn't. Rather than focusing on trying to always be this perfect example of doing everything just right I can instead be confident that I am not doing things that I know are wrong. In this way I become free of the need for perfection and can be kind to myself when confronted with the results of my unavoidable imperfections. There is a tremendous peace and comfort that comes with simply doing my honest best and accepting that the results are Gods responsibility.

## JULY 22

There is no way to get through life without experiencing its ups and downs. At times I've tried making my world smaller so I would feel less of both and all I found was increased loneliness and self-pity. Trying to live life as loner seemed to draw me further away from any understanding of what purpose my life served and the ability to find any meaning within it. I've tried to control my world through excess in an effort to feel only the "party" side of life which led to addiction and all the horrors that come with that. Learning how to be a man of character and developing an ability to find meaning and purpose in my life has come from facing the reality of life's problems and hardships rather than avoiding, denying, or minimizing them. Recovery has shown me how to no longer view the ups and downs of life as standalone events that offer some deeper meaning as to my own personal status or value. Yes, of course recovery freed me from the addiction that was ruining my life, but in sobriety I am faced with living life on life's terms, the good, the bad, and the ugly of it all. At first I tended to excessively personalize these individual events without seeing them in the bigger picture of being simply a part of life. If I got a hot new girlfriend I was clearly the greatest human ever, if we broke up I was a failure. I've learned that happiness and suffering are both unavoidable parts of living a full life and that they lose their true meaning when isolated outside of the larger context and framework of being simply a part of life. By placing them properly within the bigger picture of my lifetime I was able to gain an understanding that what I am really striving for is the feeling of contentedness that comes from doing both well. Childlike wishful thinking is good for children but as a grown man I can only be of value to myself and others by fully experiencing and learning from the lessons that life provides. As I face each new challenge or suffering that life presents, instead of losing hope and giving up, I can instead look back at the other hurdles that I've overcome in the past and approach the new one with some degree of grace and faith seeing it as part of a larger continuum. While I may not be able to control or determine how it all works out. I know that it will work out and that my Higher Power will make sure I am ok.

# JULY 23

The question of finding meaning in life is one that I largely disliked when I was younger. I felt as though seeking those sorts of deep answers was a somewhat useless pursuit as it was clear to my young immature mind what life was all about. Like many teenagers and young adults I was full of confidence about my understanding of life and simply wanted people to get out of the way so I could pursue it. I was full of overconfidence and inexperience wrapped in an unjustified hubris based on opinion rather than experience. That immature outlook followed me into adulthood as alcohol and drugs muted my personal growth. And what a mess that became as my addiction layered itself onto my sense of confident knowledge that I knew what I was doing—that I had it under control. It undergirded my denial and inability to see how insane my situation was as I mocked any attempts by those close to me to offer other ideas about how I could, and should, change and grow. Slowly I've come to realize the importance of reviewing and examining who I am and how life experiences have shaped my thinking—both in the past and present. Those experiences continue to unfold in ways that offer new understandings and insights around my beliefs and actions. Today I greatly value the depth and meaning of my life and want to make the most of my days—a goal that isn't necessarily always measured in achievements or accomplishments but rather in personal growth and understanding. The development of a spiritual focus in life has helped me to more closely examine how I live life each day and provides a capability to freely review and evaluate my actions, my choices and decisions, with less fear and trepidation about what I may find. Recovery has softened my ego about how I view myself so that I can welcome and accept my faults and failings as simply being part of the human process rather than a sign of some epic and tragic personal failing that consigns me to a place of doom and dread. Recovery affords me an ability to find deeper meaning and purpose in my life that is part of a larger sphere of being than my own individuality and yet comfortably places my sense of personhood within it.

# JULY 24

The longer I stay sober the sicker I was when I arrived in recovery. It has taken years for me to realize just how insanely out of sorts I was in active addiction or how mistaken I was about so many of my most basic understandings about how life works. About what it means to be a strong and healthy man. In many cases I've now come to believe that the reality of life is exactly the opposite of what I used to think it was. Contempt prior to investigation kept me from the truth in many ways, for many years. It is remarkable how much change has occurred in the way I view myself and my role in life. A good example of this is the ability to not only see and admit that I need help—and to then be able to ask for it. For years I viewed asking for help as a sign of weakness when the opposite is true. In addiction this problem was exacerbated by my delusional thinking and excessive fear that grew out of the shame and guilt of my actions. With each passing disaster my life continually worsened. My understanding of where my bottom was—how low I could go and the things I would tolerate as part of my life—became stranger and more desperate. It was increasingly hard to ask for help because the people who I knew truly cared for me seemed always further away with each new low. I was fearful of sharing the truth of my situation with those who could see just how far I had fallen. My new "friends" in addiction were rarely trustworthy, usually unreliable, and unlikely to be able to offer any true insight or meaningful assistance. They were in the same boat I was—suffering horribly in a downward spiral of addiction. It wasn't until those occasional moments of brief sobriety and clouded insight, often just after another debacle of some sort had taken place, that I was able to consider reaching out to the people who could actually help. Oftentimes the sad idea that I could figure it out on my own would sooth my pride and ego and off I would go again. The cartoonish childish fallacy of the man alone against the world, strong and always able, led me only to a long, hard, and lonely road. The reality of human life, throughout all time, is that it is a "we" world. Perhaps it is true that a wise man knows that it is only in the giving and receiving of help with others that humankind reaches its true potential.

# JULY 25

The true realization and acceptance of the ultimate powerlessness of my life is a daunting task. Indeed there are many ways in which I can control my own actions but the responses of the world around me always remains frustratingly unpredictable and oftentimes seemingly either randomly or even purposefully difficult. Perhaps it is human nature to focus on the memory of things that work out well however in active addiction that became more difficult and unlikely as few things were ending well. My addiction and codependency are both ways in which I try to extend my sphere of control outward from myself into and onto the world around me. As the lack of control within my own world in addiction persisted I would increasingly try to shift the emphasis away from my own actions toward the world outside of me in terms of how people, places, and things were creating the problems in my life rather than looking inward at my own thinking, actions, and beliefs. I now see how there were futile efforts— ultimately expressions of my unwillingness to accept and have faith—to trust in the spiritual element of my own life. Acceptance of my own life, my place in the world and the cultivation of a sense of authentic belonging and deserving, is a vital part of how recovery has changed my outlook and understanding of how I fit into the world around me. Addiction deluded me into thinking I was in control of much more than is possible and in time the inevitable results, the crushing isolation and failures, fully pierced that delusion enabling me to at last let go of the idea that I could someday find a way to make addiction work. Today I am better able to let go of the desire to control life around me and fully accept only the responsibility of my own actions in life. I can see how they are a reflection of my own solitude and unavoidable human individualism. I can let go of the childish need to combine my existence with the actions of others. I am indeed alone as a man and yet my life is also linked into and a valid part of the human cosmos. A spiritual connection guides and validates me. It has allowed me to fully grasp and value my own life and provides the willingness to live well for myself—because after all—it is my life to live. I alone experience being me and it is an exciting realization to fully grasp my gift of life for what it really is rather than abuse it for what it isn't.

# JULY 26

When I was a young child my family moved a lot and so I was often the new kid in the neighborhood. We often moved a long distance and so in many ways I was also quite different culturally. Having a different accent and not understanding the local customs and inside jokes of the other children meant I rarely felt like I fit in or was accepted. Instead I was compelled to prove myself and demonstrate that I was good enough or better than. I somehow needed to confirm that I was not only unique but also in some way special and worthy. I was also angry at the world. Although at a young age I didn't really understand my anger or its causes and instead would simply act out through rebellion and defiance. This need to prove I was something became a driving force in my life as I sought to excel at all things wherever I could. When I wasn't able to excel at being the best I then often worked to become the worst. Always things were framed in extremes as I sought the power and control that was lacking in the chaotic world of my upbringing. This insecurity and sense of inadequacy meant that I was sure to be the best drinker and able to consume more than anyone else. By adolescence my world was firmly rooted in the alternative and party lifestyle as I saw myself increasingly unable to fit into the normal societal frameworks and activities. In recovery I've begun to learn how alcohol and substance abuse was never really my original problem and that in fact it was my solution. Unfortunately the solution was short lived as the inevitable addiction set in and I began partying so I could remain loaded rather than as some sort of social lubricant. In an ironic twist, the solution I found that offered me the chance to control my ability to fit in with those around me quickly took control of me. In recovery I've learned to see my underlying problem—learning how to live life on life's terms without running away or distorting and trying to control my reality with substance abuse. The gift of a spiritual awakening offers me an understanding and acceptance of the idea that I am enough. That I am always enough and that the best I will ever be is an imperfect human with little control over the world around me. Instead I have learned how to control with world within me and in that way can more calmly face the unpredictable world around me.

# JULY 27

I grew up with a real disdain for spirituality. I was into concrete facts, actions, results and proof. Logic and practicality were the hallmarks of the modern world and I often mocked all of those 1960's themes of peace and love that my parents had been into. I was assured by the promise of new technologies and advancements and the advent of computers that provided a strong sense that what was needed in the world was decisive action rather than increased spirituality. Today as I look back I can see that in many ways this desire seemed to be rooted in an unwillingness to look closely at my own troubled self-image and was tied to my need to overcome a sense of internal fear. My inadequacy and insecurity became masked by self-importance and hubris. This drove an inability to connect in any meaningful way with religion which I felt was some sort of formalized aid for the weak minded who weren't strong enough to take on life on their own. Ultimately, I was my own Higher Power and that was that. Of course that never really worked out very well for me and I ended up in recovery trying to figure out what went wrong. The years of trying to control and manage the world around me as I descended further into the depths of addiction created an insanity of thinking and beliefs that left me disconnected, disheartened and deeply confused. The efforts of my journey in early recovery never took root until the day I accepted in my heart that I would turn my will over to a Higher Power and let someone else run the show. The willingness to accept a spiritual way of living was the key that opened the door to a lot of change. I remember clearly the moment when I quit fighting. It felt very odd to know that I was moving into a place which was unknown. I was afraid that even as I gave myself fully to my Higher Power I might not remain sober. It was so difficult to embrace an unknown and simply have faith—to trust in something I had only a vague understanding of and couldn't define. That moment was the first step in a spiritual journey that has allowed me to find my own path to a God that is meaningful and real to me in a way that has allowed me to begin, at last, to stop trying to be my own God.

# JULY 28

When I was in active addiction my living was centered on short term thinking and driven by unhealthy patterns of mental and physical behavior. It was a shallow existence and day to day grind for survival in which my goals and dreams simply became smaller and fewer as the confusion and mists of addiction clouded my mind and body. There was no balance in my approach to life, no accounting for the future or recognition of any responsibility to myself and others. Life in addiction increasingly left me disconnected from the world and in many ways acted to cause an internal disaggregation of both mind and body. Not only was my spiritual life drained but I also suffered tremendous physical consequences as I became less and less integrated as a person. I was literally and figuratively falling to pieces. I was in a state of confusion that prevented me from seeing any of my problems within the larger framework of my overall life and instead I would intensely focus on one small part of my problems as if by fixing that part it would somehow prove that I would then be able to fix the others. Recovery has shown me how to have a more holistic approach that deals with the bigger picture of my life and my place in the world. I have a more spiritual method that while centered on the actions of today acknowledges and prepares me for my responsibilities in the future. I am able to see myself as more fully integrated person and understand how the various parts of my being must be operating properly in order for me to live well. Like an engine, I must first be firing on all cylinders in order to then be in tune. By attempting to be aware of my Higher Powers will for me I accept that I am part of a future plan and can work to be able to fulfil it by using the steps in my recovery. I must also accept that my recovery is centered in many areas and I cannot have success in one area while forgoing the others. Spiritually based recovery must lift all the boats in the harbor of my life: spiritual, physical, mental and emotional health. It must enable my social participation through recreation, fellowship, work, and service. Together they provide a healthy ability to seek and carry out my Higher Power's will for me.

# JULY 29

Sometimes as the saying goes, the devil you know is better than the devil you don't. During my years in active addiction it was the fear of the unknown that in part prevented me from taking the risk of meaningful change in my life. My life was in a shambles and yet it was all I seemed to know. As my situation worsened the desire for the escape, comfort, and quick relief from it all increased and kept me ever more focused on drinking and using. Somehow, in my skewed thinking, I believed there was a way to continue that would work. I told myself I was afraid of losing that which I knew but in fact I was afraid of that which I didn't. This crippling fear of the unknown, of not being good enough, of failing and perhaps discovering that I was ultimately ineligible for recovery, acted to prevent me from making a truly serious attempt. In time I managed to realize that life in addiction is always just one poor decision and a short walk away. I can always quickly return to addiction and all my misery will be promptly delivered back to me. It was the unknown of how to live life sober that truly terrified me. In order to catch a new life I had to let go of the old life. For me that meant holding onto nothing but willingness for a while as I left my old thinking and beliefs behind and began the journey that would bring new ones. It meant taking a risk and having faith—believing that the hope for my future that I had gained from seeing the recovery of others could lead to something that would work me. Having faith that if I did what they did I would also find relief required me to do more than simply think about it or voice the idea. I had to incorporate it fully, accepting it as a fundamental part of who I was going to be. As I truly joined with my Higher Power and began to take meaningful action recovery immediately began to work for me as never before. It is a reminder for me today that I must be willing to risk trying new things in my recovery if I am to have any hope of continued progress and growth. It is only through the trial and error of living in new ways that I am able to continue to invigorate the future of my own personal development and spiritual awakening.

# JULY 30

Addiction was a world that held me in its grasp through the delusion of my ability to control life and the illusion that somehow I was. While it's true to say that I found getting sober quite a bit easier than staying sober it was the early failures in recovery that allowed me to begin to identify and learn how addiction schemed to keep me in its clutches. In the very beginning recovery meant facing what seemed to be a long road of repairs to my life. My inability to focus on the more profound questions about who I was meant the solution was framed in repairs that would occur to my outside world. Many of the things I heard said in meetings I only partially understood. For example it was suggested that I not compare my insides with other people's outsides and I grappled to truly get to the bottom of what that actually meant because at that time so much of what I thought was wrong with my life were things that were external to me. Legal problems, possessions, careers, friends and family were all situations that I needed to mend, overcome and achieve. Over time I've realized that the most important place for me to focus my efforts is on my inside sense of self and not the trappings of my outside world. Today I can see many people whose outside world is in great shape while inside they struggle greatly. Experience in recovery has shown me that as I improve my spirituality and personal growth—my inside work—the rest of my world becomes more satisfying. The challenge was learning how to bridge the gap between the results taking place in my life because of one set of beliefs to a new system of thought that would provide different results. Slowly I became better able to understand what was meant by terms like "spiritual awakening" and "living life on life's terms" enough to be able to leave the world of my old thinking and begin living in a new way. It was only after I became willing to let go of my current beliefs that I was able to begin the journey of finding their replacement. This shift of focus to an understanding about how to take my place in the world around me rather than trying to force the world around me to meet my terms freed me from the bondage of self. Because I am happy with who I am inside there is no longer such a strong and futile need to attempt to solve inside problems with outside solutions.

# JULY 31

Recovery is all about change. It is not only the process of discovering my progress and spiritual growth but it is also how I experience it and use it to review and shape my future. One of the greatest wonders I've experienced in recovery is the transformation that continues to take place with how I view my past. When I arrived in recovery, the wreckage of my actions in addiction framed my past in a way that was a shameful burden and an anchor in my efforts to move forward. Today my past has become a useful asset that enables me to help others and is a tool for living well. In a broad and general way, recovery has shown me how to learn from my past and make changes in how I live moving forward. More specifically, it allows me the opportunity to do it on a daily basis. The recognition of this reality is one of the more important parts of my recovery and reinforces the fundamental truth that all recovery takes place one day at a time. Ultimately, all the days that add up to a long period of recovery accumulate in the same way—individually. Each day in recovery is equally as important as the next when I allow myself to be fully engaged in the process of a spiritual awakening. I know I am walking on the path of recovery because the scenery of my life changes. I am no longer waking up and realizing that I'm in exactly the same place as I was a year ago. Perhaps it was Lily Tomlin who said, "I've given up all hope of having a better past" and I rightly don't wallow in regret or suffer my failings endlessly. However, I can learn from my past and use those lessons to drive the change and growth that takes place in my life today. And while this process is certainly at times found in the form of big shifts, displacements, occasional breakthroughs and momentous insights, it also is an opportunity that is available in many small ways each day. This has become a core essence of my recovery, living life fully day by day, and by doing so I can engage in the continual process of improving my spiritual self. It is a remarkable journey that provides space for me in the moment of each day in which I can make spiritual contact with my place in the world. Every day I get the chance to add a new element of positive value and esteem into the trail of my past that I leave behind.

# August

"We only have what we give."
— Isabel Allende

"As I walked out the door toward the gate that would lead to my freedom, I knew if I didn't leave my bitterness and hatred behind, I'd still be in prison."
— Nelson Mandela

"We have all known the long loneliness and we have learned that the only solution is love and that love comes with community."
— Dorothy Day

# AUGUST 1

The simple answer to how I live my life in recovery is found within; however, it took a long time for me to gain entry to the framework of understanding that connected me to the reality of recovery being an "inside job." For years I fed on the addictive cycle of battling with the world around me. The struggle and fight of competition and reward, defying the odds and manipulating outcomes that met my needs, was relentless and over time it became the prize rather than a pathway to it. In a way I was measuring my success in how well I was able to persevere and overcome life's many seemingly devious and unfair obstacles. This framework required me to complicate and mistrust the world around me so that I could then triumph against it. The creation of complication and the endless parade of unmanageability was a hallmark of a lifestyle in addiction that I knew well. Recovery allows me to approach each day in a simple way with my own house in order and fully aware that the opportunity of the day lies in how I conduct my own life while avoiding my desire to conduct life around me. My primary concern must be with my own motives and actions—not those of others. Today I try to find honesty and simplicity in the challenges of the day. Problems can be reframed as opportunities to learn, grow and change. I no longer have to relive my drama endlessly by constantly recreating it and can instead sort through the problems of today and then move on. I don't approach each day as a battle to be won because that sort of thinking automatically places me in the driver's seat and negates my reliance on a Higher Power. It implies that I am in fact going to "take charge" of how the world unfolds around me. Instead I am better able to focus on how to see each day as another chance to practice the principles of recovery and bring the ideas of spirituality into my daily living. It is more like an experience to be enjoyed and explored with an attempt to find a small measure of grace and dignity as I navigate through whatever part of human life arrives. I try to remain calm and contribute while I "keep it simple," like it says on the wall of the meeting hall.

# AUGUST 2

The beginning of the end of the crushing isolation and self-contained thinking of addiction began when I started doing step work with a sponsor. Before I could possibly learn how to be open and honest enough to share my truths I had to also find them within myself. The truth of who I really was had become deeply and profoundly hidden and my lack of any understanding of how this deficiency of self-knowledge was affecting me was a barrier that was formidable and incomprehensible. I had to first learn and understand how the problem even existed, to see and recognize my shortcomings, and then begin the work of addressing them. The process required a willingness to be vulnerable and learn new skills that explored the feelings and beliefs that drove the patterns of my behaviors in ways that I wasn't aware of and couldn't see. As part of becoming vulnerable and open with another man I also had to do so with myself. It was one of the hardest things I've done in recovery because it really challenged me to look hard, with a clear mind, and examine who I really am. It was desperately difficult to pierce through the hard shell of a lifetime of painful experiences and overwhelming realities about how my personality had been constructed throughout the years as a child, a young adult, and as an addict. Over time it has become easier and more routine for me to be vulnerable with close friends and express my inner-most thoughts and truths. This is because I've experienced the benefit of its unique and powerful ability to create change in the patterns and cycles of shame and guilt that have in the past controlled me. Today I am able to choose the path of willingness and use the tools I've gained and the skills in using them to continually decode and better understand how I show up for myself and in the world around me. By staying involved in active recovery I maintain the willingness and open-mindedness that is central to continued self-understanding. There was no way for me to be open and honest enough for a valid existence in the "sunlight of the spirit" without opening up to others and becoming vulnerable. It is one of the most life changing experiences I have known and a vital part of how I work to maintain a fit spiritual condition.[15] [16]

# AUGUST 3

To this day I can clearly remember in active addiction that feeling of never wanting to go to bed. There was always a drive for more, a party somewhere, people to get with, the drunken dialing—always a search for something other than the loneliness of being left with just myself. The terrible disconnected feeling of how, despite the promise of the good times of substance abuse, I was often left utterly unfulfilled. In recovery I've

---

[15] Check out the work of Brené Brown on vulnerability - Brown, Brené. Daring Greatly : How the Courage to Be Vulnerable Transforms the Way We Live, Love, Parent, and Lead. New York, New York: Avery, 2015.

[16] *Alcoholics Anonymous : The Story of How Many Thousands of Men and Women Have Recovered from Alcoholism.* 4th ed. New York City: Alcoholics Anonymous World Services, 2001. P. 66.

learned how the crushing isolation and loneliness of addiction is one of the classic symptoms of my spiritual illness that is at the root of my alcoholism. I remember as a youth when I was acting out in class a teacher rather harshly told me I needed to spend more time alone with myself. Even then I struggled with such insight and knew that the last thing I wanted to do was to be alone with myself and it was reflective of the underlying causes and conditions the left me feeling awkward and unable to seem to fit in. Slowly I've learned to be comfortable with who I am and to develop an ability to enjoy solitude. It is perhaps no surprise that throughout all of human history the search for spiritual awareness and growth has often included periods of solitary effort. This hard work of being alone with oneself, seeing and answering basic questions about who I am and what I shall be, seeing my own tenuous frailty and humanity, requires time away from the distractions of day to day living. My own search for myself and my connection with a Higher Power has come as a result of finding and holding my own soul and self closely and carefully—and sharing it with others so that in a way I am never really alone anymore. It is a remarkable feeling to understand what it is to be comfortable in one's own skin. Recovery has shown me how to be true to my own self and gather the spiritual fortitude and integrity that allows me to be a whole person. One who can truly stand alone and be comfortable with who I am and how I relate to the world around me—content in my place with nature and my Higher Power.

# AUGUST 4

One day at a time I can take it easy and let go and let God while I try to keep my thinking simple. The slogans of recovery work best for me when I'm out living life rather than when I am in a meeting. They are a reminder to let go of my efforts to control life around me and to be flexible. To leave gaps in my approach to the day. The process of recovery is so often rather abstract and confined to its own rather safe and comfortable world that I must remember to bring it with me and exercise its principles in the affairs of my daily living. I can be ready and open to taking time to see and explore what is going on around me rather than rigidly pursuing my own agenda and plans for the day so furiously that I am closed off to my surroundings. It is in the gaps in my day that I can experience the spiritual moments and be ready to hear what my Higher Power's will is for me. My willful selfish and self-centered nature wants to control, organize, optimize and drive a certain outcome or achievement and in doing so I can lose sight of the most important part of daily life—the crucial element of being present in its unfolding. Each day is a chance to experience and participate in the moments of spirituality and awakening that are a critical part of my recovery. By learning to be comfortable with the distractions, delays and detours of the day I am offered the chance to go with the flow of my Higher Power rather than forcing my will into all situations. In addiction my days were framed with a sense of purposelessness and unsatisfied discontent—I never wanted the day to end because of the feeling that there should be more. In recovery, I've learned that there is always plenty of time to enjoy the day and at the end there has always been enough. It is in the reflection of my actions with others and the world around me that I see myself more clearly and can have the chance to hear the messages of spirituality and simple meaning of daily living that are present around me all the time waiting for me to notice and value them.

# AUGUST 5

The ongoing process of working through the steps of recovery and relating that work into my daily life is a continual source of personal discovery, growth and understanding. The very act of living in recovery, actively and regularly following the path of the steps and sharing my experience with others provides a constant opportunity to further explore the depths of my own self. I have changed in profound ways through learning and gaining more understanding and insight about who I am now. Along the way I have learned more about coming to terms with my past and being honest about my present as I continue to learn how to shape and participate in my future growth. A requirement of the steps is that I learn and grow from my daily experiences so that I can enlarge my spiritual connection with a Higher Power and also work with others to carry the message. This ensures a vibrant and helpful activity level that keeps my recovery allve and healthy and is most often found through the active art of living and sharing my life with others in honest and meaningful ways. In being active and sincerely engaged both in the lives of others and also in the process of my own spiritual growth I am challenged to continue to examine my own truth about how my actions reflect my beliefs and values. It offers me the chance to enjoy the work of having a deeper grasp of my own motives, desires, and hopes in life. While I can still find myself questioning what I am doing and at times will struggle with the choices and decisions that present themselves as my life unfolds I am better able to participate in them comfortably and calmly. Those feelings of being lost, confused or fearful about my life have largely been replaced with an element of insight and patience that allows me to more deeply engage with my own feelings and thoughts. Increasingly I realize how much more powerful, interesting, and rewarding life has become. My experience is that the opportunity of real recovery is a never ending gift of personal growth, insight, and usefulness that is found through my relationships with others and guided by the ongoing work of the twelve steps.

# AUGUST 6

Learning how to have a full and varied life experience is one of the great opportunities for addicts in recovery. My addictive nature leads me toward becoming overly focused on things—maniacally so at times. When that thing is alcohol or drugs then I become completely out of control, unbalanced, and unhinged. Of course it was the insanity and unmanageability of active addiction that brought me into recovery but once I got past the drinking and using it slowly became clear that in many ways the real work of recovery had just begun. I had to learn more about how that same compulsive mind-set drove many other parts of my thinking and living. To this day, it can still quite easily dominate other facets of my life distorting my thinking and beliefs about myself and the world around me. We perhaps all know at least one sober workaholic or excessive fitness fanatic. Of course one of the ideas of recovery is that I become "addicted" to it, so in that way this compulsion can and does—perhaps somewhat ironically—save my life. The opportunity for growth lies in my willingness to take risks and try new things. To broaden my life experience and expand not only my spiritual awakening but also my life. In recovery it is the widening and increasing of my spiritual growth that has replaced my addictive behavior and is what I seek to explore and be conscious of each day. I often hesitate to find new growth in my life because it forces me to accept that there is no panacea—no great and perfectly "right" solution to my problem. That I can't work really hard at it until some magical bell rings and I have arrived. What provided me balance last month or last year will often change for me and I must once again explore the often difficult and challenging space of new growth in my life. All new growth requires a rebalancing of my associated thinking and beliefs. I've slowly learned to accept this and as a result can hold onto my thinking about life a little more loosely and remain comfortable in the understanding that the right answers are never static. They change as I do. Finding variety and balance helps me confront the limited and brief reality of my life and challenges me to live it to the fullest for what it actually is rather than chasing some idea of what I want to force it to remain or become.

# AUGUST 7

One of the hardest things in life for me—growing up and certainly in addiction—was the ability to form meaningful and honest relationships with others. It has taken years of recovery to become better able to have faith and trust within loving relationships with other people without holding them to unrealistic standards or having unfair expectations about what I think their behavior should be. It has been through acceptance of my own inevitable personal failings that I have become able to accept those of my friends, allowing me to transcend the gritty reality of human imperfection and enable a sustainable and realistic love for them. Learning how to love, while accepting the flaws and imperfections of those with whom I have close relationships, has also opened the door to my ability to accept and love myself. As it is often said in recovery "the best we get is human." It has been through the risk taking and honesty of close relationships with others that I've learned more about what it means to be human and to love in a genuine way. I've learned more about its limits and realities and how my own personal boundaries, my morals and values, must learn how to tolerate and coexist with my own humanness and that of others. For me today, that understanding is increasingly comfortable with the unavoidable imperfection of being human. Just as I make mistakes, and often find myself doing things I am quick to judge others for, I must also accept that it is that way with others. I can quickly be upset, indignant or righteous about someone else's mistake, but of course if I'm honest I must realize that I too have made the same mistake—usually more than once. The insanity of my addiction constructed an unreconciled coupling of an intolerant lack of forgiveness of others with a shameful self-pity around my own failings. Learning how to live with brotherly love and patient tolerance has opened up the door to the world of authentic loving and meaningful relationships. As I have grown in recovery my understanding of what love is has changed from a youthful and childish "story book" ideal toward a deeper and more mature reality as I better understand its role in relationships and how love's powerful values are rooted in human frailty and vulnerability.

# AUGUST 8

In my youth, when I would get stuck on a problem or task that wasn't going well, my parents or grandparents would often kindly and softly suggest that it might help if I were to take a break and come back to it later. I never wanted to do that and disliked the suggestion. I always wanted to solve the problem myself and wanted to do it right now! I personalized their suggestions and felt like it meant I wasn't good enough to do whatever it was I was trying. I felt like I shouldn't need to take a break and my desire to show them wrong, to demonstrate that I was able to solve the problem myself, would take over and drive me into further frustration and anger. Thinking back it's a reminder of how I tend to obsess and fight to have my own way. My grandiose opinion of myself was driven by a terrible fear of failure and not being good enough. It led me to thinking that cried out in my own mind thoughts like, "don't they know who I am" or "I'll show them." I wanted to deny my humanness as though somehow I am special and things that other people need to do don't apply to me—like for instance the rules. Or later in life—the law. In recovery I've learned more about being a regular average man. How things that work for other people will also work for me if I try them and accept the results. Learning how to take a break when things aren't going well has been a profound lesson in acceptance of my own human imperfections and learning how to let go of my "go it alone" ideas about independence, prideful individualism, and liberty when they are failing me. The experience has offered me a way to see and apply some perspective about what it looks like when I am trying to force my will on the world around me. When my will is properly aligned with that of my Higher Power my life tends to roll along fairly smoothly but when I am trying to exert my selfish will, or acting with poor motives, things become forced and difficult. I am able to see asking for help as a sign of maturity and strength rather than one of weakness. Taking a break allows me to review, ponder my thinking, consult with others, and come back to a task with a fresh approach that is often more helpful and effective.

# AUGUST 9

One of my core defects of character is an enlarged fear of not being good enough and of failing. This fear of not being good enough and the subsequent embarrassment and shame drives me to try to control and force my will into life around me. It also drives me to limit my efforts, my goals and dreams, and avoid taking risk or trusting in the unknown by choosing to seek easier accomplishments that I know are within reach. It has been hard to slowly uncover and see just how deeply this character defect is embedded in my personality and how it affects much more than I would care to admit. One of the great challenges and opportunities of my recovery is to learn how to "Let go and let God." In time I've learned that in many of the most difficult situations in my life my attempts to force my own fearful solutions have had poor results that I struggle with. Often I end up making a bad situation worse—which ultimately just compounds and confirms my original fears of not being good enough. However, when I trust in my Higher Power and have faith and courage to follow a path into an unknown solution, often times things tend to work out well and in ways that I could never have possibly imagined. Letting go and letting God has enabled me to follow my vague dreams and intuitions in ways that have allowed me to grow and change unexpectedly along a path I never would have found on my own. Slowly, through experience and practice, I have become better able to allow my thinking and actions to simply go with the flow of life around me. I am better able to take it easy and allow enough time for God's plan to unfold without attempting to force my own will into a situation. Today I have the patience and trust to face the unknown with grace, secure in the understanding that my Higher Power has a plan for me. One that is better than I can imagine. One that will reveal itself in time as I stay the course and allow it to happen.

# AUGUST 10

The gift of reason that separates humans from the rest of the animal world is profound and meaningful in so many ways. As a young man, alcohol and drugs kept me from the full accomplishment of the maturation stage of life from boy to man. I missed that vital adolescent process of leaving the nest and striking out on my own, not from a physical standpoint, but from an emotional one. Instead I left early on the party bus and skipped all the hard work of self-discovery and growing up. As a result I was a young man who was immature and undeveloped in some crucial ways that allowed me to fall into patterns of behaviors that were driven by faulty relationships that could never work. Becoming a mature man in recovery has meant coming to grips with the knowledge of my own mortality and acceptance of my singular existence as an individual who is alone with himself. Despite years of trying in active addiction, the fact is that I can't cheat death nor can I avoid the loneliness of being human. Accepting my mortality means confronting and making serious choices about how I live. These vital individual insights about my beliefs and morals, the search and acceptance of my place within the world, ultimately must come from me alone and are difficult and painful at times. Understanding the inherent loneliness of my individuality meant learning that I couldn't avoid it by finding "the right" relationship or person. I had to build a meaningful relationship with myself before I could have any hope of one with another person. Accepting my human fate and reality has opened the door to living life in a new way that is full, deeply rewarding, and meaningful because I am finally fully in touch with myself. I have a strong grasp of who I am and what I stand for in life that allows me to be comfortable in my human loneliness in a way that places me as a peer with all others. It drives the anchor of an understanding that allows me to be a part of, an equal, a man among other men, alone without feeling disconnected from.

# AUGUST 11

In recovery we are shown the goal of "fitting" ourselves to be of maximum service to our Higher Power and to other people. This is quite a shift from my previous thinking when the goal was usually to be of maximum service to myself. This became clear in active addiction as my behaviors demonstrated that fundamentally I was acting like an immature child whose only concern was meeting my own wants—regardless of the cost or impact upon me or others. Sobering up and beginning to walk the path of recovery allowed me to see how isolated, selfish, and self-centered my world was, and then began to expand my ability to participate in the world around me. The goal of being in a fit condition to seek and do my Higher Power's will in turn means that I must also focus on taking care of myself. The expression H.A.L.T. (hungry angry lonely tired) offers a good spot check for when I am struggling with that task. It has been clear to me that I am more effective in helping others when I ensure that my own self care is the first priority. It is a process that has taken time to become used to. Previously I was caught up in a belief system that said it was a sign of manhood and endurance that I could forgo my needs to achieve a goal. The all-nighter of cramming for a school exam quickly became the all-nighter of partying and still being able to somehow go to work in the morning. Today I am clearer about the importance I must place on my own self-care as a form of recognition and commitment to the goal of being the man my Higher Power wants me to be. Ultimately I am the only one who can choose to take the actions I need in order to remain healthy and rested. No one can do it for me and it certainly won't just happen on its own. Sometimes those actions can be as simple as a nap or a walk with the dog, but it is the ability to recognize they are needed and helpful that is the real sign of change for me. Self-care has become tightly linked to my own sense of self-worth and value. It demonstrates that I appreciate and care about myself and is an example of the meaningful action that recovery shows me how to take in order to live more fully and usefully.

# AUGUST 12

Tolerance and acceptance of others is easier for me when the "others" are members of my own group or belief system. The principle of brotherly love that undergirds the eighth step of recovery represents a call to action for me with regard to all of humankind—not just the people or beliefs that I like and identify with. Assuming a viewpoint of others that includes judgment and superiority moves me in the wrong direction spiritually. In addiction I can be very quick to judge others in part because of a deep fear of being called out on my own behavior and actions. It can be much easier for me to point the lens of criticism and oppression at the actions of others and in doing so avoid any review or reflection upon my own immoral, selfish, and hurtful behaviors. Perhaps in some ways by being embroiled in a constant dialog about the problems, faults and ensuing punishments and oppression of others I was able to justify a lack of spirituality within my own life—lest the charade of my belief system come undone. After all, given my actions in addiction, and the harm I have caused others, who I am to possibly make judgment, claim to know better, or to discount and deride another person's beliefs? Surely this situation is a two way street? And if so, then the better more useful question for my spiritual growth must become one that asks—how do I arrive in the lives of others? Experience has shown me that it is only through acceptance and tolerance of other people and their divergent opinions that I can truly confirm my own belief system. I don't have to always agree with the ideas and beliefs of others, that would be foolish of course, but it helps me to listen and evaluate them with a truly open mind in order that I may test the currency of my own ideas and thoughts. I have learned that many times that when opinions, ideas, or actions of others bring a strong emotional response from me it is because there is something inside me that still requires examination. At the core of the issue is the simple fact that, no matter what our beliefs and differences, as humans we all share much more in common than the sum of our differences. When I turn the impulse to judge inward I can often experience personal growth. I can accept without agreeing and forgo the need to correct or fight.

# AUGUST 13

In active addiction I knew something was wrong but wasn't able or willing to honestly face the truth about what it was. Addiction is a disease that centers in my thinking and it deluded me about what was real. In recovery we often hear it said that addiction is the only disease that tells us we don't have one. This misleading symptom of the disease of addiction makes recovery all the more difficult. In order to recover I had to allow that my own thinking was part of the problem and seek, accept, and rely upon the advice and help of others. This conundrum of becoming able to understand that my own thinking was at the heart of my problems—and to then be willing to accept a situation in which I would stop trying to solve my own problems and allow others to help—was very difficult to navigate. Of course in time I ultimately discovered that addiction was itself a symptom of my underlying problems of a lack of spirituality and unaddressed issues of self-identity, self-worth, guilt and shame. The addict inside that is trying to kill me has a favorite weapon and it is called shame. It wants to hide and pretend it's not there and not really affecting me. I had to become vulnerable and open myself to others in order to actually see how profound and fundamental my problems really were. To see how deeply they were affecting me—both explicitly and implicitly. My years of covering up and minimizing the consequences of shame had distorted and hidden the truth. Over time I have come to see very clearly how addressing these underlying issues of guilt and shame are the foundation and bedrock of my spiritual awakening. Until I could learn to have love for myself and accept that my self-worth was valid it was hard to accept that the love of a Higher Power (and of others) was something that could be effective and real for me. It was a slow path of learning to truly grasp and believe that I was not only fully qualified for the promise of a life in recovery, but that I was also completely eligible. The language of spirituality is love and I couldn't begin to speak it, share it, and live it with others until I learned how to love myself—even just a little.

# AUGUST 14

One of the greatest gifts of my life in recovery has been the return of personal choice. In addiction my options were continually shrinking and increasingly constrained by the results of my errant actions. I painted myself further into a corner of limited options with lies, deceit, and ever gathering consequences. Each day became more hopeless as I struggled to find something of value in it. As my addiction worsened it become impossible to fool myself with stories and tales of how I would soon be doing better. It was also more difficult to escape this truth through intoxication as I struggled to sustain my cycles of using and addiction to stay loaded. Slowly my choices all ran out and I was faced with the reality of always longer jail sentences and complete social isolation from any friends or family. Finally I was able to grab hold of the one chance that always remains for any addict—the choice of sobriety, treatment, and the beginning of a new life in recovery. The paradox of my story was that I had to ultimately lose all other choices in order to make the one I should have made long before. Recovery has allowed me to live freely again and each day presents me with a grand array of choices about how I will live. I am able to enjoy options that provide value and meaning in my actions—and in doing so increase my self-worth and esteem. Freedom from addiction has allowed me the chance to truly explore and experiment with life while discovering my own sense of identity within it. At the end of the day I can feel good about myself and see that it contained value and purpose. As a result I can finally understand that it is also my life that has value and purpose. I am able to measure that value in a wide variety of ways that aren't linked only to measures of external success. I can enjoy personal growth, free time, and introspection as much as working well and achieving a goal. Recognition of my value as a person comes from within as well as from others. It demonstrates the value I place on my participation in all aspects of daily life. It reinforces the simple truth and joy of life—that in some way or another each and every day is worthwhile.

# AUGUST 15

It has been frustrating and difficult to learn that so many things I believed about what it means to be a man were not so much completely wrong but were instead terribly incomplete. In so many areas of life I had made do with a surface knowledge and understanding of something rather than taking the time and effort to investigate it fully. I figured I knew enough to get by with and was typically more focused on questions about what I wanted to do right now—like party! The story of my life as a self-centered addict revolved around shortcuts and incompletions and so it is no wonder that I struggle in recovery with deeper questions about what it is to be a man. It has been difficult and time consuming to at first become aware of how significant these shortcomings are—how they have had profound impacts on my life—and then somehow find the courage to begin the task of resolving these gaps in my knowledge and character. More recently I've learned the powerful importance of being a more complete man who is able to share his feelings and experiences with others. I have realized that many of the things I believed about manhood were shallow and false. That the cardboard cut-out, story-book marketing version of manhood with its trite slogan for every problem is just a manufactured media device that has some elements of truth but lacks any depth or true basis in reality. The more compelling truth is that as long as mankind has been recording history there are continuous examples of how strong men share their doubts and questions about life with each other. In recovery, and in most other areas of my life today, I experience the value and truth that comes with being part of a group of men who work seriously to share, discover, explore, and improve their lives. My thinking has changed as I've learned from others and gained more self-understanding and awareness. I have confirmed that addiction is a disease that centers in my own thinking and that I can find no relief without friends who help me understand my own doubts and fears as being simply another part of the human condition that we all share. It is not the fact that I have faults and failings that matters—it is how I choose to accept and deal with them that defines my sense of manhood.

# AUGUST 16

When I arrived in recovery I felt I was different than most everyone else in the group. My experience, my story, seemed worse and more extreme than many others. It was almost a point of twisted pride that was blunt in its efforts to show that I was somehow sicker than most—for how else could I possibly justify the guilt and shame that I felt about what had gone on in my life? In some ways the vagaries and cruelties of life in general that combined with my own list of self-inflicted consequences in addiction were somehow justified and explained in a circular logic model that kept me trapped in the past. Over time I have learned to better understand the reality behind the advice to listen for the similarities not the differences with other people in recovery. While I was seeking to be judged on my exploits and the extremes of my experiences in addiction I was also partly debating, procrastinating, and avoiding the simple solution that ultimately we all face if we want to recover. The common malady we all share in recovery is our powerlessness and the need for a spiritual solution. A Higher Power to rely upon that will provide an answer to our problem—the problem of ourselves. The singularity of my problem being myself drives a repeated desire to be my own solution. Ironically though, it is only through the group that I can find and remain on the path to my individual relationship with a Higher Power. I struggled for a long time to accept something so simple and basic. I wanted to explain how my situation was different. Claiming, "You don't understand" or "Yea but ..." as I fought the requirement of giving over my own misguided death grip of control and selfishness in my life. Slowly I joined with the others in the group and followed their path. Increasingly I realized and understood our commonality in the solution. Our stories in addiction and paths in recovery all have many differences but they all find resolution and relief through an active reliance upon a Higher Power. I am repeatedly reminded that it is only with the help of the group of others who are similarly afflicted with addiction that I am able to maintain the perspective and support that keeps me properly connected to my Higher Power.

# AUGUST 17

Nothing brings me into closer contact and conflict with my desire to control and shape the world into my own design than dealing with the inevitable changes that life brings. Life happens, and the changes that occur often highlight my own powerlessness as well as the futility of my attempts to prevent and hide from, or deny and ignore, what is going on. Of course addiction was the ultimate form of denial with which to resist change as I tried to hang on to a way of life that was killing me. Despite all the evidence to the contrary I would blindly smile while claiming everything was all ok. Even though in those rare moments of insight and introspection I saw there was clearly no end game. No successful outcome. I still fought and held out against the change that recovery brings. As with all things that I practice—in time I become better at them. And so it has been with my experience of the practice of personal growth in recovery. Recovery, at its most basic level calls out to me and opens the door to change in my core beliefs and understandings about life in general and my place in the world specifically. It challenges me to let go of old ideas and understandings while constantly remaining open minded to what the future brings. Accepting change and learning to view problems as opportunities while depersonalizing difficulties as simple facts of human life—rather than viewing them as unfair and unjust events directed at me—has had a profound effect on my ability to live contentedly. Many times I have found myself back at the simplicity of the Serenity prayer as a reminder of my goal of not fighting the inevitable, or railing at it while remaining stuck in the past, and instead choosing to face life as I move forward in ways that enable my own personal growth. It is my own ego and desire to control life that provides the basis for my reluctance to embrace change. It is the fear of losing out or perhaps those faint feelings of punishment or impending doom that hold me back. Each day as I let my Higher Power guide me through the changes of my life, I progress further and am able to create more history that reminds me how the path forward has always turned out better than I expected.

# AUGUST 18

Recovery has taught me a lot about how to go with the flow in life. The fact remains though that there are many times today when I want the flow to stop! It can seem daunting and wearisome to have to deal with the unknown of the future and the loss of the present as the inevitable cycle of life goes on and some things fade from my life into my past. Of course there is no stopping time and I am frequently reminded and confronted with the fact that I often have little control over so much of what occurs in my life. My old thinking wants to cling to ideas and circumstances that are long past their due date. Often times when something expires I try to replace it exactly as it was—or my thinking becomes a shrine to my loss. It is easy for me to glorify the past and turn its memory into something that is distorted and elaborately overblown. Living in recovery allows me to better understand a goal of surfing the waves of life gracefully. Sometimes things will go well and other times not so well, but never does the exact same wave repeat itself. The art of looking forward to what life will bring next, rather than clinging to what has gone past, is perhaps at the heart of the notion of doing life one day at a time. Certainly my life is now fuller and brighter. The dreams I have today are much different than those I ever would have imagined a few years ago. When I fight with the flow of life I am placing myself in the position of being in charge and perhaps blocking my Higher Power's will. My job to do my part, to exert myself as a human into the flow of life, but then I must turn the results over to God and find acceptance at the outcomes. Facing the unfolding of life gracefully shows me that I am growing and remain a connected part of the spiritual world around me.

# AUGUST 19

The path of recovery has largely been one of self-discovery for me. I have learned so much about who I am, how I became that way, and how my past experiences direct my actions and thinking today in ways that I am often unaware of. As a co-dependent addict and adult child of an alcoholic, recovery offers me plenty of opportunity to learn. One of the more difficult and challenging aspects of recovery has been the slow and painstaking process of breaking down the beliefs and ideas about who I am and how I act that are rooted in my childhood and early addictive behaviors. The inherent chaos of addiction that became a part of my life at an early age prevented the discovery and development of my own personal integrity. The insanity of life in addiction was framed by a constant wariness and fear that was pervasive and unrelenting. I was always concerned with the keeping of secrets and attempts to minimize other people's ability to see what was really going on in my life. I desperately wanted to avoid the consequences that were always lurking nearby—held at bay by the slimmest of margins. Who I am today is no longer based on what I think those around me want it to be. It has taken the willingness to not only do the step work but to also participate fully. To open up and learn new skills within safe and trusting relationships with other men who are on the same journey. The process has slowly enabled new levels of understanding and insight into who I was, who I am, and who it is that I am becoming. Change is the measure of my personal growth. Today I am able to accept that my honest best, while always imperfect, will continue to improve as I continue to grow and learn. I don't have to be perfect—I just have to be honest with others in order to discover my own hidden truths.

# AUGUST 20

When I arrived in recovery my problems had accumulated into a huge mess that spanned all areas of my life. Socially, my only "friends" were addicts and alcoholics at the bottom of their disease. I had many legal problems that were piling on top of one another. I had no relationships that were working—with my family or anyone else. I was morally bankrupt and spiritually lost. My physical health was very poor. The inability to face my problems had created a huge mess. I instead was denying and ignoring them until they became crushingly unavoidable. I floundered in a confused state while blaming others and God for my situation. In recovery I slowly learned how to face these problems and find solutions to them. It took many years of slow progress to realize and fully accept the powerful fact that my Higher Power would always take care of me—if I trusted in the process and remained faithful to his will. I remember early on there were specific examples that clearly showed me things could be different when I fully surrendered to the process and had faith in God's plan for me. In time I've seen how resisting the urge to react based on my fears allows me to find solutions that are far more profound and compelling than I expected or could ever have imagined on my own. As the saying in recovery urges, I must learn to "let go and let God." Learning how to do this in my daily life continues to be a process of discovery as I grapple with the questions and situations. At first those questions centered on the rebuilding of my life and repairing relationships with people and society. As time has progressed deeper questions have come into play about how I choose to live my life and how I shape my spiritual beliefs. I have repeatedly been shown the simple fact that growth only comes when I let go of my old solutions and patiently work toward allowing new ones to form. Often I must leave behind the familiar and comfortable truths that are no longer working. The faith and willingness to step into the void of the unknown underpins this process of discovery and personal growth that I share with all humans as we work our way through life.

# AUGUST 21

Finding the willingness to get out of my own way and allow my Higher Power to work in my life is easier said than done. It requires that I learn how to become patient and understanding about the way life unfolds in its own time and through its own process. Often I am not able to sustain that mindset very well and want to force my own solution into the circumstances of life that are taking place all around me rather than wait for my Higher Power to provide a solution or unveil an outcome. In addiction so much of my life was focused on how I could control circumstances to meet my own needs through the exertion of my will. I would scam and scheme, lie, cheat and steal in order to meet my needs. I had no interest in being passive or waiting for things to take care of themselves and instead wanted to demonstrate how I could make things happens through my own action and plans. One of the sayings we hear often in recovery is that "time takes time" and that has certainly been true for me. At first in recovery I wanted so much to quickly "get my life back" without really understanding that what was in fact happening was that I was getting a new life. It has been my experience that I tend to overestimate how much change I think should occur in the short term while underestimating how much will change in the long term. As I look back I can see many examples of how my own solutions that I was trying to enact paled in comparison to the solutions my Higher Power provided. I've become better at being patient because I have experienced the best results that way—results that are usually better than anything I could have planned or thought of myself. I can remind myself today that often one of my choices is to take no action, to defer a decision or want, and simply wait and see if another option may present itself. This more mature approach has taken time to develop and today I realize that usually when I am trying to force a solution it is because it is not the right one. Slowly I am becoming wiser in recovery as I learn to rely more deeply on my Higher Power.

# AUGUST 22

One of the great challenges of recovery is the idea that we should "practice these principles in all our affairs." At first, enjoying sobriety was enough and I was able to hide behind the convenient adage of "progress not perfection." But soon, when I was rigorously honest with myself, it was clearly obvious that in many ways my own will was not aligned properly with that of my Higher Power. My addictive nature can evidence itself in many ways—such as gambling, smoking, and sex. My commitment to recovery and a reliance upon a Higher Power means that I cannot ignore and justify my addictive or immoral actions using the familiar tools of denial and rationalization. Over time I have become better at extending the core and basic ideas of recovery to ALL other areas of my life. It is well documented over the ages that there is a close and important relationship between one's physical, mental, social, and spiritual health. Working the steps is an all-inclusive process—it doesn't work if I only do some and not others. And so it is with my life in recovery. I have found that I must try to address all aspects of how I live and act—lest my reliance upon God falter. It is not ok for me to have one hand on the steering wheel of life trying to share God's job and deciding that some of my faults and character defects are the ones that are ok to live with. It is my job to continue to ask for his help to carry out his will—not justify my own will and live in a partial charade. In many ways it was this insight about how I choose to live that drove a strong need to integrate the principles of recovery into my life in ways that are meaningful and complete. I realized the profound difference that exists between the absence of active addiction and the presence of true spiritual recovery. It was at first easy for me to confuse the two given the remarkable transformation that occurred when I at last managed to sustain my sobriety. I was truly changed indeed. However, it soon became clear that sobriety and recovery is not the same thing. Sobriety was merely the very beginning of the journey that allowed me to discover and work on the underlying causes and conditions, the deep rooted flaws and misunderstandings that had been formed within me, that I must continue to improve and develop in recovery.

# AUGUST 23

In addiction I was in denial about my faults, my weaknesses, and my powerlessness over many aspects of life and my own addiction in particular. I was delusional about the reality of my situation and was unable to accept the futility of my attempts to continue to find a way to succeed while still doing the same things that were causing me to fail. In early recovery I was able to begin to deal with the grosser handicaps of my active addiction but it has taken longer to learn how to see and accept my many other weaknesses and flaws. The actuality of my imperfections and the situational reality of many of them, such as age, past actions, or my criminal record, cannot be denied. However, my more subtle defects of character require hard work to discover and accept. As is the case with much of my life in recovery— knowledge of the problem is just the beginning. The real challenge is answering the question that follows their discovery. What am I willing to do about these problems? It has only been when I truly accept and work to mitigate my imperfections that I begin to make real progress and change in ways that help build my character. I can become stronger and more complete when I recognize and accept my shortcomings and limitations. I will never be a professional basketball player. I will never be tall, dark and handsome. It is through accepting these facts as simple truths rather than allowing my addictive personality to form them into personal failings that I transcend them. All of us as humans have strengths and weaknesses, capabilities and limitations, and by accepting my own I am able to move closer to taking my place in life as "a part of" rather than re-justifying the isolation and separateness that is the hallmark of my addictive thinking.

# AUGUST 24

It is hard work trying to get the world to do what I want. For years I was often frustrated and angry as I struggled in the vain attempt to get life to conform to my own rigid ideas and beliefs. More often than not I was unwilling to accept that the ideas of others could also be correct or valid—in fact in most cases I wasn't really even listening as they shared them with me. My own ideas, plans, and ego were too loud in my own mind to allow me to truly listen and properly consider the opinions of others. In work life, as my business grew I had to learn to be more flexible allowing others to do things their own way and slowly I learned how to delegate authority. However, in active addiction, my focus became more rigid than ever as the fears of not getting what I needed, or suffering the consequences of my actions, drove me further toward a place of inflexible desire on one hand and an easy ability to compromise my values and morals on the other. My inability to change my addictive behavior left me fragile and weak as I repeated the same behavior again and again in ways that always brought horrible and painful results—yet I clung to those false ideas blinded by denial, isolation, and delusion. The inability to be flexible and hear the messages of others who were trying to help me, prolonged and deepened my cycle of addiction until my life became so smashed and broken that I could no longer piece it together at all. Recovery has asked me to go far further in relinquishing my addictive desire to control by clearly defining what is my business, what is God's business, and what is "none of my business." Most of life is none of my business in the sense that I mustn't try to control it, judge it, or force my opinion into the lives of others. Because ultimately I am only able to control my own response to life it has required me to become more open to change and acceptance. I am learning to more easily let go of ideas and beliefs that don't work anymore and be open to new solutions and approaches that can better accommodate the uncontrollable realities of life. Doing so better allows me to live life on life's terms rather than pursuing a futile attempt to make life always conform to my own plan.

# AUGUST 25

Fear of failure and of not being good enough was a big barrier to my ability to achieve recovery. The subtle companion point to this truth was that I often took the position that if I wasn't able to do something perfectly I wouldn't try at all. Of course I would have denied this with all the bravado and bluster my addicted mind could muster. As a result, my ability to grow and develop as a human was stymied. In recovery the same traits arrived with me and at first I wasn't willing to fully commit. I was more comfortable in the role of the suffering addict who couldn't succeed—fearful of really trying lest I fail. To recover I had to risk failure and fully assert my desire to be sober. Over time I've become more able to accept my natural human imperfections and failings because I am also working to grow and overcome them. The pursuit of spiritual growth has not always been smooth and easy. While there have been many embarrassing moments and hard facts to be faced about my shortcomings and weaknesses it has also meant the discovery of new skills, virtues, and capabilities. When I returned to college the first few quarters were very hard and I almost quit more than once. Today it is much easier for me to claim my place in the world and understand the process of growth that always includes failures and successes. When I look back I see that one of the most interesting parts of my growth has been how I have dealt with obstacles and blockages. Remembering how recovery has worked for me in the past helps me figure out how to overcome the challenges that I will continue to face in the future.

# AUGUST 26

It seems that the challenge of recovery from a disease that tells me I don't have one must be centered in honesty. Paradoxically, that honesty perhaps must originate from outside of one's self. For me, self-honesty is where my recovery truly began. In time, this has come to make a lot of sense for me although at first it was more of a *Plato's Cave* or *Matrix*-like experience in that I wasn't able to fully comprehend that the life I thought I was living wasn't what I thought it was. Despite the ample supply of clear evidence that things weren't going well, it was very difficult for me to comprehend the totality of my misunderstanding. The completeness of the lie I told myself about my life was very hard to pierce but by slowly and thoroughly working with other men I was able to open the door to progress in this area. I knew that I was a very good liar to others, but it took time for me to realize that I was the person I lied to the most. In early recovery my work began by overcoming those lies centered on ideas like "this time it will be different" or "no one will know." The initial breakthrough came when I finally quit fighting the idea of having an honest relationship with a Higher

Power. I can always successfully lie to myself, and usually to others, but if I am truly honest I can never lie to my Higher Power. Over time my recovery has evolved into a deeper understanding of my morals, values, standards, and ability to better see the truth of the motives that underpin my actions in life. Not only must I have the fortitude to be honest with myself—I must also share that experience with someone who knows me so that I am not alone in the process of understanding and interpreting growth within my recovery. It remains all too easy for me to twist the honest truth in a way that can lead me in a direction that I, and more importantly my Higher Power, don't want me to go. Getting past the implicit lies of active addiction and forging new and honest relationships with other people became a foundation for discovering the truth within me about who I really am. Learning how to be honest with myself began with a simplification of my life and an approach to daily living that relies on willingness and open-mindedness. It has become the centerline of a path of self-discovery that aligns my own will with that of my Higher Power.

# AUGUST 27

The myth of the extraordinary surrounds me constantly in advertising and marketing. I see it in the words and beliefs of others and in my own thinking about the kind of man I am supposed to be. I valued a pursuit of the extraordinary, of excess and uniqueness, and disliked the idea of being a "normie." This skewed outlook of entitlement and superiority was something that developed early as I was exposed to the culture of alcohol and partying. Being able to drink more, get higher, connect with the best deals, and generally work life to my advantage was always framed in a competitive way with others. I could do it all and still get up and go to work. At least that was the story I told myself. This pursuit of the extreme almost killed me and the process led me to believe all sorts of things about myself that simply weren't true. The simple fact is that as my addiction wore me down it became ever more obvious that I couldn't even muster "ordinary" in my ability to conduct myself in life. As my disease progressed my ability to recognize how sick I was also diminished and as life was falling apart around me I struggled to be honest with myself about what was going on. Recovery has helped me understand that the measure of my success in life is found within. The only thing I am really competing with is my delusions about who I really am and what my purpose is. Today, my life isn't framed in extremes. I can recognize and avoid the distorted heroic self-image or its counterpart, the "I am worthless" dialog, as simply a throwback to my addictive thinking. I can instead accept the simplicity of being an honest man who has taken the time to seriously examine his values, morals, and how I live my life today.

# AUGUST 28

Anytime I need a reminder of how my character defects constantly affect me, all I need to do is think about the last time I was speaking with another person who is more knowledgeable than I about a particular skill, trade, craft, or subject. My fears around self-esteem and not being good enough will often kick in to some degree and prevent me from asking questions that would show I know less than I would like to seem to about the subject. In time I've become better at asking questions to learn more, and not waste a chance to improve myself, however, I can often quite easily prefer to leave myself in ignorance rather than face the fear of appearing weak or lesser. It is ironic that while my intent is to appear as though I am competent and knowledgeable, the outcome ensures that I miss the chance to advance in either area. By following an old fashioned narrative about what it is to be a man, a narrative that I learned as a child, I miss the chance to learn what it truly is to be man. In these examples it is easy to see my self-inflicted problem but in others it is far harder to come to grips with the honesty and self-appraisal needed to truly learn the hard lessons required for spiritual growth. Instead I am more likely to simply overvalue what I think I know to be true and undervalue what I don't—or somehow magically decide that it doesn't have value for me (usually with no basis in fact or experience). As the old saying indicates, contempt prior to investigation is a sure way to remain ignorant. Overcoming the ways in which my broken ideas about masculinity keep me weak rather than growing stronger, requires that I be aware and on point—driven by honesty and humility about my lack of knowledge. For me this was a process of practice that began in small ways. I have slowly learned to overcome the discomfort of feeling weak and unknowing by learning to love the openness and excitement of understanding new things. I must maintain a willingness to yield to the idea that I can always learn more and gain a fuller insight about things I think I already understand.

# AUGUST 29

It has taken me decades to learn and accept that my role as a man is centered on being "a part of" rather than "apart from." So much of my thinking in life was self-centered and based on ideas and beliefs that created an excessive emphasis on self-reliance and separated me from others. I held on tightly to a "Go it alone" attitude that was at best intolerant of others and usually quite scornful of the average man. My own opinion of myself was inflated without any clear evidence as to why and I felt I was better than those around me. Those people I knew who were clearly successful I was keen to get close with to try and mimic, learn from, and gain advantage through association. In active addiction all these traits became more exaggerated as I churned through people as though they were a raw material that I could get what I could from and then discard. As I burned bridges behind me I grew increasingly isolated, desperate, and lonely as I slowly moved to a place where I was completely alone and hopeless in life. The more I closed myself off to others the more doomed I became and the smaller my world grew. Recovery has shown me the critical element that was always missing—the understanding and acceptance of the fact that human life is a "we" activity. Despite the songs and stories that glorify the heroic tradition of being a self-made independent man, recovery showed me that being a man means being a part of the lives of others in meaningful ways that connect with compassion, caring and shared experience. The unavoidable reality of our individual human loneliness in life is what makes it so vital that I learn how to truly connect with others. Just as in a team sport where a group works together, recovery inserts me back into life which is perhaps the ultimate team sport. Today I am a part of the lives of many other men. These relationships help me be much more content in the value of my own life. I am able to accept and understand the commonality of all of our problems, victories, sufferings and joys and include myself into the world as a person who is fully participative and engaged. The brutal and unforgiving loneliness of addiction has been replaced by a shared sense of community and purpose with others.

# AUGUST 30

It is so easy for me to get wound up about things that are ultimately out of my control. Fear can quickly take over my thinking as I create endless variations of stories about how my past will haunt me and how my future will not work out. I can "awfulize" about situations until I forget that they haven't even happened yet and lose sight of the fact that there is usually a wide range of potential outcomes that are possible—and that I am not in control of most of them. In doing so I tend to disconnect from the solutions in my life that I know are working for me while losing sight of the important lessons from the past that can guide me today. In early recovery I could spin-out for days at a time becoming frustrated and discontent until someone, usually my sponsor, helped me regain perspective. Today this loss of perspective is much less frequent or strong but still occurs fairly regularly.

It is always a reminder for me to refocus my connection to my Higher Power's will for me and my role in attempting to follow it. In recovery I learned that most of my problems were of my own making and what often drives my malcontent is "stinking thinking." This is what I must examine and ask for God's help with. Learning to trust in the process of having faith helps me let go of the worry and anxiety that is always a part of my efforts to control life. From the very beginning, the experience of recovery has shown me the path to follow. It is a path that affords opportunities for spiritual and personal growth that improves my ability to handle the problems I create for myself as well as the inevitable ones that life brings me. Ultimately the solution to my problems is always an inside job and when I'm looking elsewhere I find little relief and instead gain frustration, irritation, and unhappiness.

# AUGUST 31

The freedom I have found in recovery is breathtaking, exciting, interesting, and daunting. It is rather like entering into a new relationship but with me instead of another person. I am often excited about the potential and yet also a bit fearful of failure. The ultimate freedom to choose who I am, who I am going to be today, and what kind of man those choices are based upon requires me to understand and appreciate the challenge as it truly exists. While I can review and mimic how others approach life, ultimately it is my life and no one else's. Recovery has shown me the importance of taking personal responsibility for my own choices, my decisions, and the way in which I conduct my thoughts and spirit. I alone must make many of the choices that determine the course of my life and with that opportunity also comes responsibility. I must learn how to take my own life seriously because ultimately if I don't, no one else can. Recovery provides the ability to really take on this task by giving me the support of a Higher Power and a framework of knowledge about myself that I can build from. I am no longer like a chameleon, changing my identity to suit my surroundings while my insides floundered not knowing who I really was. I no longer lay claim to a rigidly inflexible set of knowledge, beliefs, and understandings about my life and how it should be. I instead grasp the ever changing reality of living in a pattern of growth that embraces change— some that works out and some that doesn't. By actively participating in my own personal growth both spiritually and socially I am able to grow as a human along a path of self-discovery that is mine alone to unfold. The life cycle of nature is all around me and today, at last, I can be present and participatory in my part of it.

# September

"I ponder the rhythms of letting go and embracing whatever is around the corner, trusting that the empty spaces will be filled. And knowing that sometimes community can happen only in the gaps where mystery resides."
— Joyce Hollyday

"Making amends is not only saying the words but also being willing to listen to how your behavior caused another's pain, and then the really hard part...changing behavior."
— David W. Earle

"Forgiveness is the key to action and freedom."
— Hannah Arendt

# SEPTEMBER 1

The journey from the misbelief that life is something I can control, toward a more realistic realization that I am just another ant in the ant farm, largely unaware of and unable to control the larger mysteries of the world around me, is challenging and required a major shift in my thinking. I spent years in addiction trying to pretend I was somehow shaping life's outcomes with the exertion of my will and that as a result of my efforts I was receiving rewards and successes that I had somehow earned. As the AA big book notes, it is the re-arrangement and changes in my thinking and beliefs that form a fundamental part of a spiritual awakening that provides an ongoing connection to the source of the solution to my problems. In recovery I've slowly learned how to let go of the idea that I am in control of the world around me and instead simply see how the only area I can have any real effect is that of my own actions and thinking. The great truth of recovery that I have found lies in the reality of it being an "inside job." The world will always be too large and complicated for me to try and manage or control and I must let go of the delusion and vain glory of thinking I somehow can be in charge of it. My sponsor often reminds me that there are three types of business for me to understand. The first is my business, the things I need to take care of each day that relate to my own actions, thinking and choices. The second is God's business, which is pretty much all the other things that are going on around me and then there is the third kind of business—which is non-of-my-business. Learning to stay out of other people business through maintaining healthy boundaries connects into my ability to sustain true faith in my Higher Powers plan. I cannot force my will onto the world around me but I can align it with my Higher Power. The wonderful gifts of life are readily available to all and it's my job to figure out how to shape myself in a way to receive them rather than try to change how they are delivered. Each day, when I maintain my spiritual connection with my Higher Power, I am able to see how it is only through my own growth and change that my experience with the world has improved.

# SEPTEMBER 2

The more I sit and excessively ponder my problems the larger they become. The more I sit and think about how my life is yielding little that pleases me the more unhappy I become. My experience in active addiction involved a daily "checking-out" from any sort of meaningful activity that was helpful or healthy in terms of my mental, spiritual or physical well-being. In some cases there was a social aspect to my excesses, but over time as my addiction deepened I soon lost touch with that part. I became comfortable with spending time only with others who were equally as addicted to the oblivion of substance abuse. The final stages of my addiction left me completely alone in a way that was incomprehensibly hopeless. In recovery I was shown how to take daily action in order to improve my situation. It created a vital shift from thinking and talking about how the past had been unfair to me—or what the future would be like someday—into a place of taking meaningful action. Each day I began to create the very first small and hesitant changes that opened the door to a new life. I have learned that ultimately life is a self-service experience and I must take meaningful action in order to meet life rather than waiting for it to come to me and then complaining that it wasn't what I ordered. There are many ways that I can take action, both positive and negative, and so the choice for me is always framed in the larger viewpoint of meaning and purpose. A simple walk around the neighborhood doesn't need to be tied to a goal or result. The action itself is meaningful. There are many examples of ways I can take meaningful action that are of benefit to me as I try to bring myself into a balanced well-rounded life—and isolating and obsessing aren't on the list. I have come to see how it is my actions today that are my life and the reality of keeping mind, body and spirit healthy and in balance is vital. There is no point in regularly changing the oil in my car while ignoring the squealing brakes. My mental, social, spiritual and physical natures cannot survive individually. They all need each other. Recovery has shown me how to recognize this simple truth and that by taking the meaningful action that is available to me in the now of each day I can experience more fully the entire gift of life.

# SEPTEMBER 3

It is easy for me to become overly focused on any particular problem or event in my life and give it more meaning and power than is appropriate. In recovery, the first step directs me toward a goal of being honest with myself about how I am living my life. For me this has meant learning to recognize when I am simply being unrealistic or caught in a cycle of self-pity and denial. In my lifetime there have been many chances and opportunities and that will continue to be true in the future. By staying on the path of recovery I have experienced how one single event that is taking place today will never preclude others from occurring in the future. The door that closes for me today merely means it is time for me to move towards the door that is opening for me tomorrow. It is not the end of my world. A few years ago when I had a bad test result or frustratingly difficult class or quarter at college I was occasionally ready to throw in the towel and claim I could never do it. Of course those feelings didn't last and luckily I didn't take action upon them. Today I realize that imperfection, failure, and struggle are just a part of living life fully. It would be naive to think everything will always work out just the way I want or to somehow measure or predict a lifetime on the basis of a day, week, or month. Of course my alcoholic mind loves to take that sort of insane thinking to heart. My ability to "awfulize" is unparalleled at times! Participating in spiritual and personal growth has meant learning how to accept today's reality without being sure of tomorrow's outcomes. I can't control the good things in life and mustn't fall prey to the easy trap of exerting my desire to control by taking actions that ensure a bad outcome in the future. The script of my life is never written by the outcome of a single event or two but rather holds the opportunity of a continued series of lifelong choices and chances.

# SEPTEMBER 4

It is fair to say that I have never known loneliness that was as profoundly deep and spirit shattering as when I was in active addiction. Years of wanting to avoid being alone with myself left me unable to enjoy any sense of solitude. Learning how to be truly and fully comfortable with being alone with myself took many years of work. In early recovery my mind was often too busy "chewing" on things for me to be able to relax and be calm. Even as a youngster I wasn't keen on time alone as it forced me to confront my own self which was often confusing and difficult. I much preferred the escape of books or movies, and later in life the escape of alcohol and drugs. Today I am able to not only regularly experience quiet time alone but have come to value it because of the results it brings me. The process of the steps and of being involved in recovery for a few years has allowed me to "clean house" so that when I sit quietly with myself I can enjoy the time. Like many things in life, the art of meditation is something I didn't value very much when I wasn't able to do it. My understanding of what it was and how it worked was limited. However there is no denying that often in times of great struggle, if I didn't just go get loaded, I would go for a walk or find a quiet place to think. Today I have the gift of being able to use that resource every day because my thinking and life is no longer completely insane. Meditation and quiet time provides me another form of daily exercise that boosts my spiritual and mental health. Just as my physical health only responds to active exercise so it is with meditation and the regular effort to stay healthy in my mind and spirit.

# SEPTEMBER 5

The beliefs I have in my own ability to be independent and not need other people, my stubborn ideas of self-sufficiency and individual pride, are hard to overcome. In early recovery it was fairly easy to admit, and painfully obvious, that I wasn't able to get sober alone. However, at times it is harder for me to stay connected to the reality that this fact brings me to. Acceptance of the fact that a Higher Power is what saved me is one thing but the implications of its deeper meaning are another. The fact that I am loved, that I am valuable, that I am worthy, are truths about my Higher Power's love for me that were harder to accept. At times I can find myself drifting away from simple but profoundly important truths. My old ideas are rooted in a battle of me overcoming the world's unfairness—a battle that was always doomed to failure and created a world of persistent dread. Recovery demanded that I "let go and let God" which left me in an unfamiliar place and doubting my own worth. Spiritual growth has shown me that God is in charge and there is no battle with the world around me to be fought. I am already good enough. The only battle that remains is within me and is based around feelings of fear, self-esteem, acceptance, and faith. Today my self-reliance is as strong as ever but stands with direction and purpose, clearly and squarely on the bedrock of faith and trust in my Higher Powers love for me and my willingness to be part of his plan. This foundational aspect of my new outlook on life connects me more than ever to the important role of other people in my life. It is only through sharing my life with others that I can affirm and experience the reality of God's love that is extended to me through other people.

# SEPTEMBER 6

Recovery is a spiritual process that I was skeptical about at first. The whole idea seemed so tenuous and abstract to me when I arrived in recovery. For a long time I resisted the idea of a true connection and reliance on a Higher Power. I instead tried to understand what it would be like before choosing to blindly rely up on my Higher Power. I wanted assurances and proof. As with many things in life it was something that I couldn't understand until I actually did it. In many ways this theme of stepping into the unknown—of having enough faith to trust my Higher Power and a willingness to commit to that relationship—is what stands before me as the moment of choice that will free me from a place that I am struggling with and open the door to a new place that I can't see clearly. A place that isn't fully understood and whose outcomes that aren't clearly defined. Time and again I have had to simply place my trust in a Higher Power and commit to the change that is in front of me because I implicitly understand that I can't remain where I am at. The great chasm between the desire to control my destiny and the freedom of letting go so that God takes charge of my path is something I must leap into again and again as my spiritual growth and connection to a Higher Power develops. My understanding of the supremacy of a reliance on my Higher Power is still growing and changing as I become better at participating in the relationship. Each time I listen closely to the messages, the mild discomforts and persistent disquiet that mark the need to change, I become more attuned to my spiritual connection. Today I am clearly able to see how this process has changed my attitude and outlook toward my own life and the world around me. I am increasingly able to have insights about myself that were previously infuriatingly and despairingly absent. Today the spiritual awakening occurring inside me, this intuition of self, is a quiet guide and friend that is always present and available to me. It allows me to direct my actions in meaningful ways that continue my self-discovery and spiritual growth.

# SEPTEMBER 7

I have often heard it said that in order to have a friend one must be a friend. From my teenage years onward, friendships were often based more upon a person's ability to help me get what I wanted from life than my ability or desire to be a good friend to them. They were typically a reciprocal arrangement that in the chaos of addiction was almost always limited in scope and depth. The focus for me was increasingly on partying, sex, consumption and less about shared interests, discussions about beliefs or ideas about life and finding our place in it. Those early days of casually drinking until dawn and enjoying wide ranging and interesting conversations during pleasant social times faded quickly. They soon transitioned into a fast-track world of inebriation, excess, staggering consequences, isolation and mental oblivion. In recovery I've learned how to have proper friendships that are natural and honest. Friendship, as with so many aspects of life such as love, trust and faith, is something I must first learn how to have with myself before I can have it with others. Just as it is futile to try and install a broken part into a machine and expect it to work I had to become healthy with myself before I could become able to have healthy friendships with others. The transition away from the crushing loneliness of being alone in addiction towards a more rewarding ability in recovery of being able to spend comfortable time in solitude opened the door to meaningful friendships with others. Today I can approach friendship without unrealistic needs or expectations and can accept the imperfections and failings of others along with their strengths and positive attributes. This flexible and more realistic approach has replaced the demanding and judging expectation of others that created a fatally skewed perspective of what friendship was and instead relies on the understanding of my own personal integrity and validity. When I am not a friend to myself then no friend is ever good enough but when I learn to be my own friend the whole world can also be a friend.

# SEPTEMBER 8

Learning how to build the truly deep friendships that are a vital part of recovery has taken time and a sustained effort to overcome my addictive tendencies towards fear and isolation. As I became willing to open up to others one of the hardest challenges was that I was suddenly faced with the realization that I didn't know how to do it! I didn't truly know my own feelings or who I really was. What I've discovered is that this lack of mature understanding of my own emotions and feelings was the real roadblock. The notions and stories I told myself about how I was just the kind of guy who didn't share was merely an excuse to avoid myself. The real problem was that I'd never done the hard emotional work of examining who I was and how I really felt about myself, my past, and my life in general. Emotional maturity has been one of the great benefits of recovery and for me it goes hand in hand with spiritual growth. Over time I've become able to learn the skill of sharing my emotions. At first it was with one or two very close friends and over time that group has expanded—and so has my ability to control and manage what I share. At first it was just a huge mess of stuff with little control. Today I am able to understand the boundaries that go with the process and how to share deeply or generally as needed. For me, sharing my feelings and emotions with others remains the absolute requirement for a true entrance into the "we" part of recovery.

# SEPTEMBER 9

There is a part of me that wants to personalize almost everything about life. It is a selfish, needy, and egocentric part of me that distorts the normal flow of life by making it about me—my fears, my needs, and my sense of entitlement or shame. It is a form of emotional escape that is illogical and powerful. Even though I can see it happening it is often hard to avoid. While sometimes it takes the form of elation and superiority it is more often rooted in despair and dread. Recovery has helped me understand that the ups and downs of life are unavoidable and simply exist as part of living rather than as some personal "Life-Genie" that follows only me. All of us face obstacles and challenges in life and recovery shows me how to learn and grow from them rather than suffer them repeatedly. For years in addiction I made the same mistake in a dozen different ways and never saw how I was the problem—instead I blamed others, the world, and life. Today I know that there is always hope and that the opportunity of growth and progress is an ever present part of the hurdles of life. When I remember this, and avoid my selfish childish responses to life, it gives me the courage to face my difficulties remembering that I always come through the process stronger and wiser.

# SEPTEMBER 10

As the old saying goes—"two eyes are better than one." The gift of friendship allows me the chance to see life through the eyes of another. Recovery has helped me overcome the insecurities and lack of self-esteem that drove my need to always be right and the belief that my opinions were likely better than those of others. I have become more able to truly hear and see other people's viewpoints, beliefs, and opinions as being another valuable truth that I can learn from if I am open-minded enough to consider them. The fear-laced rhetoric of clinging to a known dogma or an old idea prevents the chance to grow and learn from the process of evaluating and challenging my current thinking with ideas that differ from mine. Most importantly, friendship and close relationships require me to be tolerant and accepting of the diversity of others—without judgment or a need to correct or refute them. I can value them as equally valid and truthful knowing that we all see the world through a different focus and perspective. In this way I can multiply the array of insights and approaches that are available for me to bring into my life. Leaving behind the derision and skepticism of ideas that are not my own ensures that I am much more fully prepared to find the right solution to life's problems. When my only tool is a hammer all my problems become nails. In life I face a wide diversity of problems and opportunities. Friendships based on respect, equality, and openness with each other help me experience these events well.

# SEPTEMBER 11

Learning how to be happy with myself, as represented in the actuality of how I am today, has taken a lot of honesty and courage. For many years I was in denial about the reality of how things that I had done in my life really affected me. It was easier to take an attitude of "it's just a flesh wound" as I soldiered on in life gravely injured while pretending everything was ok. I refused to honestly face the truth of how unresolved guilt, shame, and resentment distorted and polluted my daily life. Avoiding looking within myself for answers to my problems left me with no choice but to create and habituate beliefs that my problems were the results of others. Living in this way resulted in a misguided charade that left me with a stark and confusing inability to be comfortable with myself. I was living with a constant tension and dread that was unrelenting. Working the steps and being a full participant in recovery, as well as other forms of help, has allowed me to redirect the search for answers to my problems. It has shown me that they are always initially found internally rather than externally. Slowly I've come to realize the powerful and freeing truth of the adage that "if I'm not the problem there is no solution." It allows me to face myself and as a result I can face life contentedly each day. The profound change in how I view myself has opened the door to my participation in the world around me as a man who is free from my past and fully qualified in my eligibility to be a part of not only my own life but also the lives of others. Learning how to love myself was an unavoidable part of being able to transcend the shame of my past and allowed me to truly begin to love others and the world around me. Just as one walkie-talkie won't connect to the other until both are turned on, I had to turn on an acceptance around a sense of love for who I am before I could truly connect and participate with the love of others. The sense of justice and closure that working the steps brings to my life is a powerful force that arrives each day for me when I acknowledge the fact that I respect who I am today.

# SEPTEMBER 12

It has taken years of work for me to really begin to understand just how severely my addictive and co-dependent character warped my ability to participate in any sort of truly healthy relationships with others. A good example of this was the regular occurrence of insane fighting, arguments, and the on again off again patterns of behavior that were the hallmark of all my relationships—even in early recovery. I was unable to express my anger or disagreement properly for many reasons; including a sense of guilt and shame around my own behaviors, an unwillingness to acknowledge my part in anything, and the inability to see and accept the truths that didn't fit with my illusory version of reality. Fear of being called out on my own problems left me resentfully unable to speak up about my dissatisfactions with others until they would slowly build up and then explode. Recovery has shown me the importance of expressing my feelings and given me the tools with which to do so. It has allowed me to be free of guilt and shame by learning how to find a sense of personal integrity and justice through working the steps. It has delivered an ability to keep my side of the street clean as I move forward in life. Recovery helps me overcome my fears and desire to control others so that I can have healthy boundaries and express my anger or dissatisfactions in a helpful way. By understanding my own values and expectations I can stand up for them. I no longer have to remain quiet and allow my resentments to build and fester. I am able to clear the air and move forward, which strengthens and clarifies my relationships with others. I continue to rely more deeply on my relationship with a Higher Power that helps me in soft and subtle ways to uncover new understandings of how my actions and beliefs connect to a deeper authenticity around questions of how my character defects show up in my daily life. My progress in recovery is delivered daily in a way that seems to accumulate slowly until suddenly new insights and realizations compel me to change again and dig deeper into myself as I lean forward into the often difficult process of spiritual growth.

# SEPTEMBER 13

The chaos and unmanageability of addiction was something I grew up with. Many of the intergenerational effects of addiction are simply a part of who I am. Recovery has meant finding a willingness to explore what that means in ways that are deeper than simply trying to stay sober. In the process of self-discovery and personal growth I have often been keen to ignore or sidestep some of the most basic and fundamental questions around how the reality of who I am—and how I was raised—drove my addiction and continues to impact my life today. In many cases I have learned that at times my actions in life are shaped, almost predetermined in a sense, by my childhood. In my years of active addiction I often had little insight or understanding into the root causes that drove so much of what was going on with me. For years I was likely to brush aside questions about how I was raised and how it affected me with posturing and an off-handed nonchalance as I tried to convince myself that I was past all that, that I had worked it out—that I was all good. I was not all good. The chaos and unmanageability of my life offered a powerful demonstration of that truth and ultimately it brought me to recovery. The powerful fact is that recovery and the work of the steps has shown the falsity of that claim and allowed me to find the courage and skills to face my past so that I can do the hard work of reconciling the facts of my upbringing with the values and morals of who I am trying to be today. In order for my ship to successfully sail on the sea of life I can't ignore the many needed repairs or simply pretend and hope that everything will somehow simply be ok. Living in recovery has shown me how to build relationships with other men who offer a similar role to that of being a father figure. They have the valuable knowledge and insight of how recovery has worked for them and others. It is through these relationships that I was able to begin the process of facing my past and becoming open to learning the many new skills and lessons that were for so long missing in my life. I have often heard people talk about how they "grew up" in recovery and that has been the case for me.

# SEPTEMBER 14

My constant desire for control and the accompanying unwillingness to allow my Higher Power to be in charge has been one of the most difficult areas of change in my life. My need to control is so subtle and deeply ingrained that I never stop discovering the various ways it affects me. One of the greatest examples of how I continue to struggle with allowing God to be in charge centers in the powerful feeling of control provided by my negative thinking. I don't have the personal power to always make good things happen in my life but I can absolutely make my life miserable. As I look back at my years in active addiction I can find many examples of how I managed to create chaos and drama in my life by routinely participating in cycles of behavior that I knew would ultimately have a bad outcome. Be it relationships or substance abuse, I made poor choices and decisions that again and again returned me into situations that I knew would end badly. Fear of the unknown and my inability to control positive outcomes was something I could never really seem to have the faith and courage to stand strong in the face of. My own "will power" was never enough to break the pattern. It wasn't until I truly began to have faith that I was able to at last begin to make the small steps of progress that resulted from actually trusting in my Higher Power instead of seizing control myself. When I am negative and hurtful to myself and others I am exerting a form of willful control that is clearly at odds with the wishes of my Higher Power. It has taken many years of work to truly grasp the powerful reality of shifting my way of living from fear to faith. Having true faith in the future that God will provide moves me away from fear based efforts to exert negative control in my life. Today I am better able to stop myself when the "stinking-thinking" of negativity starts playing in my mind. I have the experiences of recovery that offer recent examples of how I truly am eligible and fully qualified to enjoy positive things in my life. Time after time my Higher Power has provided me outcomes that are far more beneficial than anything I would have realistically planned for by myself. When I let go and let God I open the door to new blessings in my life by simply getting out of my own way.

# SEPTEMBER 15

I think the measure of my spiritual growth is always found in the reality of my relationships and experiences with others. While the relationship with a God of my own understanding is a very personal and introspective event— one that has profoundly changed my relationship to the world around me— the results are largely found in how I participate in life with others. This is the only way I can test how well my beliefs and ideas align with my actions and deeds. I can consider the age old cliché of being a drunken abusive husband on Friday night who is piously attending church on Sunday. It is an obvious example that highlights the often more subtle and difficult reality of honestly and vigorously approaching life in a way that provides a meaningful and truthful validation of my morals and values. In addiction so much of how I lived was framed in a confused experience rooted in denial and delusion. I almost always sought to base my understanding of self on intentions rather than actions which created an untenable and broken mental state from which I could find no respite. I was trapped in the uncomfortable place of living a lie that I could never completely hide from my consciousness. Recovery, through the group of people around me who are also on the same path, has slowly shown and taught me how to live my life with others in a manner that continues to increase my ability to be truthfully God conscious in my daily actions. It is the practical life experience, beyond mere theory, that creates spiritual growth for me and those around me as we all experience the love of a Higher Power in our actions together. Addiction isolated me from the team sport that is life. Recovery provides the training and practice with others that has allowed my own life skills and reliance on a Higher Power to slowly be regained and then improved. This reconfiguration of my beliefs and values within the context of a spiritual awakening offers a cheery and comfortable place within me that it always available when I seek it. It exists because of the relationships with others that link me to God's world and provide a keen sense of peace about my own place within it.

# SEPTEMBER 16

One of the greatest freedoms I have received in recovery is the ability to stay focused on my own path in life and avoid getting distracted, caught up in, or overly concerned with the actions and activities of others. Learning how to be concerned with managing my own business and staying out of the business of others has been a huge gift that has set me free from the trap of trying to control or direct other people's lives—and all of the resentment, disappointment, anger and general mess that results from trying. The vitally important question is how I choose to live my life. In the past the desire to involve myself in how others lived their lives was a convenient and falsely righteous distraction from my own poor choices and failures. When I am thorough in my own actions I am better able to go with the flow of life around me. I can avoid getting caught up in things that create unhealthy yet enticing and familiar feelings like superiority, righteousness, outrage, judgment and rhetoric. Life will always provide an endless supply of fuel for that fire. Recovery has shown me how to focus on my side of the street in life. I can accept what is going on around me while trying to be helpful and yet remaining largely un-invested in the outcomes and life choices of others. It is never my job to try and live the lives of others for them.

# SEPTEMBER 17

Learning how to value myself properly has allowed me to gain a lot of insight into how deeply ingrained my addictive personality is. It exposes the subtle yet harmful ways that can cause deeply rooted suffering and struggle in my life. For so many years my life was framed by struggle. A fight to overcome the odds, or more accurately, getting out of the holes I would dig myself into through poor choices and actions. In recovery the subject of self-care becomes central. At first it was the simple ideas of eating well or avoiding unhealthy people and pursuits. Over time, the importance and practicality of self-care has grown to include financial and emotional stability. I have had to learn the importance of taking myself seriously and no longer ignoring the maintenance of my own needs. Physically, spiritually, socially, and mentally I must remind myself that I am worth the effort. My Higher Power wants me to healthy in all these areas and if I want to be taken seriously by others in life I must first demonstrate that I am serious about taking care of myself. Ultimately, recovery asks that I demonstrate through example how faith in my Higher Power has changed my life. Not partially. Not only on Sundays. Not in just one area but in all aspects of my life. Sometimes it is only through example that I can truly be of help to others.

# SEPTEMBER 18

In recovery I have been able to find a new resource in the faithful relationship with my Higher Power. It continues to build and grow. And while I'm still waiting for my halo to arrive (glowing brightly above my head) there is no denying the change that has occurred in how I am able to deal with life. This change in my approach to life is often most profoundly demonstrated when I am in the midst of troubled and difficult times. During my years in addiction I regularly felt the steady pall of despair that seemed to follow me around like a dark cloud of dread—a horrible uneasiness and discomfort that was always present to some degree. Even when things were going reasonably well for me there was always this vague backdrop of worry—a sort of constant need to be looking over my shoulder as I remained vexed about what would befall me next or what painful consequence was waiting around the corner. No matter how well I worked it there was never any true sense of being okay with myself or the world around me. By building a relationship with God I have transcended that place of doom and hopelessness. Today, when I am confused or perhaps near despair I can tap into my faith and enjoy a certain peacefulness and calm. Over the years in recovery, time and again I have made it through difficult times. I know that while the future may be uncertain and how things will specifically work out always remains unclear—I will be ok. The calmness and serenity that comes with accepting this truth allows me a measure of peacefulness that is comforting and familiar. When I remind myself that my job is simply to do the best I can with what is in front of me today. When I avoid the desire to manipulate others or force my will into everything. It is then that I sit comfortably in the seat of trust. Learning to trust my Higher Power has taken time, but today I can look back and see that the results of that trust and faith have always exceeded my own petty plans and desires. This recognition that God's plan is always best for me allows me to remain calm and secure through the storms of life that inevitably arrive and that sooner or later always pass.

# SEPTEMBER 19

For a long time in early recovery I was dubious and fairly cynical about the idea of having a spiritual awakening. I was skeptical of many things that I read in the various books of recovery. I doubted the likelihood of it happening for me—at least to the same degree as it had seemed to happen for others. Often when I listened to people in meetings talk about their spiritual awakening I questioned their sincerity and authenticity. They seemed at times to be trying to convince themselves as much as anyone else—and perhaps in some examples that was the case—but for many others I could see and hear a genuine element to their experience. However, even with the presence of these doubts, the path of recovery was the only choice that seemed to make any realistic sense for me because nothing else was working in my life. All my own best efforts had yielded was the horrid and ever worsening mess that I had found myself in when I finally sobered up. I was fearful of the world of recovery because it seemed like it would be the final failure if for some reason it didn't work for me. Over time I have been able to experience the reality of spiritual growth and can still feel the excitement it brings as my growth continues. I have learned how to discover more about who I really am—the person inside who was lost for so long while being held hostage to my addiction and the insanity that followed. I can remember feeling almost giddy and excited as I realized that I was changing in some fundamental ways. It was as though I had found a great new friend within myself, or perhaps like meeting a lost son or daughter for the first time, and I realized that life would be forever changed as a result. For the first time in my life I was truly at home within myself and I knew that my faith and relationship with God meant I would never be so lost and alone again. I understand now how it is natural and unavoidable to feel anxious and unsure before such a seminal event as meeting oneself for the first time in life. I understand why it had taken so long. Experience has shown me that the only way to fail in this effort, this miracle of self-discovery is by being too afraid to try because ultimately it is a fundamental human experience that is available to us all.

# SEPTEMBER 20

Recovery forces me to examine the excessive pursuits of my natural desires and how this selfishness and self-centeredness causes my relationships with others to become twisted and hurtful to all involved. This was particularly so during my years in addiction but my struggle with selfishness continues as I follow my path in recovery. In active addiction my behavior was often appalling. Using justifications, delusional thinking, bizarre rationalization, and outright lies I contorted my friendships and placed the blame for the horrible results with everyone else and rarely at my own doorstep. It is hard for me to think of a better or more direct example of this than in my sex relations. The raw and powerful desire for sex became separated from my human reason and operated from a firmly rooted place in my animalistic core. The act itself, and all of the associated falsities, half-truths, and manipulations that went with it—many of which I was unable to see until I completed a thorough working of the steps—caused untold problems in my life both directly and indirectly. Recovery has shown me a growing ability to understand and accept these desires in ways that are well balanced and appropriate. For me, few things in life are more likely to trigger feelings of guilt and shame, or provide fertile ground in which to grow new resentments, than the tricky world of relationships that include physical intimacy. In recovery I've seen time and again how easy it is to cover up mixed motives and find convenient ways to rationalize and delude myself about the authenticity and appropriateness of my actions. I have had to re-learn and change my thinking about sex by moving away from the immature framework of understanding that my childish youthfulness brought with me into adulthood. The gift of a spiritual awakening that allows me to find true deepness and respect in my relationships with others has allowed me to expand and elevate my understanding of how intimacy is a complex component of a loving relationship rather than simply a physical means to an end. Increasingly I can appreciate and participate in an experience that explores the human bond and shared communion of life and love that sex often truly expresses.

# SEPTEMBER 21

There are several core scripts, or perhaps one might call them plot lines, that are at the heart of my addictive behavior. In the movies for example these scripts are often just as predictable—the hero always triumphs in the end (and gets the girl of course), the bad guy dies or is sent to jail, and the world is saved and remains perhaps a bit flawed but still a good place to be. My life in addiction held fast to a similar sort of scripting. The details of the scenario would change but it was basically the same story over and over again. In recovery many of those traits and storylines continue to affect how I see my place in the world. I can often to struggle to realize what is occurring as I make choices and decisions that drive toward a set of outcomes that are predictable. It is something that seems to happen unconsciously and even when I do realize what is going on it's still very hard to deal with in a way that creates meaningful change. An idea or activity occurs that provides excitement or a rush of pleasure and then I pursue it to excess—usually while creating some vaguely fantastical expectation about how it will turn out. Or another activity helps me feel more secure, perhaps it compensates for a feeling of self-doubt, and I latch onto it and it consumes me as I compulsively lose myself to its lure and reward. The underlying obsession, craving, and subsequent denial of active addiction resurfaces in some other form or activity and with it returns that familiar restlessness, irritability and discontent. There are many ways that this same plot repeats itself and re-appears in my life. It disconnects me from a proper level of emotional self-care while distorting and confusing my ability to have a balanced and spiritually healthy existence. The various scripts of my addictive nature continue to replay themselves in subtle and nuanced ways as I easily find ways to create my own problems in life. Slowly over time I have become more aware of what it going on while becoming better able to stop and adjust myself accordingly. Usually, the root cause is that I've drifted away from a reliance upon the spiritual connection to God and the gratitude, acceptance and self-esteem that it provides.

# SEPTEMBER 22

Learning how to take it easy and go with the flow is one of the parts of recovery that has been the most rewarding for me. It is fair to say that when I arrived in recovery my life wasn't flowing very well. In addiction, each day was marked by struggle and a hard to shake feeling of dread. There was a constant state of uneasiness and an urgent sense of needing to do something. I felt as though I was always either running from some ominous and impending problem or preparing to deal with the consequences of a prior one. At the best of times the past and the future always dominated the present moment leaving me constantly frazzled, tired, confused, upset or unsettled. At the worst of times I was out of control, delusional, angry, depressed, and perhaps suicidal or homicidal. Always my life took place in a pall of hopeless loneliness that sat like a tablecloth under all my actions. Recovery has shown me how to free myself of the anxiety of trying to change the past or arrange the future. Instead I focus on living well just for today. By living each day well I slowly build a better past for myself—one day at a time. In doing so I am also preparing myself to be better able to handle what the future brings. I am more likely to remain calm about my plans for the day and accept that things rarely work out exactly as I plan or expect—and that it is ok when this happens. The experience of living this way for a while has given me the confidence and understanding that I don't need to worry about much more than doing my best today. When I take care of today, tomorrow always takes care of itself. One of the biggest benefits of living this way is a newfound productivity and usefulness. By being more present in the actions I take today, I can in fact take more action today. Instead of wasting time thinking about things I can't control I spend time doing the things that are available to me. It frees me to enjoy time for myself, to enjoy the art of living, while avoiding the tragedy of mental turmoil and anguish that will disrupt my life if I let it. The addictive-like obsession to battle and control the past or the future has been removed leaving me with the simple task of enjoying today.

# SEPTEMBER 23

Sobriety confronts me with life on life's terms and offers me the tools of a life in recovery to use moving forward. At first it was shocking and difficult to face the results of many years of living life foolishly—to sit soberly and review the harsh wreckage of my past. The pressure was uncomfortable and my character defects, my moral ruptures and failings, still flailed wildly as I began the process of aligning my motives and actions with an understanding of a Higher Power. In addiction I was able to avoid, postpone, ignore, and deny simple truths about life. A good example was the idea that somehow my addictive behavior would get better on its own or that there could be some sort of magical ending where I continued my addiction without any trouble or problems. How laughable is the notion of a socially responsible addict who uses recreationally on the weekends or holidays—such a thing simply cannot occur. In those rare moments of clarity and insight I could see that the path I was on led only to disaster but I was unable to change course. Like a deer frozen in the headlights of my own intoxication I couldn't seem to move. Recovery has allowed me to learn how to face and accept certain truths about being a human man—like love, companionship, friendship, aging, and mortality. I can see that the full measure of life contains many elements and never just the ones I find easy or convenient. These truths about humanity and my participation with them is the essence of learning how to move past childish denial and take my place as a man amongst men. I have only one life to live and while I have made poor decisions in the past recovery shows me that I no longer have to continue doing so. It has shown me how to live a life that is genuine and honest with open eyes and an active heart. Each day I know how to choose to be a part of fully living what is, and always will be, my one and only life as the person I am today. Accepting my place as a human who is connected to my own life and its inherent spiritual connection to the world around me removes me from the project of fighting the world and instead frees me to flow with it.

# SEPTEMBER 24

In life we all, without exception, reach the same ultimate destination. None of us gets to live forever. I think about when I am older looking back on my life. What is it that I will value about my time here? In recovery I am faced with a similar opportunity to review my past as I reach the changing point of sobriety. I look back at the many years that were spent in misguided pursuits and at times lament the waste—finding value in the experience only in the ability it provides me to help others. I battled life each day with my will to win and worked hard for material possessions that were then easily lost—given away by my addiction. The most painful losses were the many ruined relationships and lost opportunities to live fully. Today the measure of my value as a man is centered not in my achievements or possessions but in how I live my life each day. When I look back at my life I want to be able to know that I contributed to the world around me through other people in a way that was meaningful and helpful. Instead of seeing the world as something I fight, while trying to gain my slice, I instead see the world as something I am already a part of. I have a stake in humanity and see my role within the whole. It is this sense of participation, of being a part of something larger than myself that has filled the empty and hollow part of my addictive personality. I am able to feel that today I am enough, that if I were to pass tomorrow then it would be a graceful departure made softer by the understanding that I had at last figured out how to live life in ways that were meaningful and that contributed to the larger human project.

# SEPTEMBER 25

It has taken time for me to not only understand and grasp the idea of recovery being an inside job but to then translate that idea into meaningful action and a sense of awareness in my own life. For so many years the point of view I carried around about life was centered in things that were outside of me. I was almost exclusively concerned with the external and avoided the painful work that is required for any sort of meaningful and mature introspection and personal growth. The result was that no matter how well I managed to control and contort life around me into a fashion I desired I was still vaguely discontent and disturbed. No matter how I arranged my outside life I could find no true satisfaction with myself or my life. Until I seriously and rigorously approached the task of sorting out my inside life I wasn't able to experience what it was to access a truly new level of being content. As I look back at how the transformation occurred I realize that I had no idea what it was like until it began to happen. The many years of excessive and punishing addiction had been the final capstone on a lifetime of avoiding the personal responsibility and growth of becoming a healthy adult. As my ability in this area has grown I've realized and experienced a tremendous peace and freedom. I enjoy a true sense of release from an external measure of life and instead find a comfortable reliance upon a Higher Power that validates and guides my internal life. Honestly reconciling my inner disturbances and learning how to love the "who am I am" in life today allows me to face the inevitable ups and downs of life calmly and serenely. Today when I am alone I am content and relaxed with my own company and can enjoy the pleasure of solitude. That clawing and desperate sense of loneliness and shame that used to dominate my time alone with myself is gone. It is important for me today to stay in contact with the love that I have for who I am today, flawed and imperfect, but worthwhile, courageous, and sober. As I continue to build and strengthen a relationship with God I hold onto the reminder that the absence of self-love is shame and that today I am free from the bondage of self and eligible for the full humanity of my daily life.

# SEPTEMBER 26

The drive for material security, monetary achievement and social status is a pursuit that for me highlights the tricky and murky relationship between my own personal insecurities, character defects, and the reality of how as an addict my natural instincts always tend toward being excessive. A friend once insightfully commented about his retirement planning and the question of how much is enough. He wondered if it was when one has enough to feel they don't have to rely on their Higher Power anymore. The idea that we can insure ourselves against life and ultimately exert control upon the world around us is an ingrained part of the western society that drives us to acquire and consume. My alcoholic mind will always require more and unless I address the underlying issue of my spiritual malady there will never be enough for me in life for me to be truly satisfied. It seems that contentment in life, that true sense of comfort and ease with who I am and how I live, is something that is fundamentally unable to be addressed through possessions or status—perhaps because these are things that reflect outward when the solution I seek is something that also requires an inward reflection. For me, the process of a spiritual awakening continues through the application of my slowly improving skills in the area of self-examination and discovery. They allow me to dig past and transcend my knee-jerk initial responses to life and find the deeper underlying motives, causes, and conditions that create them. I have often found that my initial answers to the simple questions of who I am and what I want in life are misguided. I often get what I have been seeking and then find it is not enough, or not what I really want, and the result is that I am confused and disillusioned. Recovery provides a framework that helps me cut through the illusions of my immature thinking and find the deeper truths about myself. Truths that can be hard to confront and reconcile because they are often painfully difficult to change. My awakening from the zombie-like world of addiction continues to require a rearrangement of my beliefs and thinking. A shift from a framework of what the world can do for me toward a spiritually based understanding of what I can contribute to the world.

# SEPTEMBER 27

Most of the problems that I struggle with in life today are rooted in experiences and lessons from my adolescence. Like many people in recovery my heavy drinking began at an early age. As a result my formative years during the journey from youth to manhood failed to provide the lessons, growth, and maturity I needed to become emotionally and spiritually well developed. My solutions for life in many areas remained juvenile, immature, and largely ineffective. I struggled to understand what the problem was because I didn't know what it was that I was missing—or even that there was anything missing. And of course my drinking and drugging clouded the entire process. In active addiction my world became increasingly isolated as my limited relationships with others degraded further leaving me ever more disconnected from the opportunity to learn effective life lessons. I spent most of my time with others who were also struggling. Most of the lessons I learned were of the wrong sort and in general I was a poor student. In recovery I have learned that I must participate in meaningful relationships with others that allow me to learn these lost lessons for life. By participating with others who are choosing a spiritual path in life I have at last been able to find the morals and values that undergird some meaningful principles in ways that guide my daily living. The process offers me the chance to learn important life lessons through living my life as a part of the world around—me as an insider and participant—rather than excluding myself from community. The idea that I must be a part of a community in order to learn how to live life properly makes sense because life is rather like a team sport. It cannot really be played alone nor can I become good at it practicing alone. Today I rely on healthy honest relationships with others in ways that at first seemed unnatural and foreign to me—because they were. Through this shared experience I grow and become more able to properly participate in the full measure of my own life and the lives of others.

# SEPTEMBER 28

I remember hearing Clancy I., the well-known AA speaker, talk about the simple fact that in recovery the very best we can hope for is to become a healthy human. And that, as such, the best we ever become is imperfect and flawed—as all humans are. Prior to recovery, life for me tended to be framed in very distinct ways. Everything was a win or a loss, a victory or a defeat, a success or a failure, and usually there was an overblown and epic framework around all these situations that seemed to place excessive importance on their outcomes. I chuckle now to myself now when I look back at how naive I was to think that any particular event or circumstance could have possibly have been the one to determine the entire course or outcome of my life. While indeed it is true that some events have had a profound and lasting impact on my life, the fact is that my place in life today has occurred as the result of a great many choices and circumstances that have all combined to determine my life. Certainly there are some actions that might qualify as crucially important forks in the road but few that were truly life altering in their own right. Instead they were most often simply out of proportion and ridiculous as my addictive personality blossomed in active addiction and my world resided entirely within the land of excess—excessive consumption, beliefs, thinking, and reactions. In recovery I've learned how to moderate and avoid the excessive fringes and extremes of life while acknowledging and accepting my own flaws, failings, and foibles. Learning how to deal with my ever present imperfection has been a vital element in allowing me to make progress past the initial year or two of step work and early task of simply staying sober. Recovery opens the door to the endless opportunity for deeper spiritual growth that continues to develop as I learn how to discover and address my always present character defects and faults—my inherent and unavoidable human imperfection. Today am I able to ask God to help me with my problems and in doing so am better able to access the help that I need to enjoy meaningful change. Change that shapes and improves the way I show up in the lives of others as well as my own understanding of what that looks like and means.

# SEPTEMBER 29

It is important for me to remember what it was like in the years and months before I found recovery. The crushing isolation of addiction was not only lonely and soulless it was also, perhaps more than anything else, despairing and hopeless. The Big Book notes that the alcoholic will "know loneliness such as few do" and I can clearly remember that desperate hopelessness that shrouded my world at the end.[17] Early on in recovery through the stories and shared experiences of others I began to see that the door was opening for hope again in my life. Over time and through working the steps I was not only able to find hope for myself but to leverage that hope into the faith and courage that allowed me to move forward in recovery. Today I remain close to that core understanding of hope and how it ignites the world of possibilities, ideas, and dreams for me. Having hope slowly combats the years of negative experiences in addiction and allows me to grasp hold of beliefs and truths about myself and the world around me.

[17] ibid. P. 152.

Hope is the basis of my participation in the cycle of life with those close to me today. It also connects me to the generations that have gone before and the ones that will come after my life is over. It cries out to me—"Life is worth doing!" For thousands of years humankind has had hope in our collective future. Hope forms our values and beliefs and drives them into reality. Today I am able to contribute my own choices in these areas to the world around me and exert the validity of my own existence. I am no longer a hopeless spectator, slave to my addictions and cut off from my own life. I can instead see past the flaws of humanity in order to be a part of the goodness, ideas, and beliefs that for centuries have allowed human life to flourish and progress. While I can change little about the entire world, by having and holding true to my own values I can definitely affect the small part of it that I am close to each day. Perhaps in the same way that the lack of self-love is shame, the lack of hope is death. Today I experience my own participation in the hope that is life both directly through my own aspirations and indirectly through witnessing the world of others.

# SEPTEMBER 30

Many years ago I worked in the emerging computer networking field. One of the unavoidable parts of that world was that the technology was always changing and improving. Sometimes it was a minor enhancement and other times it would be "game-changing." Often what had been recently new and represented the most advanced solution suddenly became instantly outdated. Occasionally we would run into people who refused to change, holding on to old technology even though with each passing month it did not work as well and would cause problems. They held onto it because it was what they knew. It was what they were comfortable with. They were suspicious and perhaps afraid or unwilling to do the work that learning new technology required. As they continued to hold on, refusing to change while all around them the world moved on with newer products, their organizations became isolated and increasingly unable to work well with others. The organizations that thrived were the ones who were open-minded. The ones who were willing to try new technology and explore the ways it could help them move forward and improve. Recovery has required the same level of open-mindedness and willingness to experiment in order for me to continue making progress. I have had to learn how to be constantly willing to examine and reexamine my understanding of how I approach life. Just as a child who is growing must always have new clothes, I must be prepared to try new ideas and concepts that add, subtract, replace or augment the approach I am currently using—or my spiritual growth will become confined, like feet trying to grow inside shoes that are too small. When I've found something that is working for me it is often very hard to be willing to even consider change—particularly if my current solution was hard won. However, I've learned I must remain willing to consider an ever changing picture and understanding of life around me if I want to stay invigorated and energized about myself and my place in the world as "a part of." Today I see many important things that I could not see a few years ago, and for me, recovery is the art of continuing that growth.

# October

"You may have to fight a battle more than once to win it."
— Margaret Thatcher

"It is not enough that we do our best; sometimes we must do what is required."
— Winston S. Churchill

"Giving up is the only sure way to fail."
— Gena Showalter

# OCTOBER 1

In recovery one of the biggest challenges I faced was finding the ability to surrender. I needed to truly let go of my old life so that I could be free to take up a new life. As long as I kept hanging on to my old ideas and beliefs I was unable to free myself from the past and begin to create a new future. It was difficult for many reasons. I didn't really know what the future was or how and when it would arrive. It was difficult to say goodbye to people, places, and things that had been an integral and profound part of my life. While it is true that in most cases these parts of my life had ultimately been negative—coming with horrible consequences and a steep price—they were what I knew and there was a certain sort of perverse comfort to be found in them. More than anything else I had to overcome the sense of being an imposter that came with trying to become a sober man in recovery. For many years my identity was tied into ideas and beliefs that swirled around in the illogical fog of addiction and the excitingly surreal rush of the world that goes with it. Recovery has shown me how to walk towards the future of my life while setting down and leaving behind the parts of life that aren't good for me. Even when I may not as yet have found anything to replace them with. This is the great step into the unknown that draws upon faith and a relationship with a Higher Power. I needed to move forward with the confidence that I am eligible, that I am enough, and that I will be ok. I have learned that I must prepare myself to be ready and able to grasp these new ways of living and thinking. That these actions, beliefs, and behaviors only become available to me when I first let go of my old ways. Sometimes it has been like breaking up with a girlfriend and ending a relationship I know will never really work out. After a while I can easily find myself wanting her back simply because I am uncomfortable. Recovery has shown me how to hold fast to my values and morals despite the discomfort and has repeatedly demonstrated how God's plans are always better than my own. My faith in a future must be strong, patient, and cautious as I let go of the past in order to face the future. A future where the man I am trying to become always resides.

# OCTOBER 2

Forming an understanding of what sort of man I want become in sobriety is the first step in my efforts to move towards that goal. Usually I don't fully understand what I need to do to get there. It is the process of trying, of experimenting and learning, which helps me expand and fill in the details of what is actually involved. In all cases I must find the meaningful actions that allow the journey to continue. Saying that I want to live in a more spiritual way must lead me to taking actions each day that are new and often seem awkward, clunky, or even silly. It is the willingness to not only accept the theory that one should take time in life to, "stop and smell the roses," but more importantly is it whether I am actually doing so. Developing mindfulness and a desire to accept a spiritual participation in daily life allows me to find many ways to experience the full richness of life in each moment. It frees me from the perpetual hamster wheel of my own selfishness and whirling thinking. By finding and practicing ways to live fully in the moment—to enjoy a diversion, thought, conversation or aspect of nature for a few minutes—makes the rest of my busy day seem less difficult and more purposeful.

# OCTOBER 3

My own self-story, the thinking and ideas around who I am in life, is often confronted and sometimes fails the only true test—my interactions with others. I like to think I am caring, considerate, compassionate and various other positive and pleasing attributes but ultimately it is only when I review my interaction with others that I have any measure of the truth. For many years I was loathe to look at my own behavior and unable to do so clearly. I deluded myself and believed things that when I honestly looked at the facts simply weren't true. The process of the steps and becoming aware of how blinded I often am to my own faults was the beginning of learning how to combat them. Slowly I have become better at being able to see how my underlying selfish motives subtly shape and propel my actions with others. I am able to recognize my own self-absorption and the result is that I can at last see and hear others as they truly are. It is impossible for me to properly hear the music of others when my own music is blasting. Suddenly I began to realize that I was never really present in the lives of others. Until I could really step away from my own world I could not be present in theirs.

# OCTOBER 4

When I try to exert my will upon the world around me or try to force an outcome or event to occur according my own plans I am usually unsuccessful. However, when my will is aligned with that of my Higher Power success seems more likely to happen. In fact it often comes easily. When my will is not aligned properly then things quickly get sticky for me. When I am struggling, recovery has shown me how to look back at my actions, my thoughts, and expectations. I often find examples of what happens when I am selfish, dishonest, or have mixed motives. I struggle, fight, coerce and become agitated, angry, or depressed about things that simply aren't within my ability to control or make happen. When I can't accept the things I cannot change then I am the one who suffers. It is a self-inflicted nonsensical suffering that I create myself from what can be an endless supply of unreasonable demands and expectations. I then feel entitled, bitter, unfairly treated and my spiritual world closes in as my disease drives me toward the escape I am so familiar with. Recovery has helped me recognize when I am chewing on the wrong bone in life and directs me towards faith. My Higher Power will always take care of me when I let go of my own petulance and simply focus on spiritual growth.

# OCTOBER 5

It seems that there are two basic paths in life often expressed in terms such as good or bad, love and hate, optimism or pessimism and the like. The unavoidable reality of human life always seems to involve elements of both sides. For me, the ultimate choice becomes which side shall I choose? My experience has shown me that when I chose the path of darkness it brings loneliness—a crushing isolation that slowly closes off all the good things in life. By contrast when I chose goodness I find light, happiness, contentment, and meaning. The two sides are not exclusive. I always experience both around me and it is a question of where I chose to sit— what I focus on. Which side shall I become a part of? In choosing the path of light I find the greatest validation and truth of those positive values in my relationships with others. The positive experience of life is always a shared one—while the negative is always rooted in crushing isolation. Today I rely on my Higher Power, many close friendships and active participation in work or other social groups to keep me in the light. It is an ongoing process described by the ancient Greek philosopher Pythagoras as, "...the art of winning the soul to good or evil."[18] Today as I practice that art I am always rewarded. I become more skilled and experienced in my ability to enjoy true and meaningful relationships with others that yield the full experience of human life.

# OCTOBER 6

[18] Yonge, *The Lives and Opinions of Eminent Philosophers*. Bohn's Classical Library. London: G. Bell & Sons, 1901.

In early recovery one of the most difficult questions I pondered was that of self-forgiveness. I had done many things in addiction that were hard to look at in the clear light of sobriety. I struggled with how to reconcile my past in a way that would allow me to move forward. What I have learned is that forgiveness is never a singular experience. By nature and definition it is something that happens between people and so the idea of self-forgiveness is a complicated one that typically masks other feelings and motives that I am struggling to see clearly. My Higher Power is always ready to forgive and encourage me to move forward living with love and kindness for myself and others. My struggle with self-forgiveness—while somewhat centered in guilt and shame—was more fundamentally tied to denial, self-indulgent remorseful self-pity, and a lack of acceptance. Until I truly gave up on the notion of somehow creating a better past I wasn't able to fully accept my own. It allowed me to clean up the mess as best I could and gain the forgiveness of others. I could begin the process of moving forward armed with a full acceptance, acknowledgement, and understanding of my own failings, imperfections, and how they had truly affected others. It was this action that helped release me from resentments and anger towards others because after all, when I looked squarely at my own past, how in the world could I judge others or assume a position of somehow being a better person? Accepting and forgiving my own imperfections and struggles was really about letting go of my anger and resentment toward others.

# OCTOBER 7

For many years I lived my life in ways that were dishonest and failed to follow any sort of moral guide. As a result I was always busy trying to protect my self-image by maintaining a front of deniability and delusion about how I affected others. I reacted strongly to any form of criticism. I wanted to fight it, prove it wrong, or find ways to justify things by turning the tables and redirecting away from my own behavior towards someone else's. Today in recovery I live differently. I often talk about how I am now able to look anyone in the eye and be honest about who I was, who I am today, and what I hope for my future. However, I am still close to those difficult feelings when confronted by criticism and my failings. I have to work to understand and cherish the opportunity presented by such moments. They are a chance to improve myself and test my commitment to the morals and values that guide me today. The steps remind me to be truly honest about my part in things and direct me toward my Higher Powers help in removing those defects of character that create them. While today I am able to be free of the urgent childish desire to have everyone like me—I must remember that I still have plenty of faults and that denying and hiding from them moves me the wrong way on the path of recovery.

# OCTOBER 8

So much of the pain in life that I created during my years in active addiction was centered in an attempt to use my personal power in ways that were in conflict with others and with the world in general. Looking back I see that I had an adversarial relationship with most everything around me. I relentlessly attempted, at most any cost, to get the things I wanted and to shape the lives of others in order to suit my deluded ideas and beliefs. In recovery I was forced to surrender my willful excess and admit my powerlessness. Ultimately, in accepting my powerlessness and inability to control my addiction, I was able to begin to resolve the problem of the proper alignment of my will—my personal powers, efforts, and actions in life. Today my understanding of what it means to examine how I show up in the lives of others is experienced and strengthened by a willingness to forgo my own selfishness. Instead I am able to concern myself with the experience of others—to truly take the time to engage empathetically in the attempt to understand another person's reality. When I take my place as a member of humanity I am part of God's world and with it comes a sense of appreciation as well as duty that encourages me to act in positive ways. I care about others and our common collective and can begin to properly negotiate the space between my own particular will and the general will of community. Beginning with new relationships in the world of my recovery, this idea of participation in something larger than myself has spread out to other areas of my life. The shopkeeper, neighbor, and stranger on the street are all equally eligible and entitled to some degree of the respect and value that I would give to those close to me. My part in life does count and yet it counts no more than anyone else's. How I behave with all others does matter because, in a way, it is a useful reflection of how I implicitly value myself. I cannot truly value myself without valuing others. The measure of the man I am trying to be is often more keenly observed in how I treat strangers rather than my friends.

# OCTOBER 9

For many years my life was framed in ways that were dishonest and insincere. My behavior caused problems of trust, guilt, and shame. It also brought a constant backdrop of stress and tension as I worried about being found out or caught and suffering the consequences that would surely follow. I spent many hours in useless circles of worry as my imagination worked through endless stories about what the future would hold. Oftentimes my fantasies seemed to become real as I convinced myself about how the future would unfold—as though I was the unlucky owner of a crystal ball of doom. As a result of the endless insecurity of the self-generated insanity and chaos of life in addiction I am very inclined towards wanting to know the answer to all things. I want to have clarity and certainty about myself and my relationships with others. This desire tends to collide with a stark reality of human existence—the fact that most often the answers to how important questions in my life will play out in the future simply aren't available to me in the present. The uncertainties of human life are frequently exposed most clearly in my relationships with others. The desire for control drives me to unfairly take away the rights of others as I make their minds up for them by assuming that I already know what they will say or do. I then up the ante and compound my error by judging them on things they haven't done. Just I grow and mature in my understanding and self-knowledge, so too do others around me. Accepting this fact is a key part of my ability to sustain the close relationships with others that allow me to share who I am today. I can enjoy the intimacy of a trusting honest friendship without clinging to or constraining it by holding onto some predetermined form. Just as I can't hold onto the past I cannot hide from the results of my personal path along the mysterious journey of human life. Today I can accept the unknown parts of me, others, and the future without being afraid of it, trying to prevent it, or spending countless hours creating and obsessing about a reality that does not yet exist.

# OCTOBER 10

Recovery has helped me understand the truth that I alone am responsible for how I feel. This idea is in stark contrast to the "blame others" framework that I lived in addiction where my problems were almost always someone else's fault. Oh how I often I would cry out that someone else "made me" do this or that, or that certain circumstances "made me" so depressed or angry that it justified my ensuing actions. It was a framework that always ensured I had plenty of reasons to be irresponsible, self-centered and selfish. Life will always present me a wide variety of experiences and I alone get to decide which ones I will focus on. While of course during any given day I experience many feelings in response to the good and bad things that may happen it up to me to choose which ones I hold onto and allow shape my life. My attitude and outlook is a choice that I must be consciously aware of and in doing so I confront the disturbances and challenges in life that I must work through rather than being blindly controlled by them. It is when I avoid and ignore them, skipping the hard work of spiritual growth each problem brings, that I can fall into a jaded weariness and become defined by an attitude of "bummer, hassle, downer" that I wear like a suit all day. Perpetuating my suffering is a way for me to reject my faith in a Higher Power and instead put myself in control of the future. It allows me to avoid working through the problems that inevitably will arrive in my life. The process of learning how to face life and remain spiritually fit enables me to grow and face new challenges more successfully. Over time I have begun to realize that it doesn't really matter what problems life brings me. I have the ability to get through them and my Higher Power will ensure I am taken care of as long as I do the work that is needed.

# OCTOBER 11

After some time in recovery I began to better understand the idea that is expressed in the Big Book where it says "And we have ceased fighting anything or anyone—even alcohol."[19] It is a place of spirituality that arrives as a result of working through the difficult tasks of the steps of recovery and represents a freedom from the bondage of self. It is one of the core gifts of recovery. Today I am better able to accept the things that are outside of my control and in doing so redirect that energy and effort toward my own spiritual growth and development. There are so many important questions and discoveries about myself—my human characteristics that shape who I am. Questions that until recovery I never did any serious work around. I simply wasn't able or willing to work on these larger questions about life and my place in it when my existence was framed in the context of battling the world to get what I wanted—or driven by my efforts to shape it in my design. I scoffed at the idea of getting in touch with my more sensitive side and derided those who spent a lot of time worrying about their precious "feelings," or do-gooders who worried incessantly about how their actions affected others. What I've learned in recovery is that in many respects when it came to life I was like a man in a garage full of wonderful tools who when solving his problems would use only the one or two he liked while ignoring the rest. I didn't know how they worked so I didn't value them and I never bothered to invest the time to learn. Recovery has shown me a spiritual toolkit and gives me the daily practice in its use that brings me into a relationship with a Higher Power that solves my problems. By relieving

---

[19] *Alcoholics Anonymous : The Story of How Many Thousands of Men and Women Have Recovered from Alcoholism*. 4th ed. New York City: Alcoholics Anonymous World Services, 2001. P. 84.

myself of the need to battle the world around me I am able to discover and explore parts of myself that I previously chose to avoid. It is a process that has yielded an entirely new outlook and understanding of who I am that undergirds the faith and acceptance of the validity of my own place in the world around me.

# OCTOBER 12

I no longer have ridiculous illusions and delusions about the devastating consequences of my active addiction. I remember clearly where it brought me and with each passing day in recovery I move towards a better understanding of just how the insanity and unmanageability of active addiction shaped my life. Each morning I remind myself through prayer and meditation that I, on my own, am powerless. I was clearly unable to solve my problem of addiction without the help of my Higher Power and that it was only through the program of recovery that I was able to find a way to learn how to access that help. Overcoming my denial and honestly accepting my addiction allowed me to at last connect with the authentic thankfulness and gratitude required to remain free of the bondage of selfishness that propelled my addictive behavior. Until I was willing to fully surrender to the belief that I must, to the best of my ability, life my life in a way that is in alignment with the will of my Higher Power I was completely unable to stay sober and on the beam of recovery. It is clear to me that relief from my addiction is provided only on a daily basis. I must position myself to receive and ask for that help each day. This is one of the great truths that recovery reminds me of—that I will always need to be connected to my Higher Power because I will always be an inherently flawed and imperfect addict who is subject to my own weakness and failing. Left unchecked, my own thinking will always slowly drift off course and lead me astray. Regardless of how many days, months, or years the battle of my recovery from addiction is always fought in the moments of today. I don't play around with these facts of my life and I don't harbor or coddle any misbeliefs, hopes or suspicions that it will ever be fundamentally different for me. Instead, each morning, I simply get on my knees in clear subjugation to a power that is greater than me, thankful for the new life that has been freely given, and ask for the help to complete another day successfully.

# OCTOBER 13

I try to be mindful of having a lightness of spirit and finding ways in which I can express and participate in the moment. Sometimes being able to step back and remind myself of the bigger picture can get me out of the concern, frustration, or worry about a particular event or problem and free me to lift my head, enjoy what is around me and contribute to my own happiness. The grim reality of my life in addiction is often a source of a chuckle and smile when I think of how different my problems are today. However, while the relief from the ravages and insanity of active addiction is indeed a wonderful tonic, the fact of the matter is that today I still have problems that affect my ability to remain in the "sunlight of the spirit" of recovery.[20] While of course life may never be an endless series of wonderfully happy days—it is important that I continue to use the tools of recovery on an ongoing basis. One of the ways that I have repeatedly found offers me a pathway to lightening my load and lifting my spirits is the freeing and liberating feeling that comes with sharing my problems with another. At times I still want to carry a burden, often the result of some personal selfishness, resentment, dishonesty or fear that will distort my ability to remain on a spiritual path. When I share these feelings honestly with another person I liberate myself from them in a way that is different from simply praying about them. I regain my sense of integrity and contentedness. It is through actively keeping my side of the street clean in recovery that I retain the opportunity to remain spiritually fit. Given where I was and where I am today I should be enjoying a spring in my step and a song in my heart now and again! Mindfulness and gratitude are always available to me and I try to remember to use them as tools that help me let go of the narrow focus of certain problems and value the bigger picture of my faith and hope that the experiences of recovery continue to provide.

# OCTOBER 14

How often have I heard that it is better to give than receive? How often did I in the back of my mind question the logic of such a statement and feel that it was one of those things in life that might be good for the average guy but not for me! For me, I wanted to receive not give. As with so many other things in life, my mind's eye, clouded by addiction, was unable to accept that, like all others, I was a relatively unexceptional and yet important part of life and that the "rules" of life also applied to me. It was another fine example of how my own selfishness corrupted my ability to hear the truths about life that are age old and wise. It is a perfect example of how my childishness and lack of maturity carried into my adulthood as I laughed in the face of such a truth and tried to get more of what I wanted at the

[20] ibid. P. 66.

expense of others. The childish and naive notion of individual exceptionalism and the self-generated righteous hubris of some unjustified sense of manifest personal destiny drove my behavior in ways that were juvenile and immature. Having a spiritual awakening has meant revisiting my beliefs not only in theory but also in practice—and then having a commitment to pursuing an exploration and fuller understanding of the reality that new thinking can create. I must put it into action in order to experience the truth of these things. Today, I live in a life that is so much more expansive and rich. By developing an ability to view my life experience in a more mature and sensible way I have opened more choices, paths, and routes to all sorts of new experiences and value. They result from approaching life from the perspective of a truly two way street that I am a part of rather than a one way path that I use to try and extract results from life with. Life is not some abstract problem that I am working to solve from the outside—it is an experience that I participate in by being a part of. By opening myself to others, bringing and sharing the fruits of my experience to the table, I am able to enjoy and participate in the full feast of life.

# OCTOBER 15

One of the nicest things about my life today is the feeling of integrity and security that I have. I can look anyone in the eye and am no longer living in fear of what is going to happen next. I have learned how to live with a good deal of hope and faith that allows me to face life without a great amount of fear. Years of life in active addiction were a great trauma that left me fearful and constantly worried about the future as I careened from one chaotic emergency to the next. The process of cleaning house in recovery allowed me to get past the wreckage of my past and the secrets that kept me sick. Sharing my entire story with another man allowed me to finally be free from the deadly grasp of the past and begin life with a new freedom and insight. It took a while to no longer feel like an imposter in my new life. I was fearful that people wouldn't accept me because of my past. What I've learned is that most people are concerned with how my behavior is today rather than how it was in the past. Slowly I've become better at understanding how to be ok with being ok. As I've grown more content with who I am and experienced the reality of recovery I've steadily built a new life. With each new positive experience and outcome the understanding of what it means to be hopeful and excited about the future has grown. People told me that as I changed how I was behaving, by embracing a spiritual outlook and positive actions, my life would also change. That reality has become a simple and powerful truth that I can truly accept today. It allows me to live calmly while facing the future without fear of the past.

# OCTOBER 16

Increasingly in life I find that I am concerned with understanding, enabling and expanding feelings of connectedness, value, participation, and meaning in my life. By focusing on the internal rewards that occur as a result of living life in a way that is aligned with core values and morals I have begun to answer the question of "what is enough?" For many years the answer to that question was quite simple—there was never enough. The classic response, "My drug of choice was more," reveals how ingrained and central this thinking is within addiction, but also within many other parts of life. For many people the measure of their success is tallied in units of material possessions that validate and delineate their understandings of self. I have moved away from the external measures of success and achievement that in our modern consumerist society are commonly linked with possessions and the attainment of goods, prestige, competitive achievements and the need for feelings of superiority and entitlement. What brings me the most satisfaction are the feelings of belonging, acceptance, and calm that arrive as a result of understanding who I am and how I want to live. They provide a sense of security and stability. I am no longer struggling and fighting to get somewhere because I have already arrived. Each day has become its own simple destination and I am present within it enjoying the elements of life that are here now rather than mentally scurrying around for something in the future.

# OCTOBER 17

Recovery has helped me be progressively more flexible about how I understand my life. At first I struggled to honestly see and admit that my addiction was a problem. Looking back now it's remarkable how much I struggled with that first basic step given the insanity and the numerous clear examples of profound and self-inflicted problems in my life. Slowly I've become able to make room inside the jar of my mind for new beliefs and ideas that replace my old thinking. The experience was often a bit disheartening as I realized how little I really understood about many of the most important aspects of life like love, relationships, spirituality, and honesty. It was frustrating to see how, in so many ways, I had failed to mature into a healthy adult and I sometimes became depressed and fearful that I would never figure out some of these things. The turning point began when I fully grasped hold of the willingness needed to be ready to let go of what I thought I knew in the hope of finding an improved and more helpful belief. Today, while holding my values and morals quite tightly, I can hold my beliefs and understanding of what I think I know about life a bit more loosely. Each time I am wrong or learn something new it represents an opportunity to grow. So today I welcome these events rather than deny or avoid them. They are lessons and signs, sometimes painful and difficult, sometimes delicious and joyful that demonstrate meaningful progress and growth.

# OCTOBER 18

The life changing reality of having a spiritual awakening has been something that is often hard for me to express. In early recovery the notion of such things seemed far away and while perhaps not completely unattainable it was certainly a distant, undefined, and unlikely goal that I struggled to understand. Like many newcomers I was more focused on how in the world I might stay sober long enough to get the judge off my back and fix some of my bigger problems. I really struggled with the idea of a spiritual experience. Looking back I see that I lacked any meaningful way of connecting to the idea. This inability to see a path toward spirituality in my life really hindered my early recovery. However, I kept going and tried to have faith that as the saying goes—more would be revealed. My experience has been that by actively participating in a program of recovery I at some point found myself having the realization that it was happening. It had started to happen slowly in small ways without any great fanfare or announcement. I simply realized one day that I was experiencing a spiritual awakening and that I had an active and real relationship with a power greater than myself. It is this experience that leads me to believe that a spiritual awakening, like happiness, is not one of those things that can be pursued directly in life. It is something that occurs as the result of doing other things. Today my faith in the power and truth of my own spiritual awakening, and the source of change it has become in my life, is very strong. It grows stronger each day as I build and express in my life a greater reliance on the spirituality of the world around me.

# OCTOBER 19

As I continue along the path of recovery, remaining active and involved in the growth of myself and others, I learn new things. Sometimes they are hard truths that arrive suddenly and jarringly. Other times they arrive softly and slowly develop as the passage of time allows me to understand things I've learned already in deeper and more meaningful ways. Just as it is impossible for me change my past it is also impossible for me to unlearn things or return to the place I was before some new insight occurred—though sometimes I kind of wish I could because the discovery often requires me to change. I am then called back to the crux of recovery as I face choices about what kind of man I truly want to be. Facing new found faults and unhealthy behaviors requires the often painful and hard work of change. Invariably these changes involve how my actions affect others and the outcomes that result. My efforts to control life in response to my fears cloud my relationships with others. It prevents me from honestly accepting their truths as I instead cling to my own designs. The subtlety of my delusions around motives and actions is often hidden quite deeply. And when discovered often confronts my willingness to always do the right thing because there are time when I'd rather pretend I hadn't noticed. Experience has shown me that learning new things about myself is one part—choosing what to do about them is another.

# OCTOBER 20

There is no avoiding the complexity of life—no matter how hard I work on having the right friends, job, schedule or activities. Sometimes I can be quite frustrated that even in recovery my life can become so complicated and challenging. My days of addiction offered a daily selection of poor choices and complex problems that seemed impossible to decipher. In recovery I've made great strides in my ability to make good decisions, develop boundaries, and participate in only healthy relationships. Be that as it may, the fact of life is that there will always be those confusing and disheartening events that occur. I can easily become muddled and unsure of what is going on and how it will work out. This is when my ability to have faith is tested. I must resist the urges to force my will on the situation and perhaps make things worse. I have learned to focus on my side of the street and allow things to run their course. Past experience has shown me that I can trust in my Higher Power to take care of me and so I can also do that with others. Instead of being hurt, angry, resentful or trying to get my way by being "helpful" I can instead allow other people the time and space to find their own path. I can simply be available and helpful should they ask. My discomfort and uneasiness is quieted when I have faith and take a broader perspective that allows me to watch how others resolve things without my direct involvement.

# OCTOBER 21

The world of recovery has given me the gift of a new life. It is easy for me to look back at where I was and see the truth of this. The challenge today is for me to be able to sustain the willingness, open mindedness, and honesty that are needed for continued spiritual growth and ongoing personal development. There are always opportunities to be more honest with myself about who I am, how I behave, and the fears or selfishness that lurk within my character defects. The rough edges of how I treat others offer clues to my own insecurities that I must have the honesty and courage to follow. They lead me to new opportunities for growth should I have the acceptance and insight needed to pursue them. I must find the willingness to overcome my own skewed beliefs and justifications that I often use to minimize and blur the truth. Ultimately my ability to be useful and helpful to others is rooted in the sincerity and thoroughness of the ongoing efforts to know myself.

# OCTOBER 22

There is a curious relationship between my natural human flaws and the understanding of my faults as they relate to addiction. It is easy for me to focus on my days in active addiction—with their resulting periods of chaos, unmanageability, and dishonesty—and see those faults as simply the results of alcoholism. In some respects they were, but largely they are simply excessive and extreme examples of the same faults that exist within me in sobriety. For me, core questions of spiritual values, self-esteem, and the fear of failure or loss always center on basic beliefs about my place in the world and how I link those beliefs to the ability to hold true to the concept that we are all equally eligible and valid in our creator's eye. No matter how smart, dull, or flawed a person is, we all get only one vote in God's world and I am due only mine—no more or no less. When I accept my own validity and focus on voting well in life through my actions and deeds I can free myself from the need to judge others or measure their value. When I remove the confusion of addiction I am left with the results of my own actions and thinking around the faults of others. They often provide opportunities that direct me toward my own faults—faults that are often hidden behind my excited review and judgment of others. This process opens the door to a deeper recognition and reconciliation of my own fears and failings.

# OCTOBER 23

Spending some time each day thinking about spiritual growth as a concept helps me connect to the bigger picture of my journey on the path of recovery. However, it is when I review my plans for the day and commit to trying, one more time, to live according to my principles and moral values that I make the connection between the conceptual and the specific. At night when I review my day I may gain insight and direction about how things went. Then, in the morning I can ask for help as I try again. During the day I can take time to pause and relate the underlying principles of the steps to the various tasks at hand. Will I be able to be honest and kind in a discussion with another? Am I able to listen helpfully or will I prefer the sound of my own voice? How can I be useful and yet have the faith to allow others to find their own solutions rather than trying to control life through my own ideas. The daily practice of a spiritual approach to life in thoughtful, specific, and meaningful ways guides my own growth and tests the question of whether I am merely talking the talk, or indeed walking the walk. I've learned that the real work of the long journey of self-discovery and growth takes place mostly in the process of living well today.

# OCTOBER 24

I remember the relief of early recovery as I began to realize that I was truly gaining freedom from the addictions that shaped and controlled me. It was a tremendous feeling to be able to start over again on a new path and have confidence that I wouldn't be creating those sorts of problems in my life again. It was during that period that I slowly came to truly believe and have faith in my Higher Power. Then I began to face the difficulties and hard work of living life on life's terms and learning how to rely on faith as the realities of human life confronted me in small and large ways. I had to choose to either rely more completely on my Higher Power or turn back towards my own will. This was the time when I learned about the difference between what it takes to get sober versus what it takes to stay sober. Slowly I begin to experience how the gifts of success in recovery accumulate in ways that build and increase my faith. As I faced the inevitable challenges of life and got through them I added another "win" to the faith column. Each of these wins helped overcome the sense of fear and doubt that was rooted in my addictive past. It was important that I remembered those early victories because they gave me strength in the more difficult struggles that came. With each of life's passing trials and tribulations I have learned more about how to find assurance and refuge in the actual practice of my spiritual faith.

It is a practice that I work at each day when I kneel and pray to ask for help, or when I pause and reflect in gratitude or appreciation. With routine daily effort, and deliberate practice through meaningful action, I am able to maintain the spiritual connection of recovery.

# OCTOBER 25

Recovery offers the notion and reminds me that today I am "a part of." It is a simple idea that over time has grown in meaning and value to me. The realization that no matter what is going on in my life—be it good, bad, or indifferent—I am still always a part of the world around me acts like an anchor that hold my spirituality in place. When I go for a walk with my dog, share a smile with a stranger or pause to admire the majesty of Mount Rainier, I am participating in the world in a way that transcends my individual problems and connects me to a spiritual constant that is always present. The spiritual fabric of life is always nearby and available. It helps me see the temporary nature of my own personal struggles and points me towards the longer arc of my own part in human life around me. Today I am able to be open to these moments, to tap into them, and in doing so help alleviate the domination and fear created by my thinking and worry about life's uncertainties. The gracious spirit of life around me is far more powerful and constant than any of my fears.

# OCTOBER 26

Finding meaning and purpose in life is one of those wonderful philosophical questions that we all face in our lives. Addiction gave me purpose, albeit a horribly distorted and ugly one, but offered no meaning that extended beyond myself. In some ways it promised the enjoyment of a life shared with others in a special and exciting way but ultimately left me, confused, isolated and demoralized—an outcast who had become unable to participate in the society of people around me. This is a fairly ironic observation for me today considering the stories I often enjoyed about how drugs and alcohol would offered some sort of spiritual connection that sobriety couldn't. I was left disconnected, desolate and utterly alone. Today I am able to participate and add value to the world around me. I believe in the human nature of a shared experience and community that is helpful. One that works together for the benefit of all. By taking my place in community I am able to find actions that are outside of myself and in many small ways amplify what is good in life. Over time my cynicism has given way to hope. The blunt and unavoidable truth of my experience confronts my doubts and selfish traits. I cannot deny that I feel better about myself because of how I live my life today. I have tasted and experienced the "Good Life" and it is more than I ever imagined—leaving me forever changed.

# OCTOBER 27

Recovery has opened a door to love that I never saw before. It has allowed me to walk through it and begin to grasp a love of life that is accepting and broad. My notions of love have typically been very rigid. They were framed in themes of loyalty, self-righteous ownership, blind duty or perhaps the unquestionable love of family. These were the things that were the ends of life, the results or rewards of my successful pursuit of life. Being so utterly focused on only the results of my actions led me down a slippery slope of moral decline and lost values. As addiction took over I found I couldn't lower my standards fast enough to keep up with each new bottom that arrived. I became less and less able to look at how I lived and lost complete sight of why I lived. Today I am able to appreciate a deeper love of life itself, the means of life rather than its ends. Through the slow process of learning to accept and love myself I began to find a love of the imperfect, the incorrect, the flawed, and the failed. Having a love of life is today a much broader and deeper proposition, a sort of magical pair of glasses that allows me to see the love that is life that is almost always present in some form, no matter what the circumstance or event. It enables and invigorates my participation and connection with the fundamental purpose and goodwill of our shared human experience together.

# OCTOBER 28

Recovery asks me to form new habits based on new ways of thinking about myself and the world around me. In early recovery I struggled for quite a while as I tried to grab ahold of these changes because I had not fully let go of my old ways. It took time for me to be able to really believe in the ideas of recovery that were being presented to me. I struggled to understand and believe that they were valid for me. It took a lot of slow and tentative trial and error before I was truly able to let go of the old and grab onto the new. I fully discovered the truth in the statement that, "Half measures availed us nothing."[21] Looking back now it seems so odd that I would want to hold onto things that were so negative in my life but I think it was because in many ways I wasn't able to believe that I could actually have a better life. The repeated failures of addiction had left me without hope or belief. Overcoming that situation was a long haul and provided one of the lessons that I have learned to rely on heavily—time takes time. There is no magic donut that will provide the lessons of recovery and it took me time to slowly learn them in ways that connected with my own experiences and thinking. Today I realize that we are all fully qualified and 100% eligible for recovery no matter how bad our lives have become. I see clearly how there is always opportunity for more lessons and improvement for me on the path of spiritual growth—that this is my life experience, mine alone, and that obviously I can pursue it. After all, no one else is going to live my life for me now that I am free from addiction.

# OCTOBER 29

There is a certain comfort that arrives for me when I simply focus on doing the next right thing that is in front of me without spending too much time worrying about how I can control or affect longer term outcomes. I know that I have a choice, an opportunity, to do the tasks of today to the best of my ability. This focus on living in the now of life allows me to avoid wasting the time of today in ways that aren't productive or helpful. The angst of negative thinking, created when I try to predict the future by projecting forward the negative outcomes of the past, prevents me from creating positive history today. The hope of recovery and of life doesn't require that I quantify, predict, or try to arrange the timely arrival of things that I want or think I need. It instead quietly reassures me that by doing a good job today I will advance a little bit further along a path of positive growth and progress. Allowing negative thinking to create a negative outcome takes no courage. It fuels my faithless, fearful, and insecure need to control and distances me from the principles of recovery. This balance between positive and negative, between fear and faith, between control and trustful open-mindedness creates freedom from my disease and represents the daily work of sustaining my recovery. Remaining positive and hopeful often takes great courage when facing life's challenges and it always strengthens and deepens my connection to a meaningful spirituality and faith in life.

---

[21] Ibid. P. 59.

# OCTOBER 30

Today I see my own experience clearly—the past, present, and possible yet unwritten future of my own story—and I am in the middle of it. The biography of my own existence surrounds me and I tend to view the world with me at its center. However it's hard for me to understand my life when I view it only from this perspective. The world and society that I live in have a profound effect on my reality. Am I in the city or the countryside? Did I attend a good school or grow up in a loving household? Is my family tradition one of poverty or wealth? Are there good jobs nearby or are many people out of work? All these factors are part of the history and structure of the world in which my life exists and I must see how the two relate in order to have a fuller understanding of its meaning. When my view of the world is confined to my own circles of understanding, the facts of my own knowledge and truth, then I am less likely to gain a new perspective that increases my worldview. It is when I encounter things that are perhaps beyond my understanding or beliefs, when I remain open to possibilities that seem impossible, that I truly become open to the realm of the spiritual. I must look outside myself and my own truths of today to increase my ability to find the deeper truths of spirituality that grow my conscious contact with God. Today, the crux of my spiritual growth centers on the ability to navigate between the larger worldview and that of my own personal experience in a way that gives context and meaning to my life. Having a spiritual connection with the world around me provides a gateway to a perspective that eases and enriches my daily life.

# OCTOBER 31

The trick or treat world of being able to wear a costume and in one day get lots of free candy exists only for children—but the lesson it shares persists throughout the modern consumer culture. The frame of our media driven world focuses on unrealistic outcomes and creates expectations that breed dissatisfaction and confusion when I fall into the trap of believing that they are completely real. For most people, life simply doesn't work that way. Many people I know work very hard and make good choices in their lives yet struggle to get by. A "get rich quick" mentality coupled with the myth of widespread economic mobility leaves many people frustrated, despondent, and demoralized. In early recovery I wanted to operate from a similar framework by hoping for great spiritual progress in a matter of months as I quickly worked the steps. What I've learned is that time takes time and progress has arrived for me in many ways, sometimes quite quickly and other times agonizingly slowly, but ultimately it is all about an ongoing journey rather than the attainment of a point of completion. The practice of spirituality is an art that offers me the chance to improve over time but with an often varying degree of success. What is important is that I practice each day. In this way I am able to not only look back and see progress but also better understand the meaning and purpose of my daily life in a frame that is realistic and free from confusing expectations created by the alluring "trick or treat" candy of the modern marketing driven society around me.

# November

"The resting place of the mind is the heart. The only thing the mind hears all day is clanging bells and noise and argument, and all it wants is quietude. The only place the mind will ever find peace is inside the silence of the heart. That's where you need to go."
— Elizabeth Gilbert

"The function of prayer is not to influence God, but rather to change the nature of the one who prays."
— Søren Kierkegaard

The poverty in the West is a different kind of poverty — it is not only a poverty of loneliness but also of spirituality. There's a hunger for love, as there is a hunger for God."
— Mother Teresa

# NOVEMBER 1

There are many ways in which I can find a spiritual connection to the world around me. That connection also exists in the biography of my own experience within it. My life has been full of experiences and memories and many of them are powerful and pleasant reminders of the spiritual nature that is part of living life. In addiction I became trapped in a cycle of false memories and make believe stories that keep me isolated and disconnected from everything. Life became the same hopeless, dreary, and shabby story told a dozen similar ways. The story followed a familiar path, a false promise and shallow belief of a good time based on an unrealistic expectation that always turned for the worse and ended badly. I repeatedly demonstrated that there are few problems in life that a few drinks can't make worse as I wondered how I had ended up in abject defeat yet again. Living in recovery allows me to remember and reconnect to the meaningful spiritual experiences of my past while I am at the same time participating in similar ones in the present. This boundless range of human experience is powerful and profound. Sometimes it thoughtful, reflective, happy or carefree, sometimes sad or melancholy, but it is the collective memory of these similar experiences that can offer me choice in how I live my life today. Recovery brings me closer to my own spiritual capital delivering its experience and expertise into my daily life and allowing me to more easily offset and balance the accounts of my life in addiction. Today I can better realize when I am feeling a lack of spiritual connection, take a little break, and through a variety of simple ways reconnect to the basic spiritual underpinnings of my life that help me navigate through the often tiring, difficult, and confusingly frustrating day to day experiences that are always a part of life on life's terms.

# NOVEMBER 2

The experience of spiritual growth in recovery helps me better learn how to be honest with myself about myself. My human capacity for self-delusion and wishful thinking was of course exaggerated extremely by active addiction but it still persists for me in many ways. Recovery allows me a chance to build honest open relationships with other men who at times are willing to care more about me than my feelings. There have been many times when I was confronted by the honest opinion of other friends and I had to reconsider my own thinking as a result. This sort of honest friendship helps me develop important skills and experience that guide a deeper understanding my own motives, fears, and self-deceptions. Sometimes it was very painful and difficult while other times it was simply a helpful chance to view a situation or belief from an alternate and more realistic viewpoint. It is a two way street and today I am able to be honest with others about what I see. In order to have a friend I must be a friend and I've learned that a real friend is kind yet honest and direct about sharing his views. For me it is not about my opinion and being right or wrong. It is about taking the time to be considerate, thoughtful and plainly truthful about what I see going on and sharing how my own experiences relate to similar situations that others are working through. This shared process of spiritual growth underlines the important truth that spirituality is always grounded in community and friendship.

# NOVEMBER 3

When I think back to those first days and months of early recovery I can still feel the cold serious chill of fearful confusion and hesitancy. The problems I arrived with were significant and I questioned if I could really free myself from them. The relationship I tried to form with a Higher Power was framed in desperation and fear as I struggled to find hope where I had only hopelessness. It wasn't a lighthearted situation at all. I chuckle today as think about how my relationship to a Higher Power has grown and changed. As recovery has freed me from the dark oppression of addiction I once again see the humor and lightness of life. There is a certain comedy to my Higher Power's world that today I can share in. The fun side of life had been returned and I can be playful and lighthearted with others, and perhaps most importantly, with myself. As the famously quoted joke goes, there is only one rule in Alcoholics Anonymous and that is rule #62, "Don't take yourself too damn seriously."[22] Today I can laugh at my flaws and foibles without fearing they will kill me. I have seen how my Higher Power has led me to an improved and changed life and I have confidence in the ongoing journey that lets me laugh at my own imperfections as I continue to walk life's endless path of progress.

# NOVEMBER 4

Recovery has taught me how to live each day for its own purpose. I have no idea how my future will ultimately unfold, however, I do understand

[22] *Twelve Steps and Twelve Traditions.* New York: Alcoholics Anonymous World Services, 1981. P.149

the simple fact that today is the only day I ever get to really live in. The today that is here now is where I spend my entire life and in recovery I have the chance to value and participate in each day as its own unique opportunity. This is such a contrast to how I lived in addiction when each day became a foggy blur punctuated by miserable and traumatic events that soon rolled past into an ever growing slideshow of vague horrors—any one of which a regular person would have been shocked into action by but which for me were just random scenes in an endless bland and grey world. The zombie like life of addiction was defined by a lack of any higher purpose or meaning that consumed each day to the point that even their names didn't matter. Who cared what day it was? It didn't really matter. Recovery offered me the escape from a lifeless existence and brought color, meaning and purpose back into the world of each my days. By choosing to live well according values and morals my actions provide esteem and worth as I add another day to the journey that my Higher Power has placed in front of me. This morning I prayed for God to direct my thinking and help me live this day well. As I look back I can see how these days add up and create progress in my life. I know I am heading in the right direction without having to know the exact destination. The daily commitment to faith in the relationship with my Higher Power shows me how to find the value of my entire life within the journey of a single day—today.

# NOVEMBER 5

Learning how to live life on life's terms has meant changing my own. This simple fact has opened the door to great change in how I view myself and the world around me. I am no longer able to live in the illusion of having all the answers because the experience of addiction and recovery has shown me the fallacy of such thinking. As I've gotten past the fear of being wrong, of not having all the answers and let go of the unrealistic notions of what being a man is all about I've been able to move towards a much deeper and meaningful understanding of who I am while broadening and maturing my view of what being a man is all about. It is hard sometimes to reflect on how are far from the truth I was for so many years but the reality of spiritual growth requires that I keep my attention on the future I am creating through my life today. I must learn to let go of my fascination with the past so that I can continue the journey of recovery in ways that bring meaning and growth into the framework of my actions and thoughts today. Understanding that I don't set the terms for how my world arrives each day frees me to work on the opportunity and solutions of today's challenges rather than needlessly determining their definition or causes.

# NOVEMBER 6

My decisions and choices during my days in addiction were usually spectacularly awful. At the time I was keen to avoid accepting responsibility for them and found all sorts of ways to blame others for the problems I was creating. In the end there was no avoiding reality as the consequences of my actions overwhelmed even my most skillful attempts at self-denial. At a certain point the accumulation of wreckage in life become so evident that I could no longer deny that I was the problem and my thinking shifted into a resigned acceptance of the hopelessness of my condition. Recovery in a way allowed me to begin again and I did so quite timidly. Not surprisingly I was quite wary of life and my own ability to make good choices. I at last learned how to follow direction and not fight against life. As those early months of recovery have become years my confidence in making good choices has grown. Today I am more able to safely follow my heart and allow my individual character to express itself in ways that often require a lot of courage. I have gained a new understanding of my own right to be me as I participate more fully in the experience of life. My dreams and horizons have returned and I have a moral underpinning that allows me to make the choices and take the risks of pursuing them without fear of not being good enough. I will not always succeed in my efforts but today I am clear about my eligibility to be an honest part of God's world.

# NOVEMBER 7

I was chatting with a friend about growing old and he joked that in the game of human life Father Time remains undefeated. Just as I cannot escape my own mortality, or the changing of the seasons, there is no way for me to avoid the limits of my own ability to control the world around me. Instead, my only option is the choice to develop and improve my ability to go with its flow. The intersection of my will to control and the frontier of my ability to do so leaves me standing at the edge confronted with a profound choice. Am I willing to accept the things I cannot change and work on those things that I can change? In my addiction I constantly battled with life to force my will upon it and create the outcomes I desired. My alcoholism smashed any ideas of my power or entitlement to direct others as I faced the crushing realization that I couldn't even control my own drinking. I fought this truth as successfully as a man trying to stop the turn of the tide or the changing of the season. The spiritual lessons of recovery help me become rightsized in the scale of human life and provide perspective about my own small yet important part of the many generations of people who all must learn to flow with the inevitable changes that time brings through history to our own doorstep. Recovery has shown me how to accept the continuous process of change with acceptance, grace, and purpose.

# NOVEMBER 8

Living in the moment is an interesting proposition that continues to expand in meaning and experience for me. I recently enjoyed a class on "mindfulness" that emphasized the goal of being present and fully participating in what is taking place in the "now" of my life. I am reminded of how I can sometimes be driving and suddenly realize that I've gone off course following some other route I often take. Or better still; suddenly realize that I have no actual recollection of my driving for the past few minutes. Examples like these demonstrate that clearly I am sometimes not fully present in the activity of driving. A realization that is rather disturbing when I consider how it offers clues about how I may not be fully present in other areas without even knowing it. I can also experience this in my conversations with others when I find myself realizing I've no idea what someone just said to me because I was thinking of something else. Often times when I actively listen with focus and intent I see and hear not only what the other person is saying, but connect more deeply with what they are meaning. It seems that much of my life experience offers a chance to be more present in the moment in ways that allow me to find deeper meaning and see more of what is right in front me. The goal of spiritual growth propels me toward the slowing down and exploration that is required to ensure that I am more fully present in my own life—to be mindfully aware of the ocean of reality that resides below the surface of my daily experience.

# NOVEMBER 9

Recovery has shown me how to not only understand but to also enjoy the crucial and transformative difference between loneliness and solitude that arrives with sustained periods of recovery. From early on in my youth I can remember a certain discomfort with solitude. I was ill at ease with myself during quiet times and rarely enjoyed or valued periods of reflection or the difficult internal questions that often came with it. My response was to avoid it through any means—and getting loaded was the best way. The failure of personal development and normal maturation that resulted from my early entry into addiction left me with a mysterious gap between the general, undeveloped, and basic ideas of who I was and what I thought I stood for that was in constant conflict with the reality of how I was living my life. The chasm between the justifications I relied on in my mind and the underlying vague truths I felt in my heart swiftly opened up and become flooded with confusing feelings of guilt and shame that further propelled my addictions. The process of working the steps and pursuing spiritual growth has allowed to at last do the hard work of truly learning who I am and what I stand for in life. It has also shown me ways to understand and achieve them that resolve and transcend the guilt and shame of my past. The disconnect between my core beliefs and my actions has been closed as I have grown in my ability to live life in a way that brings esteem and value. The result is that today, quiet times and periods of reflection and meditation are when some of my most enjoyable and meaningful life experiences take place. The pleasure I feel as a result of being an active part of the spiritual connectedness to my place is the world brings a profound contentment.

# NOVEMBER 10

The crazy cycle of addiction brought a roller coaster of extremes to my life. I could shift with ease between an exaggerated belief in my own importance and worth to a despairing self-doubt and shameful guilt in a matter of minutes. The framework of all or nothing was always excessive, dramatic, and reflected the nature of addiction with its inherent highs and lows. Learning how to be a regular guy meant letting go of both sides of this good guy/bad guy dynamic which was ultimately a symptom of ego and pride. In order to somehow justify my addictive actions I needed to be anything but regular, after all, "if you had my problems you'd drink/use like this too." Recovery, and particularly the process of the steps, has helped open the door to an understanding and insight that allows me to take my place as simply another man among men who works to remain in the middle ground. I am not all that bad, nor am I all that good. I am committed to my values and morals and making spiritual progress. There has been a meagre amount of humility for me in becoming "right-sized" about my place in the world and gaining a better grasp on who I am and what is true about my life. Today, the extreme highs and lows are few and far between and the arrival of a spiritual awakening has tempered those ego driven ideas of exceptionalism and uniqueness. The often unrecognized need and effort to prove to others that I am good enough has been replaced with a soft and stable acceptance that who I am today is enough. That I am enough.

# NOVEMBER 11

Taking responsibility for my own actions in life has been a ticket to freedom from the peculiar mental twists of my own addictive thinking. Recovery has shown me in life that if I'm not the problem then I have no solution. For many years in addiction my childish thinking viewed the idea of personal responsibility as some sort of burden that life was trying to impose on me. In my mind I mocked those "normies" who conformed to the rules and were missing out on the excitement and full flavor of life. The misplaced belief that I was superior, a crucial and implicit yet unconscious way of covering up my feelings of inadequacy, found a convenient home in the world of partying and addiction. Of course when everything went wrong either nothing was ever my fault, or it was all my fault—but rarely did I have the courage to face the core questions about who I was and how my own choices, my approach to life, were at the root of my problems The process of growing up emotionally that recovery has led me through has shown me how to be a man for my own sake and no one else's. I have taken full ownership of my life and how I live it—no longer relying on a childlike disconnection from this core human responsibility. I take the task of my own life somewhat seriously because I must. After all, I'm a grown man and no one else can, or will, do it for me—and if I don't take myself seriously then how can I expect anyone else to?

# NOVEMBER 12

At one time in my life I had gone for many years without any drinking. Over the course of those years my understanding and grasp of the memory of the various compelling reasons that had caused me to stop drinking had faded. One day, in a fairly innocuous way, I suffered that "strange mental blank spot" they talk about in the Big Book.[23] The idea that it would be ok for me to have a drink arrived in my mind and I agreed. In hindsight I remember an almost out of body experience as I somehow realized the gravity of what I was doing while I watched myself do it—unable to cut through the fog of my actions. Within hours, despite nearly seventeen years of abstinence from alcohol, I was blindly drunk and behaving insanely. I stayed that way for several years afterwards. What I realize today is that I had failed to maintain the fitness of my sobriety. Today, as a result of this

---

[23] *Alcoholics Anonymous : The Story of How Many Thousands of Men and Women Have Recovered from Alcoholism.* 4th ed. New York City: Alcoholics Anonymous World Services, 2001. P. 42.

experience, I am clearly conscious of the need to work on my sobriety every day in order to ensure that the next time my alcoholic mind tries to convince me its ok to take a drink I am prepared and ready. The truth I know today is that my sobriety is measured in a daily increment. I must be vigilant each and every day in order to sustain the spiritual awakening that keeps my connection to the "sunlight of the spirit" in place and allows me to keep my sobriety intact. [24]

# NOVEMBER 13

The beginning of recovery came when I was at last able to fully admit that I was an addict and alcoholic and also become willing to surrender to the idea of letting go of my old way of life. I often speak about how I was unable to grab hold of a new life until I completely let go of my old one. There was a part of me that fought to the bitter end the idea that I must let go of my childish selfishness and grow up. My sense of entitlement was profound and I clung to it tightly. I wanted to bargain and negotiate some sort of partial compromise what would allow me to bring parts of my old life with me. I learned that having a Higher Power with whom I am honest is rather like being pregnant. There is no partial measure. You either are or you are not. Once I had made the full concession and started really doing recovery the battle become one of sustaining that commitment. More than once I came very close to relapse however I quickly became quite stable and then found that my struggles were centered on the path of self-discovery that recovery offers as I learned to live sober rather than simply trying to stay sober. Over time I became more comfortable with understanding that the journey was centered on an inside path rather than an external one. My goals shifted from the specific to the more general as I deepened an understanding of the expression that recovery is an "inside job" that occupies the measure of my journey not my destination.

# NOVEMBER 14

There are many ideas that in some way seem to have become clichés in recovery. As I progress along the spiritual path of growth it's interesting to reflect on how these clichés can show me the change that has taken place. While the sayings are repeated regularly and continue to express the same unchanging adage—the way I think about them has changed. Often quite

---

[24] ibid. P. 66.

surprisingly so. Over time I have grown better able to understand their meaning and have had experiences in recovery that demonstrate their underlying truth in ways that are personally informing. The idea that "The mind that got you here won't be the one that fixes you" is a good example. Early on I interpreted it as a comment that underscored how my own mind was clouded and unhealthy after years of addiction and that in time it would clear up and guide me to recovery. While it is true that my brain has cleared from the effects of sustained substance abuse, the deeper understanding I have today is that it is my Higher Power that ensures my recovery. The critical change hasn't been the physical healing of my brain. What has changed is the way in which I view the world and an ability to connect myself with a sense of spirituality that was largely absent from my thinking when I arrived. Whenever I am trying to force my will upon the world it seems that I am in conflict with a power much greater than myself. Recovery has helped me learn how to become part of the spiritual world around me in a way that is smooth and natural. I am no longer always fighting to exert my own design into the world around me but instead can flow with the will of my Higher Power. My mind, clearly, isn't the one that I arrived with nor has it fixed me. However, it does help me stay on the correct path in life—one that is connected to a sense of spirituality and Higher Power that does offer me a solution and keeps me free from the willful self-destruction of addiction and despair.

# NOVEMBER 15

My addictive nature is prone to extremes and excessive thinking that often have the effect of distorting my view of what is really going on in my life. I can easily succumb to denial or excessive dissatisfaction. As a man I often feel compelled to be strong and in control about the struggles that are part of all our lives. I can see my role as being the one to fix a situation or to solve a problem—to make things better. However many of the most difficult problems in life aren't ones that I alone can solve. This is a situation which in the past has led me toward the convenient oblivion of addiction in order to escape my powerlessness. Spiritual growth allows me to understand there is no valid path away from the difficulties of life through the escape of addictive behavior or substance abuse. In recovery I've learned to be more honest with myself about what is going on and yet this clarity often increases the need to stop and consider how my feelings and emotions may be out of balance. It is vital that I remain linked to an accurate grasp of my feelings and emotions rather than falling into the trap of a childlike search for a perfection that never exists. When I face what it really going on I am then able to connect to a sense of acceptance and participate in a relationship with a Higher Power that offers a path to acceptance and coexistence with the always present struggles of life. Learning to live in the real world on a more spiritual basis offers a validation of my existence regardless of the unavoidable unfairness and pain of life. It opens the door to finding ways to live that provide meaning and value through actions like service, meditation, and other healthy activities that connect me to the always available spiritual reality of daily life. In living my life in meaningful ways I avoid the grey darkness of gloom, doom, and dread that accompany the isolation of selfishness. Over time I have become less likely to obsess with or become overly focused on the endless array of problems in the world that are beyond my ability to impact. Pain and suffering are an unavoidable part of all human life and I am not some sort of special exception to the experience of difficult feelings and personal struggles. However, today I am able to use them as a reason to connect with a Higher Power rather than an excuse to avoid one.

# NOVEMBER 16

In early recovery I disliked birthday meetings for many reasons—like getting yet another 30 day coin/chip while knowing it wasn't entirely valid. The coins had that saying on them, "To thine own self be true," which seemed like salt in the wound of my failure to stay sober.[25] Ultimately it represented what was the greatest challenge of my early recovery—learning how to be honest with myself and my Higher Power. It was impossible for me to have a relationship with a Higher Power until I was willing to be honest with myself about it. It opened the door to yet another new truth— that it was hard for me to be true to myself when I didn't know myself. Years of addiction had distorted my understanding of self. I'd done and become things I couldn't understand or justify as my addiction worsened and I moved farther away from who I had been. It was no wonder that I had trouble being honest with myself. After all perhaps no one really wants to take a good hard look at themselves when they know that what they will find there is troublesome and ugly. Recovery has been a slow process of finding the inner values and integrity that allows me to live in a way that is true to my understanding of the spiritual world my Higher Power provides. Today I can look anyone in the eyes and calmly accept them for who they are because today I accept myself for who I am.

---

[25] Cantor, Paul A. *Shakespeare, Hamlet*. 2nd ed. Landmarks of World Literature. Cambridge ; New York: Cambridge University Press, 2004., Act 1 Scene 3

# NOVEMBER 17

It is fair to say that during my years in addiction taking care of myself in healthy ways wasn't a priority. I certainly wasn't fit spiritually, mentally, socially or physically. In recovery I've become more aware of how my physical health is just as important as my mental health. Mind and body are two sides of the same coin and the health of one certainly affects the other. While my early focus in recovery was of course simply staying sober, over time I began to work on other important considerations. I soon began to consider how devious and subtle my addictive nature really was in terms of the many ways in which I struggled with powerlessness. Quitting smoking cigarettes, beginning to exercise and lose weight, learning how to meditate and find quiet reflective time while on walks or gardening are all ways that I can demonstrate how I belong and participate in life. The sense of being responsible and accountable for how I conducted myself provided some of the earliest lessons in the areas of understanding how I alone can set the boundaries of my behavior that are based on my own values, morals, and beliefs. And, that these are not rigid things. They can, and will, change as I continue make progress in my own path of recovery. For me, recovery is more than simply staying sober and going to meetings. It is about expressing myself through healthy living that reflects the meaningful results of an active spiritual connection with my Higher Power.

# NOVEMBER 18

I will not forget the hopelessness of addiction. As my disease progressed I cycled down through stages of despair and circumstances that always continued to get worse. The unacceptable actions of a year ago become the better days of last month as I fell lower into an abyss of dread and pitiful remorse. The reach of any hope I might have had continued to be reduced—crushed repeatedly by my own actions. One of the first elements of recovery that I remember was the rekindling of hope. Like a trembling tenuous candle flame the idea that somehow I could begin to recover and make a new life, that it was something that could happen for me, began to become real. As I look back today I realize that in a few quick years of recovery my life changed dramatically in many ways. Through faith in a Higher Power and the steps of recovery I've been shown that the reality of life ahead of me is beyond what I can ever imagine. I have learned to no longer fear hope because I am living my life in a way that creates a proper foundation for life. I don't have to know what is coming or try to force life into my design. Instead I work on ensuring that my daily life is in order so that the door to hope, and what the future will bring, remains open and available. In this way I ensure the progress of tomorrow through the actions of today.

# NOVEMBER 19

When I close my thoughts and ideas off from other people I run the risk of my thinking becoming circular, unbalanced, distorted, and obsessive. The more I hear myself think things, the more real they become. The process tends to reinforce and exaggerate my fears and anxieties. It usually creates a self-inflicted hubris and excessive overconfidence of understanding and perception—for good or bad—that becomes increasingly out of touch with what is real in my life. I become all wound up about ideas and experiences in a way that is entirely out of proportion. There are many times when I have spent hours rationalizing a certain plan or idea and then as soon as the words come out of my mouth I realize that they are ridiculous—they only seemed like a good idea while they resided in my mind. They were a great idea right up to the moment I opened my mouth. Sharing my thoughts, ideas, and experiences with another person, a friend or mentor, helps me keep my thinking grounded and right-sized. It offers me new perspectives, more context, and solutions or suggestions from another viewpoint. This is perhaps part of why there is truth in the old saying that, "a problem shared is halved and a joy shared is doubled." Remaining alone with my own troubled thinking usually results in me trying to fix a problem with the same tool that is creating it.

# NOVEMBER 20

Each morning I kneel down and connect with the God of my understanding—the spiritual element of human life that is always present. I acknowledge how grateful I am. I am thankful and ask again for help today with living another day well. I accept the belief that there is a spiritual guide inside us all, and that this is part of the nature of being human. Appreciation of the mountains or the sea, the love I can clearly between two people I don't know or the fall leaves in the crisp morning light; all serve to enliven the connection to this part of me that I share with the billions of human souls who have lived before me and all those who will come after me. This powerful feeling of connection is the polar opposite of the most central part of life in addiction—the crushing isolation and aloneness that is ever present and relentless. Recovery allowed me to end this isolation and replace it with connection—connection to others and a power greater than myself that is always available. Despite the sometimes seemingly meaningless parts of my life and the powerlessness of my own place in the world—the immortality of my humanness brings a responsibility and knowledge that requires no study or learning. It only requires that I be willing to allow myself a connection to it. Once I am aware and open it leads me, filling my head with faith and my heart with love, as I take my place today in the gift of human life.

# NOVEMBER 21

History shows that finding balance between the natural human needs of self-reliance and the slippery slope of self-centeredness is often difficult to do very well on one's own. For an addict like me it represents a fatal flaw that drives my disease. Addiction blinds me to my own part in the problem and disables my ability to react to it. By trying to find and sustain a solution using the very tool that is creating the problem I simply repeat and reinforce the cycle of self-centeredness while preventing progress toward a healthy solution. The old saying that "two eyes are better than one" points to a more realistic approach that allows help from outside of my own thinking. This basic premise of recovery, that it is a "we" program, continues to be a fundamental component of my ongoing spiritual growth. The mind that created my problems isn't going to be the mind that solves them. I must find new sources of knowledge, experience, and insight that help me change the mind that I arrived with. I must be open-minded and willing to consider new ideas when I hear them, to seek out new solutions and approaches to my problems when my existing ones are no longer working. By listening to others and allowing their perspective to assist me I find solutions to my problems that aren't clouded by my own unclear, selfish, dishonest, and deluded motives and thinking. I often tried to control my drinking so that it wouldn't be as big a problem but of course ultimately it was the problem. I couldn't fix my drinking problem with my own approach to better drinking. The same holds true for my thinking. The solution requires the help of a Higher Power, and friends in recovery, to guide me.

# NOVEMBER 22

In the natural world most things rarely stop growing or changing. As they say back home, "The only difference between a rut and a grave is the dirt on top." I often seem to want to fight change rather than accept it. Perhaps the problems in my life that were caused by addiction have left me wary.

Perhaps they are a result of my fear of the lack of control that is often an inherent part of change. Either way, if I can accept that change is a constant then the question centers on which ways I extend the boundaries of what I know and believe. Recovery offers me the opportunity to see how other people explore this path of growth and how their values shape their morals. I can see how they, and other people who I admire, live their lives. This helps me to understand my own values and moral boundaries. I have come to believe today, that in general, if I don't take the choices about how I live my life seriously I undercut my own feeling of value and participation in the world around me. In order for me to be a man I enjoy seeing in the mirror in the morning I must do the work of taking meaningful thought and action. I can no longer sit in the moral discomfort that arises from my own actions and say, "Oh well, that's just the way I am." In order to actively pursue the goals and outcomes of the eleventh step I must continue to explore and grow the values, morals, and spirituality that form the house of my daily life.

# NOVEMBER 23

The search for my place in life, and the sense of meaning and purpose that comes with it, seems to take a path that is somewhat circular. It follows a pattern that starts with my own view and understanding of the world around me. It moves outward into the shared experience and participation of life and then returns to my own reflection, reconciliation and growth. The context of my travels guide the results and upon each return I review who I am relative to the world around me—and I have the chance to experience personal change and growth. When my search is based on meeting my needs through external measures of life like wealth, prestige, and control I learn little about who I really am. When my path is guided by an internal sense of a spiritual need then the result is a greater understanding of my place in the world. I return to myself with new ideas about what it means to be me that are different from the understandings I had when I began. The process of working the steps and finding new ways to experience and understand my place in the world has profoundly changed how I view myself today. It has opened new opportunities for my future and perhaps most importantly it has allowed me to experience a profound change in how I view my past so that my present is no longer controlled or dominated by it. Overcoming the blockages of guilt and shame that are rooted in my past enables me to transform their meaning and reframe their role in my life. I can truly see how my past uniquely qualifies me to work with others and create value where there was once only hopelessness.

# NOVEMBER 24

In my life today I've learned that feeling good about myself in a lasting way begins with an honest review and acceptance of my own morals. I must value them and relate them to my choices and actions. In addiction I regularly took actions that were counter to my own beliefs about what I knew was right and how I should live my life. The pursuit of things that are morally questionable to bring temporary relief from my unhappiness is not the same as increasing my happiness—it instead creates shameful consequences that deepen my despair. It is a circle of growth that can spin in either a positive or negative direction depending on how honest I am about my motives. In addiction my motives were always, at the most basic level, suspect and self-serving. They resulted in actions that created a self-view that was demeaning, callous, and shameful. Recovery has shown me how to create self-respect and esteem by avoiding actions that I know I ought not to do. When I pursue the "Good Life" I can then feel better about myself which in turn opens the door to my ability to enjoy the happiness that is always present in life. Doing the things I ought to moves my life in a positive direction. Feeling good about who I am begins with my own good actions and helps me take measure of the man I am today. It opens the door to a better understanding and expanding view of who I can be tomorrow.

# NOVEMBER 25

When I am confronted with the consequences of my addictive behavior it is usually a shameful and painful moment. It strikes to heart of my own sense of self and I squirm in self-loathing. My first reaction is often to find a way to deny the truth. This was the response that kept me ill for years, trapped in a repeating pattern with the same results. As the results of each repetition added up, the wall around my addiction grew higher and more difficult to look over. The powerful ability of honesty to pierce through the denial of addiction is always the crucible of my moment of choice. Shall I face the strain and chose the path of growth and progress offered by my Higher Power or will I instead ignore the truth and cover it up with spurious justifications and self-pity? Recovery has shown me that the dramatic moments of early recovery are powerful yet represent simply the first of many moments when I am faced with my own human imperfections. When I honestly accept my flaws I no longer have to run from them. It opens the door to a maturity and self-awareness that allows me to welcome such difficult moments as opportunities that can help me grow. They are starting points of continued progress—not places to sit and dwell. They remind me of my humanness and my connection with a Higher Power and others so that I can continue on with the progress, not perfection, of recovery.

# NOVEMBER 26

In early recovery it often felt like I didn't really have much to be thankful for and I was often pretty ungrateful. Sobriety allowed the chance for my head to clear and I was confronted with a clear view of the wreckage I had created in my life. It seemed unrelenting and hopeless. It took me several attempts to be able to get past this point and accept the hope and faith that the experience of recovery, that I knew had taken place for others, could and would also take place for me. The challenge became centered on learning how to build and utilize a functional reliance upon a Higher Power. As my own recovery become real I began to accumulate small examples of the ways in which a Higher Power was working in my life—examples that I was truly thankful for. I began to develop gratitude for a Higher Power that was rooted in actual experience rather than theory or the stories of others. Today I try to be grateful to my Higher Power through my daily actions. Gratitude it is a part of how I live my life rather than a collection of specific things I am thankful for. For me it is one of the most fundamental elements of how, "The spiritual life is not a theory. We have to live it."[26]

# November 27

Sometimes I struggle to keep things simple in my life. It often seems like there are so many forces that push or pull me in one direction or another. Choices I've made in the past, or perhaps even yesterday, determine the events of today and I can feel a bit trapped or overwhelmed. Perhaps I've not achieved some goal I set for myself and I become overly focused on things I can't really control—things that perhaps haven't even happened yet. Things that may never happen! Of course in active addiction this sort of thinking and "awfulizing" was constantly present. I was always obsessing about what seemed to be an endless cycle of complicating even the most simple of situations into a thousand stories about what was going to happen or the many possible ways to explain some of the things that had already

[26] *Alcoholics Anonymous : The Story of How Many Thousands of Men and Women Have Recovered from Alcoholism.* 4th ed. New York City: Alcoholics Anonymous World Services, 2001. P. 83.

happened. Situations were baffling as I searched for some sort of secret meaning or inferred message that wasn't ever there. Spirituality helps me put down the crystal ball of my self-absorbed mind and become more present in the moment that is going on today. There are basic truths that I understand today about who I am, where I have been, and how my faith in the future is centered on principles not specifics. Taking a deep breath, relaxing, and letting go of my worries allows me to enjoy what I have today. I can be thankful for my life as it is and trust in God's plan for me.

# NOVEMBER 28

A willingness to redefine my understanding and acceptance of what it is to be a man can be quite an abstract proposition. It is often hard to relate to my everyday life. I can think about traditional roles of manhood, for example the classically stoic and patriarchal provider for the family who is defined by his work or background. There are many of these simple and traditional frames and stereotypes that are familiar but often quite limiting. Expanding my life into other areas of relationships and activities broadens my perspective and allows room for growth. If happiness results from the proper pursuit of life, then I've a greater chance of being happy if I have more avenues in which to live my life. By breaking out of a single frame of how I look at myself that rigidly defines my role with others I have been able to experience growth in ways that seemed very unlikely, in fact impossible, when I was in the throes of addiction. I am amazed when I look at how my life is today compared with when I arrived in recovery and the biggest change is perhaps in my thinking. For many years my thinking was centered on sustaining my habits and actions and so it is no wonder that I was suspicious and fearful of any sort of new thinking that might threaten my addiction. I was defensive and quick to shut down any sort of thinking that would open the door to meaningful changes. Today, I am open-minded about how I can participate in life. Many of the "truths" that I thought knew about myself have long since gone and been replaced with new beliefs. Change is obvious hallmark of progress in recovery. And so, my understanding of what it means to be me continues to shift and grow. When I loosen my grip on what I think I know and stay on a spiritual path I allow more of me to be revealed—it is not about good and bad, it is about being the man my Higher Power leads me toward.

# NOVEMBER 29

For many years my problems became worse, more intractable and difficult, because of my inability to be honest with myself about the choices I was making in my life. The story of my growing problems, the increasing severity of them, and the sense of inevitability of more to come dominated my thinking and ensured an ever present sense of dread and doom. Recovery has shown me new ways to face the problems in my life rather than avoiding them through denial and procrastination. While I am not always able to solve them the way I would like, learning how to at least not make them worse has been very helpful. More than anything I am able to avoid the morbid self-pity and exaggeration of problems into excuses I used to justify my absurd behavior. I am able to connect with my faith to find the calm and peaceful understanding and grace that comes with reflection about the bigger picture of life. It helps me place today's problems, worries, frustrations, fear or pain within the perspective of the larger story of my life. While today's problems often have an overwhelming sense of urgency, I am able to understand that regardless of the outcome I will be ok. That my future still lies ahead—that the inevitable low spots of life's road no longer have to define my identity or crush and remove my hope. The saying, "This too shall pass," is a reminder to avoid judging my future life based on the moments that trouble me today. Over time my problems fade while the memories of the good things in my life remain bright.

# NOVEMBER 30

There is an art to being content with myself that I must practice. There will always be some time or another when I feel badly about my actions and behavior. About how I've treated others or myself. In the past I've been fond of avoiding these truths. Recovery has shown me how this sort of self-denial is hurtful to my spiritual condition. No matter how I work to negotiate a justification, or comfort myself with denial, I ultimately still know when I've acted badly—and it sits with me, festering, and polluting my spirit until I "come clean." Mature reflection on these feelings reminds me of the powerful force of honesty that recovery begins with in Step One. Honesty with others is always good, but honesty with myself it is a lifesaving requirement. It affords me a better understanding of what action I should take to correct relationships around me. It is a process that renews the vital freedom from denial and enables the personal integrity that provides esteem. I try to softly and accurately embrace my own negative feelings, examining them in order to see what response might be indicated or to better understand how motives, expectations or anger may be involved. Too often in the past I would just beat myself up excessively as a way to avoid true reflection and thereby and miss the entire point of the exercise.

Recovery has shown me that when I have the courage to truly face my feelings the truth of my heart always triumphs over my mind's fearful and false thinking. Today, being able to like myself is a gift that I must care for and maintain through clear and honest action.

# December

"The best way to find yourself is to lose yourself in the service of others."
— Mahatma Gandhi

"Until we can receive with an open heart, we are never really giving with an open heart."
— Brené Brown

"You are what you do, not what you say you'll do."
— C.G. Jung

# DECEMBER 1

Today I am reminded of the idea that without great lows there can be no great highs—that the full measure of life brings both to my door. There have been many times in my life when I felt lost and hopeless. In my addiction, life became ever more extreme and desolate. I had very little hope at all and was increasingly resigned to living with the crushing isolation and darkness of spirit that always seemed nearby, punctuating the daily cycle of my addiction. Today I am able to look back at those difficult times and clearly see the moment when I chose to accept hope and commit to having faith in a Higher Power. Recovery has shown me how hope can bring me through most any crisis. The simple truth is that it was only when I became open to accepting that I was truly eligible for the good side of life that I was able to find a way to overcome the really bad side of my life. I had to accept that I was not in charge of what it would look like and instead be in charge of simply believing it would happen. By choosing to be open to God and living fully in faith I found much more than I ever expected. Today I see both the good and bad in life that is part of the human condition and have learned that the real tragedy is to fail to live fully, to shy away from my heart and to end up missing out on them both.

# DECEMBER 2

Taking personal responsibility was something I was often fond of talking about for others but not very good at for myself. The classic case of wanting to be judged by my intentions rather than my actions afforded me a convenient way to blame others and avoid seeing my part in the problems of my life. Recovery has shown me how to be more mature and grown up about many aspects of life and one of the most difficult lessons was the hard truth that I am responsible for how I feel. At the time things happen they may affect me—but on a daily basis it's up to me to choose how I feel. As a grown man I must remember that once the moment has passed no one "makes me" feel anything. In recovery I get to choose how I feel, react, and act in life. It is a serious task that is part of being the man I am today. Most of the persistent and challenging problems in my life are ones that I have created for myself through my own choices and decisions. For years my addictive sense of denial flourished by feeding on the idea that the people, places, and things in my life made me drink and drug. It was a self-fulfilling circle of justification that ensured my problems were never my fault. Today I am better able to see how my own mistakes and imperfections represent a never ending opportunity for me to grow and learn.

# DECEMBER 3

I can find a sort of comfortable woe in the pastime of self-pity. I have to remind myself that imperfection and struggle are simply a part of life, that it is nothing personal—it's just how life is. It is a fact of human life that there is always plenty to eat at the table of self-pity. The hubris of excessive self-absorption and addiction cuts both ways for me, to pride or to pity. It is the middle ground of reality that I am usually trying to avoid. Self-pity leads me into a comfortably controllable place of isolation where I console myself with stories of unfairness and distorted truths while blaming others for my problems, resentments, and shame. "Poor me! Poor me! Pour me another drink," as the old saying goes. Self-pity ignites and fuels the stinking thinking of dissatisfaction and judgement that leads to discontent and irritation. Gratitude is a good counter to it. Each morning when I pray I take a moment or two and remember how my life in addiction was and that I am grateful because it's not like that anymore for me. "Grateful drunks don't drink" is something my sponsor is fond of saying and the sense of gratitude that is always present as this base level of recovery helps me alleviate feelings of self-pity. Just as there is always something to feel bad about, there is always something to feel good about—and that choice always remains mine. I ask my Higher Power for help to guide my thinking in positive ways that move me toward meaningful and positive action today.

# DECEMBER 4

It has taken real courage to learn how to be honest and truthful with myself. My fears and problems are usually rooted in selfish self-centeredness and the crushing isolation it brings. Learning how I really feel, what my true motivations actually are, has only been achieved through honestly and fully sharing my thoughts with another close friend. Truth is something that I can rarely confirm alone—perhaps because the nature of honesty and understanding seems to be based in a mutual experience. It has taken time and practice to open myself to this process and get better at it. It has been the most powerful and effective form of self-discovery I've ever found. Learning how to share openly and honestly with others was hard. In the beginning it was something that was hesitating and unsure. Often I listened to my own voice as though it were a stranger's. I had to learn how to be a real friend to myself, and another person, before I began to courageously express myself in ways that allowed the powerful force of honest truth to overcome my fearful confusion and fully emerge. Over time those fearful beginnings have led me to a wonderfully comfortable practice that I enjoy and look forward to as the truths inside me are revealed. It is exciting and rewarding to learn more about who I am and to grow in new ways. It is fair to say that the self-discovery of recovery has become one of the best parts of my life today.

# DECEMBER 5

Like many people in recovery I have struggled with close relationships most of my adult life. I was unable to really open up to anyone and never learned how to fully participate in a loving and honest relationship. I was more focused on my addiction—it always came first—and I grew accustomed to the selfishness and isolation that resulted. In many ways recovery has meant learning things later than most people do. Some of these lessons are very difficult. It has been really hard work learning how to love, to be truly honest about myself, and understand and express my vulnerability. Being vulnerable in my relationships with others has required much willingness, work, and practice. It is an idea and experience that I traditionally framed as a weakness and a threat but I've learned that it is a key component for growth. The seed must crack open its hard shell for the first sprout to appear and it will be vulnerable until it grows stronger. In a close loving relationship I must honor my partner and myself. It takes courage to be honest and open with another about those deepest thoughts and feelings. But if I don't trust, open up, and risk putting myself and my real feelings out there, then I remain stuck in my shell like the seed. Learning to express my vulnerability has helped me to overcome the shame and guilt that kept me ill. It has helped me be a more mature, responsible, honest, and loving participant in healthy relationships with others.

# DECEMBER 6

In addiction my world grew very small as I withdrew into myself. Over time I was less involved with others and had little interest in the activities and pursuits that I used to enjoy. Today my world is healthier as I participate more fully with life. I believe that how we show up in other people's lives is the measure of our own spiritual fitness. How I choose to participate in life and with the world around me can make my life more full and complete. This theme of being present for my own life has widened my understanding of what life is. How I choose to spend my time, engaged with life more fully, has evolved a lot for me over the years in recovery. I find that when I bring myself to the world in a positive way I am more likely to find experiences that are rewarding, interesting, and meaningful. The truth of my life is found in the space I share with others, with nature, and with my Higher Power. What real knowledge or experience of being considerate, patient, tolerant, happy, sad, loving, or useful can I have if I don't share my life with the world around me? Without others I am left only with the illusion of who I think I am that arrives from remaining alone and apart from life. It is in the time I spend living life with the world around me—when I am actively present and participating—that I see who I really am.

# DECEMBER 7

One of the great truths of the disease of addiction is the delusional thinking that accompanies it. The handmaiden of delusion may well be illusion and for me I allowed one to convince me I was attaining the other. The delusional pursuit of an unattainable illusion in my relationships with others kept me lonely and unhappy. It created unrealistic expectations, fueled resentments, and denied the reality of human imperfection. Learning how to participate in an honest and "real" relationship with another person—working with others—is at the heart of my experience in recovery. In the past it was hard for me to be real or honest about myself or the other person. The truth was evasive and when it did appear I often denied it. When relationships become difficult, or my emotions painful, then I would disconnect from them through the fantasy world of my addiction. Unsurprisingly, until I become healthy I couldn't successfully participate in a healthy relationship. I had to learn how to love and respect myself. Understanding and accepting my own flaws, learning how to "grow up" emotionally, allowed me to understand the imperfections of others and avoid the illusory vision of perfection in relationships. It opened the door for me to be able to participate realistically in relationships—which always includes a full range of experiences. I have learned that—within any relationship—to enjoy and sustain the "good" I must also be able to withstand the inevitable flaws, difficulties, doubts, fears and imperfections that are part of the journey.

# DECEMBER 8

Recovery shows me that I don't always have to know how or why things work in order to accept that they do work. There are many things in life that

I don't need to understand—to know how they work or what they mean precisely—in order to know that they are so. To know that they are true. I was driving yesterday and Mount Rainier was so incredible. I thought of the local Indian tribes and how many generations of humans had also viewed it in awe. How in the world did it get there? How much of human life has it seen? I was reminded of a quote in a Big Book story by St Vincent Millay, "Pity me the heart that is slow to learn what the quick mind sees at every turn."[27] It calls to me to accept and enjoy what my heart feels instead of only relying on what my mind thinks and reasons. For many years I tried to think my way to a solution for my addiction and failed miserably as my situation worsened at each turn. The modern world emphasizes the scientific method that defines facts only as things that are measurable and the idea that all things can be known. The mysteries of the human condition and the natural world are larger and older than any logical thinking I can try to rely upon. To begin to overcome my addiction I didn't have to know how recovery worked. I didn't have to know why recovery worked. I just needed to know that recovery did work. Many parts of human spirituality, like the majesty of a mountain or my appreciation of a winter sunrise, defy my full understanding—yet they undeniably connect deeply to my sense of humanity.

# DECEMBER 9

Participating in life means experiencing its highs and lows and having the courage to face all that life brings. Because life will inevitably bring me pain as part of its journey it is foolish for me to try to avoid that pain by attempting to control the world around me by not living fully. As the old saying goes, "It is better to have loved and lost than to have never loved at all," and there are many ways this is true in my life. I cannot pick and choose which parts of life to live in an attempt to avoid its pain and loss because pain and loss is part of the joy of life. Accepting this paradoxical truth and learning how to live with it in a healthy way is a part of everyone's struggle. Embracing this fact has meant growing up and discarding childish ideas about fairness and fear. Because I am part of life I only cheat myself when I try to cheat life—and the result is isolation, frustration, and hopelessness. Addiction at times seemed like either a repetitive attempt to recreate a moment from the past or a way to avoid the pain of the present. Today I can understand and accept change, loss, and pain as part of the

[27] *Alcoholics Anonymous : The Story of How Many Thousands of Men and Women Have Recovered from Alcoholism. 3rd ed.* New York: Alcoholics Anonymous World Services, 1976. P. 534.

ever evolving tapestry and story of my life. Just as no man can stop the tide—none among us can prevent the cycle of life of which we are all a part. It is the acceptance of this spiritual fact, my own powerlessness in life, which brings me the strength and courage to live life more fully.

# DECEMBER 10

The modern social construct of what it really means to be a man seems overly focused on themes and ideas that aren't always helpful. Perhaps it is similar to a woman's struggle with self-image when faced with the extreme and unrealistic promotion of the "ideal" female body. I have often struggled with common ideas about manhood—notions of strength through being tough, not showing feelings, or viewing life only in the frame of "winning and losing." This type of clichéd thinking kept me away from my own feelings. By trying to live in such a one dimensional framework, with overly simplistic values, I was frustrated and ill equipped for dealing with the complex realities of human life. Today I see how my true value and strength as a man is found in my relationships with others. By knowing myself, my values and moral code, I am able to be compassionate and helpful to people, open and loving to those close to me. Chasing the ideal of the "Marlboro Man," or some other fiction, leads me away from the truth of a man's role in life. When I try to pick up ideas for life that are the product of a stereotype or fashion I am left unfulfilled and strangely discontent. They aren't really mine and I feel uncomfortable and rather like an imposter. For me, spirituality and meaningful manhood are clearly linked—they represent the key to learning and understanding the true nature of being my own man. Today I find my path through spiritual reflection that directs my thinking and prepares my ability to live in meaningful ways each day.

# DECEMBER 11

An important reminder on the path of serenity is that I must choose how I think about the troublesome problems in my life. I have no real control over the fate life brings me—but I do choose the frame that I view life's troubles within. Am I the helpless victim crying "Why me, Why me?" Or do I see problems as opportunities to grow my life skills as a man? My happiness is rooted in the acceptance of life on life's terms and faith in the validity of my own place in life—however it unfolds in front of me. This acceptance of my problems as a constructive part of life links to the idea that in recovery my addictive past has value in enabling me to help others recover. Recovery reframes my view of life's difficulties as opportunities not problems. The idea, nicely expressed by Santayana when he said, "Those who cannot remember the past are condemned to repeat it," reminds me that the troubles in my life are always lessons for growth.[28] In addiction my life was dominated by the repetition of the same sorts of mistakes and poor choices driven by unwillingness to change my thinking. In recovery I have learned how to be open-minded about my thinking, beliefs, and understanding of who I am, what I stand for, and how I conduct myself. This flexibility of outlook empowers and elevates my human capacity to flow with life rather that struggle with it.

# DECEMBER 12

I've never been eager to examine my faults. In fact I'd often rather pretend they don't exist, or if they do, that they aren't very large or noticeable. Yet, if I have a commitment to spiritual growth and self-discovery I understand that working on my faults must be a goal. It is about being honest with myself and welcoming the knowledge of my faults—discovering and accepting them. And then seeking to find the value within them. Obviously I will never have none, but they are easy for me to avoid, and even easier to minimize or dismiss. However, working the steps has shown me that until I am honest about them I'll make little progress in understanding their effects on myself and others. I may never fully correct my flaws but I can understand and mitigate them. For instance I often interrupt and talk over people, I try not to, but it still happens more than I like. What I've noticed is that when I choose to listen instead of speaking I often hear some of the most helpful and important things that I might otherwise have missed. In my recovery today, making a claim like "that's just the way I am" is no longer a valid choice for me because I see it for the excuse and self-justification it is. Self-honesty today means I no longer knowingly accommodate my denial—instead it represents opportunity for spiritual growth.

# DECEMBER 13

The idea of "detachment" in recovery is perhaps not well served by such a clinical name. It sounds cold and quite standoffish. As I have worked to

---

[28] Santayana, George. *The Life of Reason*. Great Books in Philosophy. Amherst, N.Y.: Prometheus Books, 1998.

understand and practice detachment in my relationships I've found that it brings me closer to people in powerful and meaningful ways. It is a vital part in my true participation and helpfulness in other people's lives. For many people in recovery, including myself, relationships with others were typically codependent and enmeshed because of over-attachment and a lack of proper boundaries. I can't help someone else find their truth by giving them mine and denying them the chance to develop their own. Understanding that we are each alone with our own understanding of God in our journey in life means I can stand with you but not be a part of you. Nor can I make you a part of me. Each of us must drink from our own unique cup of life. This insight has also provided a framework for understanding how my own desire to control others works. It has helped me become able to accept people for the way they are now rather than hoping, expecting, or "helping them" become something I think they should be. Playing God in the lives of others while ignoring his role in my own life was a chronic problem during my years in addiction and it continues to be subtle area of opportunity that I get to work on in recovery. I am increasingly able to step back from my desire to mansplain the world to others in ways that disguise my desire to control as help.

# DECEMBER 14

I found the obsession of addiction to be brutal and relentless. It absorbed my free time until the only time I spent not actively using was the time I spent finding ways to get back to it. Work became harder to sustain and soon I wasn't sober even there. All my life force was absorbed by addiction. It was a rut that became ever deeper as I lost sight of the exciting possibility and hope that exists in life. In recovery I've learned how to live more fully again. I have hobbies and interests that have been renewed. Removal of the zombification of addiction has allowed me to explore new ways to be creative in my life. I enjoy how creativity can exist as an expression of the reality of participating in the process of a spiritual awakening. For me, having a spiritual experience contains lots of elements of participation. It isn't about sitting around on a pillow with my legs crossed, eyes closed, and trying to force a spiritual experience. It is about interacting with the fullness of life, be it happy or sad, play or work, easy or hard. It is about trying new things and realizing that the time to explore and expand my world is always found in the today of living. Being creative in my day allows me the chance to tap into themes of growth and change that are the antithesis of my self-destructive life in addiction. Today I can connect in meaningful ways with the experience of living fully and trying to make a positive contribution to the world around me.

# DECEMBER 15

The truth of my future is found in the moments of today. Recovery has shifted the focus of my thinking away from the unknown of the future and the unchangeable events of my past into the reality and opportunity of the now. I can only live fully when I am living in the today of my life. Today, there are many things that I know are true about how my life has unfolded since becoming involved in recovery. I know it is true that since I started to get on my knees each morning—thanking God and asking for his help in living—my world keeps getting better. This truth of my reliance on a relationship with God is something I can safely hang on to. Most everything else in life is changing and often quite impossible to control. This realization allows me to cease trying to forge the world into my own design. Today I trust that when I do the right things, the simple things of living well each day, like avoiding what I know is wrong, letting go of what I know is gone and being open and flexible in my thinking about the future, life will be what it will be and I will be ok. While the events of my past remain fixed and unchanging, the framework of how I understand them today is more flexible—kinder, less judgmental and more helpful. That opportunity to better understand my past, to better grasp at the new truths of my life that emerge in the today of my spiritual awakening in recovery empower and enable a new potential for my future.

# DECEMBER 16

Sometimes the lessons I learn contain a message I don't want to hear. However, despite my often belligerent defiance, I have to grudgingly admit they make sense though. The greatest questions in my life, the ones that bring the most difficulty, are the questions that center in my heart. I feel that in so many ways recovery has allowed me to understand the great relationship that exists between the logical reasoning of my mind and the naturally intuitive feeling of my heart. In life, learning to live wholeheartedly enables me to consider the deeper questions of my part in the greater world of life around me. I have had to learn to accept and enjoy that I have questions about myself that aren't answered yet—and some that may never be answered. When I was young I thought I knew it all. Today though not so much and that's ok. The maturity that recovery brings has brought a deeper understanding of how addiction allowed my narrow, shallow, and youthful grasp of life's meaning to last far too long in my life. It has opened me up to a much wider vision and understanding. Today, I can be open to finding many examples of growth, change, and discovery in my life. Certainly I'm not the man I once was, or thought I was, or thought I would be. As long as I'm willing to be open-minded there is always more to learn. I am glad I'm no longer a grown up version of that "know it all" kid who is blindly unable to see what he doesn't know.

# DECEMBER 17

Finding purpose and meaning in life is one of those great philosophical questions that we all face. The world we live in today is very focused on personal consumption and the values of self-propulsion and reward that go hand in hand with it. In some ways my life in addiction was the ultimate extreme of this approach. I hustled everyone around me while sacrificing my morals. I valued an ability to go to any length to "get mine" and meet my own selfish needs. The result was an epic failure—a miserable and crushing isolation that was framed in a complete loss of meaning, purpose, and self-worth. My world today is a much brighter and happier place because of a shift in thinking about how I live—from a focus on selfish individual consumption to meaningful participation in the lives of others. I can feel good about who I am today because I am useful to myself and others. I am holding true to my morals and valuing things like honesty, hope, service, and faith. This approach provides a meaning and purpose that connects with my own spirituality and connects with a growing sense of personal ownership and self-esteem. I have grown to understand that happiness is not something I can create on demand. However, it is something I can easily exclude and remove from my life. Lasting and persistent happiness is a byproduct of other choices I make in life—it is not something I can achieve directly.

# DECEMBER 18

Having healthy boundaries in my relationships is a recurring theme of life in recovery for me. I learned the caretaker "Captain Save-the-World" dynamic very early on in my relationship with my mother. It is a part of my formation as a man and I can't remove it now. I have learned to recognize that many aspects of the family relationships I experienced growing up act as a sort of default setting in my life today. I am better able to see and understand the ways they impact my relationships with others today. It is not all bad, but I have to remember to maintain my own self—my own needs and rights. In addiction I spent many years in that "suffering servant" role with the accompanying feelings of self-pity, lack of appreciation, and justification that it can bring. Self-care was not something I was really very good at—meeting my needs yes, but caring for myself was harder. It is hard to care for someone when I don't respect or love them and so my own self-loathing, guilt, remorse, and anger—the things that fueled my addiction—also prevented me from caring for myself. Working the steps and living in recovery has shown me how to overcome those feelings so that I can at last love myself in ways that are meaningful and healthy. This opens the door to proper self-care. I have learned that caretaking others as an excuse or balm for my own internal issues is not healthy, for them or me.

# DECEMBER 19

Sitting on the porch watching the sun come up. It is a simple thing I enjoy on the winter mornings when the sunrise arrives each day right in line with the magnificent spectacle that is Mount Rainier. It seems timeless and quite spiritual—and on a chilly, crisp and clear morning it is very inspiring. The reality of today's life for me is just that—reality. I've learned to be more accountable to having a real life, not fantasy. There have been times when it was all fantasy and nothing was real other than the long list of things I was in denial about. Understanding and reliance on a relationship with my Higher Power, the world around me, and my own small place within it, lets me do the things each day that are in front of me rather than the fantasy of what tomorrow will bring or live in denial or what has happened in the past. In recovery, more choices arrive each day, and I have the ability to accommodate my interests, learn what I really like, and take the time to pursue them. Like the sunrise, each day is a real thing with real life for me to live and in doing so tomorrow brings me much more than the fantasy world I imagined. Understanding how to live fully in the today of my life has unlocked the door to an ability to create a meaningful and stable future.

# DECEMBER 20

Faith is a wonderful thing. It has carried me through many of the most difficult parts of my life but it was when I lost faith that things became the darkest. I have found faith to be one of those tricky concepts that has required a re-thinking and the experience of living it in a new way to really grasp how powerful a force it has become in my life. The whole society and world around me is built on many forms of faith and integrity. My recovery centers on a willingness to participate in life with others who share a faith in a power greater than themselves. This common sense of spiritual connection creates an experience of binding agency within those who participate together—to those who give up the attempt to live my life alone in self-sufficiency. I saw that a spiritual path worked for others and had to be willing to have faith that, in time, it would also work for me. As I started in recovery I found that it worked right away—a little—but I couldn't maintain the honesty and integrity of self to keep it. As I kept trying I learned how honesty and integrity were faith's companions. I became truly free from my own self and free to be myself. Today I know that having integrity, remaining true to my values and morals, is the work of the true faith needed to give me the peace I enjoy each day.

# DECEMBER 21

There are some things in life that move only in one direction or the other, where there is no middle ground or resting point. Either I am taking good care of my health or I am becoming less healthy. Either I am becoming more honest or I am continuing to justify being dishonest. It is also like this with my spiritual condition. I must take action each day in my efforts to be a spiritual man. I often think of paddling a canoe up river. As long as I keep paddling I continue to make progress but if I stop then the river slowly brings me back the way I came. While of course there are days when I am very busy pursuing my interests and activities—living the life that I have been granted—I am still very conscious of how spirituality undergirds it all. My recovery is not a separate activity that I perform in the morning like the dishes and then move onto the rest of the day. It is part of all my day, evident in my thinking, words, and actions—in how I show up in the lives of others. It is found in the actions of my daily living rather than the stories I tell myself or others. For me today, putting my recovery first in life has become simply living my life spiritually. It cannot be separated or parsed out of my living and requires taking regular meaningful action to keep it active and vibrant. It is part of the daily behavior of my living. Sometimes I behave better than other days but it is always present in some form because I can no longer leave it behind. If my living of life is truly comprised only of today, then today is the day I must live well—If not today, then when?

# DECEMBER 22

No matter how dark my world gets, I can always find hope when I make the effort to persevere in my choice of recovery. I strongly value the idea that I should do what I ought to do in life. I should work to be the man I want to be. When I remind myself of this goal it is only a start. It becomes real when I make the right choices during the day. Today I can look back at times when part of me wanted to be less than fully honest, to take a lazy shortcut, or indulge an unhealthy desire and I am reminded of where that path led me. Today I am on a path that instead encourages me to choose the next right thing. I see that these moments of doing the right thing increase my self-worth and esteem. Even just a small thing has meaning and value in my imperfect journey. Increasingly I see that I am becoming the man I want to be today as a result of taking many small steps in the right direction. As a result of my practicing this sort of principle I am able to grasp how despair and discouragement are normal feelings that I can alleviate by choosing hope. It is clear to me today that even in the worst, most horrible situations, people find ways to have hope. The human spirit that chooses life is always available to me and I must be willing to do my part—to reach out and grasp it.

# DECEMBER 23

The experience I have had through being willing to participate in and enjoy true and lasting friendships has relieved me of the crushing loneliness of my past. So many times in recovery I've had to face certain beliefs and ideas about who I think I am and become willing to let them go as I adopted more realistic and helpful approaches. Many of my ideas about being a man were convenient clichés, often quite childish and one dimensional, almost comic book parodies. They were beliefs and ideas that kept me from working through my problems and addictions. I had to overcome the fallacy of society's "strong unfeeling man" and learn that true manhood is found through sharing and caring. Today I understand the difference between loneliness and solitude. In addiction there was a sense of total isolation and disconnection from the world that left me alone in the company of others. It is perhaps ironic that in order to learn how to be happy alone with myself I had to learn how to not be alone and live fully with others. It is only through the honest relationships with other men—built through the process of recovery and step work—that I have been able to truly begin the journey of self-discovery and understanding that relieves me of the burden of my own skewed thinking. I have come to realize and accept the difficult process of holding my thinking loosely, being open-minded and willing, so that I can allow new ideas in while letting others go.

# DECEMBER 24

In active addiction I remember how hard it was at times for me to participate in celebrations with the rest of the world. I wanted to do the "party" and yet not be responsible to my family or loved ones. It strained my already meager finances and I resented having to buy gifts instead of meeting my addictive needs. It highlighted and exposed the painful and harsh reality and truth of my addiction as I avoided family events because they impinged on my using. I reacted with a false sense of not deserving to participate, of not being worthy, or perhaps mocking it all in some way—all of which were simply ways of remaining selfish and isolated. And it was during those holiday evenings when the world was celebrating and I was alone that the crushing isolation and dark hopelessness of my life in addiction cut the deepest. Today I choose to be a part of the celebrations with others in life. At first I learned how to do that with other people in recovery, at the celebrations and party's held in AA halls or my home group. I attended the gatherings I was invited to. When attending family events that were stressful or difficult I would try to focus on the good parts, the positive elements, and let the frustrating parts go. I slowly learned how to overcome the associations and stories of the holidays of the past and began to build new ones. Today, I am willing to find the goodness in myself and others who make an effort to celebrate life together. The holidays have been a difficult time for me in the past but each year I am better able to truly join with others in the celebrations in life. I am better able to do so because each year I continue to become more a part of my own life.

# DECEMBER 25

It has taken time and regular effort for me to develop a relationship with a Higher Power, a God I understand and can relate to. In early recovery, I struggled for a long time to gain a truly valid connection to a power greater than myself. Yes, time takes time, but at some point I realized it had become real. It had to become both honest and also be one of the most important things in my life. It wasn't until I was able to be honest and true to my Higher Power that I was able to achieve any meaningful spiritual growth. Today that relationship is always within me and I have peace and faith in my place in the world around me today because of it. It has shown me how to enjoy and find meaning in life through participating in relationships with others. It reminds me to be aware of the folly of trying to possess things that can't be possessed. It has helped highlight the futility of trying to find happiness through consumerism and controlling others. The gift of a relationship with a Higher Power has enabled me to learn how to find the peace I used to seek always in outside things and instead realize how lasting and sustainable happiness can only be found through the pursuit of inside things. It is a powerful truth that by turning my will and life over to a power greater than myself I have found a tremendous freedom and joy within myself. The "inside job" of recovery truly began for me only when I became able to trust and have faith in an outside source.

# DECEMBER 26

The lesson of learning how to let go of the material world as a source of validation, value, and self-worth is one that came painfully for me. When as a successful local entrepreneur I lost my business and was suddenly left with nothing it was a sea change. I felt destroyed and worthless, guilty and a failure. I quickly learned to live more simply and was confronted with the reality of letting go of my grand ambitions for life. Then round two came with my drinking and I truly went to zero—spiritually, physically, mentally, and socially. As my life has reformed in recovery I've learned to be better able to let go of my need to control. I have loosened my grip on "things"— material possessions, possessive relationships, as well as many of my core ideas and beliefs. I increasingly realize that for me, the gift of true freedom in life is a simple appreciation and participation in daily living while living daily. I truly had to live my way into a new way of thinking and give up the attempts to think my way into a new way of living. Being honest and straight with myself is all that I really need. I have never had this profound sense of freedom before in my life—despite having much outward success. Understanding and accepting the power of living in a way that I fully respect is the greatest reward I've yet found in life and it requires no "things" to achieve and sustain it. It is a spiritual gift that comes from within and because of that it is always available.

# DECEMBER 27

Christmas time has a wonderful theme of family, caring and giving that is easy to lose track of in the modern materialistic world of the latest gadgets, shopping for gifts and spending of money. It is fun and exciting to participate in all the activities of the holiday season. It brings a wonderful sense of connectedness and community that offers a comfortable feeling of truly being a part of life—of being actualized as a person—that is validated through engagement with others. However, while all of that may be well and good, it is also a reminder for me that peace of mind is an inside job. Using external achievements of gifts, work, success, and popularity provide only fleeting comfort that fades when I'm alone, leaving me feeling empty and shallow. It was an utterly confusing experience to have attained the things that I thought would make me happy only to find that I was still disturbed and discontent. Pursuit of better life values such as honesty, friendship, integrity, and humility. Forming true relationships with others, nature, my Higher Power and the world around me. These things allow me to have an understanding of who I am that comforts and satisfies me when I'm alone. It replaces that empty feeling with a worthy, peaceful, and valuable ability to find contentment, even in solitude. The understanding and commitment to participating in life as a whole and contributing individual with integrity and spirituality means that I must understand my own self as a person first.

# DECEMBER 28

For me, and for most people I know in recovery, the profound change and spiritual awakening that is at the heart of their transformation happens a little bit at a time. I've had a series of spiritual experiences, each of which is a bit like a small light bulb that turns on. Over time they add up to create and illuminate a new view of not only what is around me but also who I am and who I am becoming. I'm often unaware of the change in me when it happens, noticing it only later as I realize I've grown and changed again. Learning about myself and who I am allows me to become more aware of my actions and motives. The process gives me a deeper understanding and insight into the causes and conditions that underlie those actions and motives. It enables me to add to my grasp of who I am today, to learn new ways of doing things, and to see and act in the world differently. I love that one day at a time I create a new future and in doing so I also create a new past. Today I'm proud of who I am, and who I've been these past few years. There are many people who only know the person I am today. What a wonderful gift that is. For so many years in addiction I desperately asked that I be judged on my intentions rather than my actions. Today I am comfortable and content in having my actions be the currency of my self-esteem and the sense of self-worth that is reflected in my relationships with others and in the way that I understand and think about myself.

# DECEMBER 29

Perseverance sprung to mind this morning as I thought about failure and the human trait of getting up and trying again. My tendency to "awfulize" my shortcomings and view them in ways that are extreme prompts me to think about failing and trying again in grand terms and dramatic storylines. Certainly in addiction there was always an overly dramatic and excessive framework around even the most simple of things. The desire to be constantly in the middle of some sort of battle or struggle that could be heroically overcome was always just another way of keeping my addictive nature engaged and active. Hero or victim were the two master narratives of my insane plot for life. However, in the new world of recovery it is the little things that often count the most each day for me, reminding me of the true nature of progress not perfection. Accepting, for example, that I'll never be perfectly honest, always caring and unselfish, or a good listener all the time is vital to the truth of being honest about the reality of things. The truth of my reality is that usually my imperfections have consequences that I prefer to ignore rather than acknowledge. The gift of my spiritual awakening is that I can be aware of these daily failings and recommit to trying harder. I can persevere in my efforts with a cheerful acceptance rather than using my imperfect reality to beat myself up while wallowing in self-pity, guilt, and remorse. The only true failure would be to quit trying and give up. Little by little I have come a great distance, yet each day there is more ground to cover, more work to be done, and more life to enjoy as I follow my path of growth.

# DECEMBER 30

"It is always darkest before the dawn," and that's how it was for many of us—certainly that is how it was for me. It is always interesting to listen to others share about how they reached their bottom and what that looked life for them. So often the stories are similar with common themes of isolation, loneliness, broken lives and despairing families. Despite years of reaching new lows my bottom finally arrived and I was able to become truly open and willing to engage in an honest relationship with a Higher Power. I found the willingness to engage with the ideas of recovery and at last reached a point that enabled me to surrender my willful childlike selfishness and start to grow up and become the mature adult my Higher Power had always intended. It was a process that addiction had stymied and stunted. I was defiant to the last—like the way a child fights the end of the day crying out for "one more TV show" or just a bit longer before bedtime. It is still very easy for me to fall into in a similar sort of petulant thinking and so that's why every morning I remind myself that I chose to be in recovery today— and I affirm what that choice means in specific ways. Today, I choose what kind of man I am. No longer am I blown by the winds of the childish whims of willful selfishness, defined by its lack of real value, purpose, and ultimately tragic consequences. I chose to be "ok" with living life as it really is instead of choosing fantasy, denial, and illusion. In time being "ok" has become a comfortable and satisfying place on the path to true freedom and contentment.

# DECEMBER 31

For quite a while I had a hard time getting my recovery to really work. I was making a lot of the right moves and noises but wasn't being completely honest with myself. It took some time to really look in the mirror and truly see past the obvious—that I was an addict—and get to the deeper question of what I was willing to do about that fact. Until I was truly honest with myself about being done getting loaded I continued to struggle with relapse, grinding along, neither really in nor out of the program. Today I can look back on the years through the lens of the steps using the principles as my guide. Am I fully honest with myself? Where might I be deluding myself? Do I have hope and faith? Is my courage to face the truth about myself and share it with another man maintaining my integrity? Am I willing to let go of resentments and have the humility to do so in a spirit of brotherly love that leads me to a balancing of the scales of justice in my life? Do I persevere in my daily house cleaning and continue to grow spiritually in my life? Am I of service to others? When I ponder these questions the answers may vary—there will always be areas I need to work on—but the big picture becomes clear. It helps me answer two critical questions. Am I on the path I know to be good, heading in the right direction—or not? Do I want to go back in the direction I came from or stay the course and in another year's time once again look back and see, not perfection, but surely progress?

# ABOUT THE AUTHOR

For many years William Flynn has lived in the beautiful Pacific Northwest. As a strong advocate for social justice, William works in the nonprofit and social services field. He is also a graduate researcher studying community and social change. William is very involved with local recovery groups and is currently working on a new book that discusses how the underlying principles of each of the twelve steps work together to invoke and sustain a spiritual awakening.

Learn more at www.ayearofdays.org

Made in the USA
San Bernardino, CA
01 September 2016